Word Power

Handbook of
American
English
Spelling

TEXT EDITION

Lee C. Deighton

HARCOURT BRACE JOVANOVICH
New York Chicago San Francisco Atlanta Dallas *and* London

Lee C. Deighton has over 40 years experience as a publisher and editor of educational materials in English and language arts. He was the editor-in-chief of the *Encyclopedia of Education*. Mr. Deighton is the author of *Vocabulary Development; Vocabulary Development in the Classroom; A Comparative Study of Spellings in Four Major Collegiate Dictionaries;* and *Handbook of American English Spelling.*

ISBN 0-15-320202-5

Contents

Pattern Finder

1

Make This Handbook Work for You

We might as well be frank at the outset. English spelling is not easy. It is filled with traps and ambushes. Many words are not spelled the way they sound—or to put it correctly, there are many ways of spelling the same sound.

Don't be discouraged by spelling difficulties. Very few people can spell all the problem words in the language. After all, almost no one has an infallible memory. If you do not recall how a word is spelled, you don't need to avoid it, and you don't need to guess.

The Word List in this *Handbook* probably contains all the ordinary words you are ever likely to use, 20,000 in all. A look-up in this book is quick and easy, much easier than in a dictionary. Just to be sure of this, try a time-test with your friends. Match this *Handbook* against any dictionary on any words they find hard to spell. Then, note how long it takes to find them! The *Handbook* will always be quicker.

The Word List contains only words from the common language. There are no scientific, technical, or professional terms. There are no place-names like *Mississippi* or biographic names like *Antoinette*. But for nontechnical words, make a habit of using this *Handbook* for *your* spelling problems.

English spelling may seem confusing, but it is not chaotic. It is built on regular patterns that have been worked into the language for more than 500 years. In medieval times, for example, it was decided that no English word should end with *u* or *v*. That is why there is an *e* at the end of *have, live, true,* etc.

A pattern is a regular way of doing something. A spelling pattern is a regular way of spelling. It is not a rule or a law. It is simply a statement of the way in which most words of a particular sort are spelled. There are usually a few exceptions, but if you know the pattern *and* the exceptions, you are the master of a great many words.

The patterns will help you organize your knowledge of spelling. They are great time-savers because they help you learn a whole group of words together instead of learning them one at a time.

Usually, a pattern covers a large group of words. If it covers only a small group, in this book it is called a *guide*.

The first part of this *Handbook* contains in brief form all the patterns, guides, and other information presented in the Lesson Books of this series. If you have forgotten a point, or if your Lesson Book is not handy, you can easily find what you want in the *Handbook*. There is a Pattern Finder to help you.

One final point: if you are typing a letter or report, you may have to divide a word at the end of a line. The Word List shows you the points at which each word can be divided. This word division is not a guide to pronunciation; it is to be used only in writing. You can imagine how helpful it would be in a business office.

The Patterns of American English Spelling

2

Patterns

I. English Speech Sounds

For convenience we may classify the 39 sounds of English speech as vowel sounds and consonant sounds. In general, consonant sounds are represented by consonant letters and vowel sounds by vowel letters.

In this book vowel sounds are classified as *long open* (LO) or *short checked* (SC). The sound-letter relationships of importance in spelling follow.

Vowel Sounds

Long Open		Short Checked	
Spelling	Example	Spelling	Example
a	m*a*te	*a*	c*a*p
a	f*a*ther*		
e	b*e*	*e*	g*e*t
i (*y*)	h*i*gh, m*y*	*i* (*y*)	h*i*t, m*y*th
o	g*o*	*o*	h*o*t
u	br*u*te	*u*	c*u*p
u	h*u*ge /yu/	*u*	p*u*t

* Scientists who study language make a distinction between the long open sound spelled *a* in *father* and *calm* and the sound spelled *a* in *call*. The point to remember is that the long open sound in *mate* is not the only long open sound spelled *a*.

The letters *i* and *o* cross over to represent other sounds:

> *i* represents the long open sound
> > for which *e* stands: po*li*ce, mach*i*ne
>
> *o* represents the long open sound
> > for which *u* stands: pr*o*ve, l*o*se
>
> and one short checked sound
> > for which *u* stands: s*o*n, w*o*n

Notes:

1. Symbols used to represent sounds are placed between slant lines to distinguish them from letters: /yu/, /ə/, /k/, etc.
2. The letter *y* is a consonant only at the beginning of a word: *y*et, *y*es. Elsewhere in a word, *y* stands for the sounds of *i*.
3. The symbol /yu/ stands for a glide between two simple sounds (*i* + *oo*): h*u*ge, c*u*te, f*u*el.
4. The symbol /ə/ represents *schwa,* the indistinct vowel sound heard in unstressed syllables: *a* · go′, *o* · blige′. The schwa may be spelled by any of the vowel letters and may appear in any part of a word. It occurs only in unstressed syllables.

> *a* · go′   qui′*e*t   pen′c*i*l   *o* · blige′
> > cir′c*u*s   mar′t*y*r

Diphthongs.   A diphthong is a combined vowel sound produced when one vowel sound glides into another. Two diphthongs are of special importance in spelling:

> ou (ow):   cl*ou*d, *ow*l
> oi (oy):   *oi*l, b*oy*

Digraphs.   When two adjacent vowel letters stand for only one sound, they form a vowel digraph. Both the long open and short checked sounds may be spelled by digraphs.

Long open sounds

Single Vowel Spelling	Digraph Spelling	Example
a in m*a*te	*ai* (*ay*)	p*ai*d, s*ay*
	ei (*ey*)	w*ei*gh, ob*ey*
a in b*a*ll*	*au* (*aw*)	h*au*l, cr*aw*l
	ou	c*ou*gh
e in b*e*	*ea*	m*ea*t
	ee	f*ee*d
	ie	n*ie*ce
	ei	c*ei*ling
i (*y*) in h*i*gh, m*y*	*ie* (*ye*)	d*ie*, b*ye*
	ei (*ey*)	h*ei*ght, g*ey*ser
o in g*o*	*oa*	b*oa*t
	ou (*ow*)	s*ou*l, gl*ow*
u in br*u*te	*ui*	fr*ui*t
	ue	d*ue*
	oo	b*oo*t
	ou	s*ou*p
u in h*u*ge	*eu* (*ew*)	f*eu*d, f*ew*
	ue	val*ue*

Note that *y* interchanges with *i* and *w* interchanges with *u*.

Minor Additions

*ai*sle	g*au*ge	br*ea*k	matin*ee*	s*ew*
		st*ea*k		
		gr*ea*t		
		y*ea*		

---

* The vowel sound in *ball* is somewhat different from that in *father* and *calm*. The digraph spells the vowel sound you hear in *ball, haul, crawl,* and *cough* rather than the sound in *father* and *calm.*

Short checked sounds

Single Vowel Spelling	Digraph Spelling	Example
e in g*e*t	*ai*	s*ai*d, ag*ai*n
	ea	h*ea*lth, m*ea*sure
i (*y*) in h*i*t, m*y*th	*ei*	forf*ei*t, surf*ei*t
	ie	misch*ie*f, s*ie*ve
	ui	bisc*ui*t, circ*ui*t
u in c*u*t	*oo*	bl*oo*d, fl*oo*d
	ou	r*ou*gh, t*ou*ch
u in p*u*t	*oo*	b*oo*k, w*oo*d
	ou	c*ou*ld, b*ou*levard

Minor Additions

pl*ai*d   br*oa*d   b*ee*n

breeches

Doubled vowels

aa   does not appear in native English words.

ee   occurs at the end of approximately 100 words, often with the meaning of "one who is" (*absentee*) or "one who has been" (*nominee*). It appears initially in a few words such as *eel* and *eerie*. It may also occur as a result of adding prefixes: *de-emphasize, de-escalate, reelect, reengage.*

ii   appears in five words as a result of adding ***ing***: *taxiing, skiing, shanghaiing, alibiing, piing,* and in a few words such as *radii* which retain the Latin plural. Elsewhere *ii* is avoided.

oo   represents either the short checked sounds in *blood* and *good;* or the long open sound in *food.* It occurs initially in only one word in the common language:* *ooze;* but finally in a number of words such as *shoo, woo, tattoo,* and *hoodoo.*

uu   appears in only a few words: *vacuum, continuum, residuum.*

---

* The term *common language* refers to the language of ordinary use excluding technical, professional, scientific, or trade terms.

Consonants

Most consonant sounds are represented by one letter: *l, m, b,* etc. For a few consonant sounds there is more than one spelling.

Sound	Spelling	Example
/k/	*c, k, ck, ch, qu*	*c*ost, *k*in, ba*ck*, a*ch*e, physi*que*
/s/	*s, c*	*s*end, *c*ent
/g/	*g, gu, gh*	*g*et, *gu*ide, *gh*ost
/ǰ/	*j, g, dg, di, du*	*j*et, *g*em, fu*dg*e, sol*di*er, gra*du*al
/z/	*z, s, x*	*z*eal, ri*s*e, dog*s*, *x*ylophone

Consonant combinations. Consonant letters may be combined with other letters to represent consonant sounds. For each of these sounds, there is a symbol with the mark ˇ written above it.

/š/	*sh*ip, mi*ssi*on, no*ti*on, etc.
/č/	ma*tch*, ques*ti*on, *ch*est, ac*tu*al, etc.
/ǰ/	bu*dg*e, gra*du*al, sol*di*er, etc.
/ž/	a*z*ure, lei*su*re, vi*si*on, etc.

Syllabic consonants. In the last syllable of words such as *bottle, button,* and *acre,* the vowel letter is unpronounced. There is no true vowel sound, although in the speech of some people, the schwa sound occurs; thus, *bot'təl, but'tən,* etc. The final consonant letter becomes the nucleus of the syllable. It is called a *syllabic consonant* and is shown in dictionaries in two ways: bot''*l* or bot'ə*l*.

Syllables and Stress

A syllable is a word or word part pronounced as a unit and without interruption.

In every English word one syllable is spoken louder and with more force than the other syllables. This syllable is

9

stressed. In some longer words there is a major stress and a minor stress.

A center dot is used to indicate the end of a syllable; an accent mark is placed at the end of a syllable and slightly above it to show that it is stressed. To indicate a syllable given minor stress, the accent mark is narrower and lighter. When an accent mark is used, the center dot is omitted.

cer′tain·ly   cu′ri · os′i · ty

II. Markers of Sound and Spelling

Since all vowel letters and several consonant letters may stand for different sounds, certain letters are used as markers to indicate which sound is intended. The marker occurs after, usually immediately after, the letter to which it applies. Any marker is an integral part of the spelling.

Markers for Vowel Sounds

1. In most one-syllable words, final *e* marks the long open sound for the preceding vowel. It may appear right after, as in t*oe*, d*ie*, and h*ue*, or it may be separated by a consonant, as in h*ole*, r*ide*, and c*ame*.

   In a few common words, final *e* is not a marker after the letters *m, n,* or *v*: *come, done, have, live,* etc. In words ending *nce*, final *e* marks the sound /s/ for *c* but does not mark the preceding vowel sound: *since, dunce, dance*. Nor does it mark the preceding vowel sound in words ending *nse: sense, rinse, response*.

2. In some longer words, final *e* marks the long open sound for the preceding vowel, but nearly as often it does not. Compare:

10

	LO	SC		LO	SC
	eng*age* —cott*age*		prof*ile* —fut*ile*
	rev*ise* —prom*ise*		def*ace* —pref*ace*

3. At the end of a word, the consonant clusters *nd, ld, gn* and *gh* mark the long open sound for *i*.

desi*gn*	fi*nd*	bri*gh*t
chi*ld*	si*gh*

At syllable breaks in longer words, each letter in these clusters may be pronounced. When this happens *i* stands for the short checked sound.

si*g* · *n*a · ture	wi*n* · *d*ow
wi*l* · *d*er · ness	bi*g* · *h*ead

4. At the end of a word, *ll* and *ld* mark the long open sound for the preceding *o*: po*ll*, stro*ll*, fo*ld*.

Exception: do*ll*.

5. Other consonant clusters at the end of a word usually signal the short checked sound for the preceding vowel.

sp:	cla*sp*, li*sp*	*nt*:	le*nt*, sti*nt*
st:	ne*st*, ru*st*	*lt*:	be*lt*, hi*lt*
sk:	a*sk*, ri*sk*	*lk*:	mi*lk*, su*lk*

Exceptions occur in *pint* and in words ending *ost*: *ghost, host, most, post;* in words where *a* appears before unpronounced *l*: wa*l*k, ta*l*k; and in some regional dialects when *a* precedes an unpronounced *l* or *r*: *half, cart.*

6. In one-syllable words, a single vowel letter between two consonant letters represents the short checked sound: c*a*t, r*i*d, l*o*t, unless the word ends with *e*. In longer words, the vowel letter may represent the long open sound.

h*o*mer	f*a*tal	r*e*gion
r*i*val	f*u*tile

7. A doubled consonant usually signals the short checked sound for the preceding vowel.

a*pp*le	swi*mm*er	e*gg*
le*tt*er	su*nn*y	o*dd*

Exceptions: words ending *oll*.

Markers for Consonant Sounds

1. The letters *i, y,* and *e* mark the sound /s/ for *c* in any part of a word.

c*e*ntral   rec*e*nt   fenc*e*

2. Final *e* and final *y* always signal the sound /ǰ/ for *g,* but *y* is not a marker after *gg*.

wag*e*   biolog*y*   so*gg*y

but

ima*g*e   eulo*g*y   fo*gg*y

3. At the end of a word, *c* represents the sound /k/. To preserve this sound when suffixes beginning with *e, i,* or *y* are added, the letter *k* is inserted.

panic + ed → panic*k*ed
frolic + ing → frolic*k*ing
garlic + y → garlic*k*y

but note

magic + ian → magi*c*ian
politic + ian → politi*c*ian

See Section X for a list of words ending *c* in which *k* is inserted to preserve the sound /k/ for *c*.

4. The letters *a, o,* and *u* mark the sound /k/ for *c* and the sound /g/ for *g*: c*a*t, c*o*t, c*u*t, g*a*p, g*o*t, g*u*st.

5. Final *e* always marks the sound /ǰ/ for *g*. At other points

in a word, *3* does not always mark this sound: *ge*t, to-*ge*ther. This is also true of *i*: *gi*ve, han*gi*ng.

III. The Spellings of /š/

The common spelling of this combined consonant sound is *sh*: *sh*ip, *sh*ell, wi*sh*.
The sound is also spelled in a variety of other ways.

su	*su*re	*ce*	o*ce*an
ssi	mi*ssi*on	*ch*	ma*ch*ine
sch	*sch*wa	*ti*	men*ti*on
si	expan*si*on	*xi*	an*xi*ous
sci	con*sci*ous	*ci*	ra*ci*al

The Letters *ci* and *ti*

The letters *c* and *t* combine with the *i* of the suffixes *ian, ion, ial,* and *ious* to represent /š/. The result is a single sound: /šul/, /šun/, or /šus/.

ian
The regular spelling is *cian* as in *magician* and *technician*. Only one word in the common language ends with the sound /šun/ spelled *tian*: *dietitian*.

ial
The spelling *tial* is more frequent than *cial*. The words in the common language ending *cial* are the following:*

artificial	financial	provincial
beneficial	glacial	racial
commercial	judicial	sacrificial
crucial	official	social
fiducial	prejudicial	special
		superficial

---

* Also, the derivatives *biracial, bifacial, interracial,* etc., in which the ending is not affected by the addition of a prefix.

13

Guide 1: In most words ending *tial*, the sound /n/ precedes /šul/, and the spelling is *ntial*: *residential, substantial, essential*. A limited list of words ends *tial* without the preceding /n/.

impartial	martial
inertial	palatial
initial	partial

Guide 2: With two exceptions, nouns ending *nce* change to *ntial*:

sequence → sequential   province → provincial

but

essence → essential   finance → financial

Guide 3: With two exceptions, nouns ending *ce* with no preceding *n* change to *cial*.

race → racial   space → spatial

but

commerce → commercial   palace → palatial

Guide 4: Five words end *ficial*. No English word ends *fitial*.

artificial	official	superficial
beneficial		sacrificial

ion

Before this suffix, /š/ may be spelled *ci, ti, si,* or *ssi*:

intention	compression
dimension	suspicion

Guide 1: Only two words in common use end *cion*:

suspicion   coercion

Guide 2: *ss* is followed by *ion*. The *ss* occurs in a few readily recognized stems.

cess: suc*cess*ion   *sess*: pos*sess*ion

	miss:	mission	press:	impression
	gress:	digression	pass:	passion
	cuss:	discussion		

Guide 3: In most words ending *sion*, the letters *si* represent the sound /ž/.

vision   illusion

ous

There appear to be no guides to the spelling choice between *cious* and *tious*. Words with these endings must be learned individually.

IV. The Digraphs *ei* and *ie*

The sounds represented by the digraphs *ei* and *ie* are as follows:

		ei	*ie*
LO	*a*	weigh	
LO	*e*	ceiling	niece
SC	*e*	heifer	friend
LO	*i*	height	die
SC	*i*	forfeit	sieve

Guide 1: The long open sound represented by *a* in mate is spelled *ei*:

weight   eight   sleigh

Guide 2: The long open sound represented by *i* in high is spelled *ie* only in three-letter words:

die   vie   tie

Guide 3: The short checked sound represented by *e* in get is spelled *ei* or *ie* in only four words in common use:

he*i*fer	fr*ie*nd
he*i*r	pim*ie*nto

Guide 4: The short checked sound represented by *i* in h*i*t is usually spelled by the digraph *ie*: *frontier, fierce, sieve.* The spelling *ei* for this sound occurs infrequently:

counter*feit*	w*ei*rd
for*feit*	
sur*feit*	

Guide 5: The long open sound represented by *e* in *be* is usually spelled by the digraph *ie*:

s*ie*ge	y*ie*ld	rel*ie*ve

This sound is spelled *ei* in the following instances:

caff*ei*ne	s*ei*ze	*ei*ther
c*ei*ling	inv*ei*gle	n*ei*ther
l*ei*sure		

and

in words based upon the stem *ceive*.

con*ceive*:	conceived, conceiving, conceit
de*ceive*:	deceived, deceiving, deceit
per*ceive*:	perceived, perceiving
re*ceive*:	received, receiving, receipt

V. Suffix Spellings

A suffix is a word part added to the end of a word or word stem. A word stem is a word part that cannot stand as a word by itself: *fer, mur, sist.*

A vowel suffix is one that begins with a vowel letter: *an, ing, or,* etc. A consonant suffix is one that begins with a consonant letter: *ly, ness, ment,* etc.

ful

This suffix is always spelled with one *l*.

cupful   armful   roomful

The plural form of words ending *ful* is spelled with *s* at the end.

cupful*s*   armful*s*   roomful*s*

Vgy

This symbol stands for "any vowel letter before the letters *gy* at the end of a word." The vowel letter in approximately 100 words is *o*.

apology   ecology
biol<i>o</i>gy   eul<i>o</i>gy</p>

Only four words in common use vary from this pattern:

effigy   prodigy
el<i>e</i>gy   strat<i>e</i>gy</p>

ly

When the suffix *ly* is added to a word ending *l*, that *l* is retained.

awful + → awfully   gradual + ly → gradually

When *ly* is added to a word ending *ll*, one *l* is dropped.

dull + ly → dully   ill + ly → illy

When *ly* is added to a word ending *consonant* + *le*, the *le* is dropped.

able + ly → ably   noble + ly → nobly

ing

When the suffix *ing* is added to a word ending *e*, the *e* is dropped.

bake + ing → baking   move + ing → moving

Exceptions: ey*e*ing, dy*e*ing.

When *ing* is added to a word ending *y*, the *y* is retained in order to avoid two *i's* in succession.

marry + ing → marrying   bury + ing → burying

When *ing* is added to one-syllable words ending *ie*, the *e* is dropped and the *i* is changed to *y*.

vie   + ing → vying
untie + ing → untying
lie   + ing → lying

When *ing* is added to longer words ending *ie*, there is usually no spelling change.

stymie + ing → stymieing   sortie + ing → sortieing

Exception: caddie + ing → caddying.

fy and *phy*

In the suffix *fy*, the *y* stands for the long open vowel sound you hear at the end of *terrify*. In the ending *phy*, which is not a suffix, the *y* stands for the short checked vowel sound you hear in *pin*. Dictionaries show *phy* as though it were pronounced *fee*, but linguisits maintain that /fĭ/ is correct.

VI. Prefix Spellings

A prefix is a word part added to the beginning of a word or word stem. There is no spelling change in the rest of the word when a prefix is added.

18

mis, dis, and *un*

A doubled consonant occurs when the last letter of these prefixes is the same as the first letter of the stem.

$$mis + spell \rightarrow mi sspell$$
$$un + natural \rightarrow u nn atural$$
$$dis + semble \rightarrow di ss emble$$

Errors may be avoided by writing the stem first, then adding the prefix.

Prefix Changes

The final consonant of some prefixes changes to match the first letter of the stem to which it is attached. The result is a doubled consonant. No change in meaning occurs with the spelling change.

in becomes *il* before *l*: *il*legal
ir before *r*: *ir*regular
im before *m*: *im*mense
and *im* in some words before *b* and *p*: *im*bue, *im*possible

com becomes *col* before *l*: *col*lect
con before *n*: *con*nect
cor before *r*: *cor*rect

ad changes before nine different consonants.

ac: account	*al*: allot	*ar*: arrest
af: affront	*an*: annex	*as*: assign
ag: aggressor	*ap*: approve	*at*: attend

Prefixes and hyphens

In general, prefixes are joined without a hyphen to the following word element. Hyphens are inserted in the following situations:

1. If the second element begins with a capital letter, insert a hyphen.

ante-Roman	pre-Christian
anti-Nazi	pro-British
mid-Victorian	un-American
non-Arabic	trans-Canadian

In a few words, the proper adjective does not begin with a capital letter, and no hyphen appears.

transatlantic	subarctic
transpacific	unchristian
transalpine	

2. If the prefix is *self*, insert a hyphen.

self-made   self-educated

3. If the prefix has the meaning "former," use a hyphen.

ex-champion   ex-governor

4. In a few words after *anti*, use a hyphen.

anti-icer	anti-hero
anti-ballistic missile	anti-intellectual

5. In some words to prevent confusion, use a hyphen.

co-op
de-emphasize
de-escalate

6. When the prefix *re* means "again," in order to prevent confusion with other words similarly spelled, use a hyphen.

re-coil (coil again) — recoil (draw back)
re-collect (collect again) — recollect (remember)
re-count (count again) — recount (tell)
re-cover (cover again) — recover (get back)
re-create (create again) — recreate (give new life)

re-dress (dress again) — redress (set right)
re-lay (lay again) — relay (pass on)
re-lease (lease again) — release (let go)
re-tread (tread again) — retread (tires)
re-treat (treat again) — retreat (withdrawal)

The hyphen is not used when there is no possibility of confusion: *reengage, reelect, retry,* etc.

VII. Final *e*

Final *e* is pronounced in approximately 40 words, with the long open vowel sound heard in *be*. Apart from six one-syllable words (*be, me, we, the,* etc.) which are native English words, the rest are borrowed from foreign languages; for example:

abalone	cadre	fettucine	machete
adobe	cicerone	karate	tamale

In another 200 words which end *ee* or *ie*, final *e* is part of the final vowel sound: refug*ee*, calor*ie*. Otherwise, final *e,* occurring in several thousand words, is not pronounced.

Final *e* as a Marker

In words ending *ue* and *ve,* the *e* is a tag assigned to the final position by Middle English scribes in order to avoid words ending *u* or *v*: val*ue*, ha*ve*. In a great many words, however, final *e* serves as a marker for a preceding consonant or vowel sound.

1. In words ending *re* and *le*, *e* marks the *r* and *l* as syllabic consonants.

acre	table
ogre	ladle

2. Final *e* marks the sounds /s/ for *c* and /ǰ/ for *g*. See Section II.

3. Final *e* marks the long open sound for the preceding vowel letter in most one-syllable words and in many longer words.

cave   immu*ne*

ri*de*   releg*a*t*e*

4. Final *e* marks the sound of *th* in *clothe, breathe,* etc. to distinguish it from the sound of *th* in *cloth, breath,* etc.

Final *e* with Suffixes

When suffixes are added to words ending *e,* the *e* may be dropped, retained, or displaced by another letter.

Pattern: Final *e* is usually dropped when vowel suffixes are added but retained when consonant suffixes are added.

Vowel Suffixes	*Consonant Suffixes*
place + *i*ng → placing	place + *m*ent → placement
noise + *y* → noisy	noise + *l*ess → noiseless
like + *a*ble → likable	like + *l*y → likely

The suffixes *ial, ian,* and *ious* are variant forms of *al, an,* and *ous.* Final *e* is dropped when these suffixes are added:

commerce + ial → commercial   grace + ous → gracious

finance   + ial → financial   space + ous → spacious

college + ian → collegian

reptile + ian → reptilian

Final *e* Changed

In a few words, final *e* is replaced by *u* when the suffixes *ous, al,* and *ate* are added.

sense + ous → sens*u*ous	reside + al → resid*u*al
sense + al → sens*u*al	grade + al → grad*u*al
use + al → us*u*al	grade + ate → grad*u*ate
rite + al → rit*u*al	

Exception Groups

Some exceptions to the basic pattern are individual instances; others occur systematically. The latter may be considered as subpatterns, as shown in the following guides.

Guide 1: Final *e* is dropped when *ment* is added to words ending *dge*.

> judge + ment → judgment
> lodge + ment → lodgment
> abridge + ment → abridgment
> acknowledge + ment → acknowledgment

Guide 2: When *ing* is added to one-syllable words ending *ie*, the *e* is dropped and the *i* is changed to *y*.

> lie + ing → lying
> die + ing → dying

Guide 3: Final *e* is retained when *able* is added to words ending *ce* or *ge*.

> trace + able → traceable   change + able → changeable

The *e* is required in these words to mark the sound /s/ for *c* and /ǰ/ for *g*. In all other words, final *e* is dropped when *able* is added: *movable, likeable, usable,* etc.

Guide 4: Final *e* is retained in seven words ending *ge* when *ous* is added.

> advantageous   gorgeous   rampageous
> courageous   outrageous   umbrageous
> disadvantageous

Guide 5: Final *e* is retained in five words before the suffix *y*. See Section VIII.

> cagey   gluey   homey
> dopey   holey (full of holes)

Individual Exceptions

Final *e* dropped before a consonant suffix

argufy	fledgling	truly
argument	loathsome	truth
awful	nursling	wholly
duly	ninth	width
		wisdom

Final *e* retained before a vowel suffix

acreage	lineage	ogreish	roseate
dyeing	lineal	orangeade	singeing
eyeing	linear	phraseology	tingeing
hateable	marbleize	pixieish	spareable
limeade	mileage	plebeian	veng3ance

VIII. Final *y*

The letter *y* comes at the end of more than 8,000 words in the common language. Suffixes may be added to more than half of these. When suffixes are added, the *y* may be dropped, retained, or changed to *i*.

Final *y* Dropped

When final *y* is dropped, the sound it represents either disappears or is represented by *i* in the suffixes *ic* and *ist*.

chivalry + ous → chivalrous   history + ic → historic
calamity + ous → calamitous   apology + ist → apologist

Final *y* Changed to *i*

Pattern: If preceded by a consonant letter, final *y* is usually changed to *i* when suffixes are added.

Vowel Suffixes	*Consonant Suffixes*
try + al → tr*i*al	merry + ment → merr*i*ment
company + es → compan*i*es	merry + ly → merr*i*ly

Final *y* Retained

Pattern: If preceded by a vowel letter, *y* usually does not change when suffixes are added.

$$
\begin{array}{lll}
\text{annoy} & + \text{ance} & \rightarrow \text{annoyance} \\
\text{journey} & + \text{ed} & \rightarrow \text{journeyed} \\
\text{defray} & + \text{ment} & \rightarrow \text{defrayment} \\
\text{money} & + \text{s} & \rightarrow \text{moneys}
\end{array}
$$

Exceptions

day + ly → daily	pay + ed → paíd
gay + ly → gaily	say + ed → said
gay + ety → gaiety	lay + ed → laid
	slay + n → slain

Guide 1:   In a few one-syllable words, final *y* is retained before the suffixes *ly* and *ness*.

dry: dryly, dryness   *spry:*   spryly, spryness
shy: shyly, shyness   *wry:*   wryly, wryness

Guide 2:   Final *y* is retained before the suffixes *ish* and *ing* to avoid two *i's* in succession.

worry + ing → worrying   boy + ish → boyish
annoy + ing → annoying   gray + ish → grayish

The Adjective Suffix *y*

Pattern: When *y* is added to a word ending *e*, the *e* is usually dropped.

able + y → ably	ease + y → easy
choose + y → choosy	smoke + y → smoky

Dictionaries often show two spellings in this situation without indicating preference or frequency of occurrence. A comparative study of current usage indicates that final *e* is dropped before the adjective suffix *y* in all but five words: *cagey, dopey, gluey, holey, homey.*

When the suffixes *er* and *est* are added to these words, the *e* is dropped and the *y* is changed to *i*.

cagey:	cagier, cagiest	*holey:*	holier, holiest
dopey:	dopier, dopiest	*homey:*	homier, homiest
gluey:	gluier, gluiest		

In a few words, the adjective suffix is *ey* rather than *y.*

clayey   mosquitoey
gooey

IX. Other Vowel Endings

Words Ending *oo*

There are no spelling changes when suffixes are added to words ending *oo*. The plural of these words is formed by adding *s*.

woo + er → wooer	voodoo + ism → voodooism
hoodoo + ing → hoodooing	boo + s → boos

Words Ending *ee*

When a suffix beginning with *e* is added to a word ending *ee*, one *e* is dropped in order to avoid three *e*'s in succession. No spelling changes occur when other suffixes are added.

e Dropped	*No Change*
free + er → freer	free + ing → freeing
wee + est → weest	agree + ment → agreement
agree + ed → agreed	foresee + able → foreseeable

Vowels Before Final *e*

The symbol *Ve* means "any vowel letter before final *e*."

Pattern: Final *e* is dropped from words ending *Ve* when suffixes beginning with *e* are added.

shoe + *e*r → shoer	dy*e* + ed → dyed
true + *e*st → truest	vi*e* + ed → vied

ie. Final *e* is retained before all suffixes except *ing* and those beginning with *e*. See Section VII, Guide 2.

die + *i*ng → dying
lie + *e*d → lied
tie + *l*ess → tieless

ye. Final *e* is retained before all suffixes except those beginning with *e*.

eye + ing → eyeing	eye + less → eyeless
dye + *e*d → dyed	eye + *e*d → eyed

oe. Final *e* is retained before all suffixes except those beginning with *e*.

hoe + ing → hoeing	toe + *e*d → toed
woe + ful → woeful	shoe + *e*r → shoer
canoe + ist → canoeist	

ue. Final *e* is dropped before all vowel suffixes, but retained before consonant suffixes.

blue + ish → bluish	blue + ness → blueness
glue + ing → gluing	oblique + ly → obliquely
value + able → valuable	value + less → valueless

Exceptions:

duly	argument
truly	argufy
truth	gluey

27

Other vowel endings. In words ending *eo*, *io*, and *uo*, there is no spelling change when suffixes are added. See Section XV.

cameo + s → cameos   duo + s → duos
radio + ed → radioed   studio + s → studios

X. SOUND-ALIKE ENDINGS

Word endings similar in sound but different in spelling occur because the same sound may be spelled with different vowel or consonant letters. While the spellings of particular end sounds are far from uniform, definite patterns and preferences appear in American English.

able and *ible*

Nearly 1,200 adjectives end *able*. It is a living suffix; that is, it is currently used to form new words or nonce words from verbs: *skiable, playable, machine-washable,* etc. The suffix *ible* is no longer so used. The Government Printing Office *Style Manual* lists just over 200 words ending *ible,* but nearly half are such incredible items as *cognoscible, indocible, ineffervescible, marcescible, putrescible,* and *thurible.* The *ible* suffix occurs in words taken directly from Latin verbs ending *ere* and *ire.*

Usage has definitely fixed such words as *eligible, fallible,* and *feasible,* which must be learned as separate items. The great preponderance of *able* is the only clue to the choice between these endings.

ant and *ent*

Both endings appear in adjectives: *defiant, insistent;* and in nouns: *accountant, resident.* There is no satisfactory clue for which ending is required in particular words.

It may be noted, however, that if a word ends *ent,* the parallel forms end *ence* or *ency.* Similarly, if a word ends *ant,* the parallel forms end *ance* or *ancy.*

| reverent — reverence | relevant — relevance |
| diffident — diffidence | compliant — compliance |

The suffix *ence* is added to all verbs ending *fer*. See Section XI.

cede, ceed, and sede

The regular ending is *cede: recede, precede, secede,* etc. Only four words end otherwise:

exceed   supersede
proceed
succeed

c and k

The final sound /k/ is spelled *k, c, ch, ck,* and *que.* The ending *ch* is infrequent: a*ch*e, stoma*ch*; *que* occurs in a few words of French origin: *antique, pique, physique,* etc.

Final *c* occurs in the ending *ic:* att*ic*, pan*ic*, etc.; and in a few words borrowed from other languages: hav*oc*, bivou*ac*, *sac*. When suffixes beginning *e, i,* or *y* are added, the letter *k* is inserted when the sound /k/ for *c* is retained. The following are the words in common use with *k* inserted:

antic	anticked, anticking
bivouac	bivouacked, bivouacking
colic	colicky
frolic	frolicked, frolicker, frolicking
garlic	garlicky
havoc	havocked, havocking
mimic	mimicked, mimicker, mimicking
mosaic	mosaicked, mosaicking
panic	panicked, panicking, panicky
physic	physicked, physicking
picnic	picnicked, picnicker, picnicking
politic	politicked, politicker, politicking

shellac	shellacked, shellacking
sic	sicked, sicking
traffic	trafficked, trafficker, trafficking

cy and *sy*

The ending *cy* is an active suffix used to form nouns. It occurs in approximately 150 nouns in common use. In many instances, *cy* has been added to a word ending *t: idiot—idiocy; recent—recency.* In all such words in common use, the *t* is dropped when *sy* is added. The single exception is *bankruptcy.*

The ending *sy* occurs as a suffix only in familiar pet names as in *Betsy,* or in an adjective as in *tipsy.* In some adjectives, *sy* occurs as a result:

1. Of adding *y* to words ending *s: newsy, tricksy, folksy,* etc.
2. Of adding *y* to words ending *ss: messy, brassy, fussy,* etc.

The ending *sy* and *s* representing the sound /s/ occurs in the following nouns in common use:

apostasy	discourtesy	jealousy
argosy	dropsy	leprosy
autopsy	ecstasy	minstrelsy
biopsy	embassy	patsy
catalepsy	epilepsy	pleurisy
clerisy	fantasy	poesy
controversy	heresy	
courtesy	hypocrisy	
curtsy	idiosyncrasy	

Note: The word *prophecy* is a noun while *prophesy* is a verb.

eer and *ier*

The noun suffix **ier** meaning "one that is or does something" occurs only in words borrowed from French. The active English suffix used in forming new words is **eer**. It occurs in both nouns and verbs: *to domineer, to profiteer, to electioneer, a junketeer, an auctioneer,* etc. The following are the words in the common language with the suffix *ier:*

bombardier	chandelier	frontier
boulevardier	chevalier	gondolier
brigadier	chiffonier	grenadier
cashier	croupier	premier
cavalier	financier	

el and *le*

In final unstressed syllables, these endings sound alike. With a preceding consonant, *le* occurs in nearly 2,000 words; *el* in a few more than 100.

The choice between *el* and *le* depends in large part on the consonant sound or the consonant letter immediately preceding.

el. The letters *m, n, r, v,* and *w* are followed by *el* rather than *le:*

m:	ena*mel*, tram*mel*		*r:*	quar*rel*, squir*rel*
n:	fun*nel*, flan*nel*		*v:*	no*vel*, mar*vel*
			w:	to*wel*, vo*wel*

When *c* represents the sound /s/, it is followed by *el.* When *g* represents the sound /ǰ/, it is followed by *el.*

can*cel*	an*gel*
par*cel*	cu*dgel*

Note: In *angle, dangle,* and *jangle,* etc., *g* represents the sound /g/.

le. The letters *f, g,* and *t* are regularly followed by *le* with only these exceptions:

duf*fel*	hos*tel* (inn)
ba*gel*	man*tel* (shelf)

31

Note: A man*tle* is a hood or covering. A man*tel* is a shelf, usually one over a fireplace.

The letters *b*, *d*, and *p* are regularly followed by *le* with these exceptions:

b:		*d:*		*p:*	
deci*bel*		cita*del*		cha*pel*	
la*bel*		infi*del*		gos*pel*	
li*bel*		mo*del*		scal*pel*	
re*bel*		yo*del*			

The sounds /k/ and /z/ are regularly followed by *le* with these exceptions:

nic*kel*	ea*sel*
snor*kel*	wea*sel*
yo*kel*	ha*zel*

eous and *ious*

The ending *eous* occurs in many scientific terms. In words in the common language, *ious* appears far more frequently.

The following are the words in common use ending *eous*. Since the ending appears after a limited number of consonants, it is convenient to consider them with the consonant letter.

aqueous	erroneous	instantaneous
beauteous	extemporaneous	nauseous
bounteous	gaseous	piteous
consanguineous	extraneous	righteous
contemporaneous	heterogeneous	sanguineous
courteous	hideous	simultaneous
curvaceous	homogeneous	spontaneous
cutaneous	igneous	vitreous
duteous		

ceous. This ending occurs often in scientific and technical words but in only one word in common use: *curvaceous*. The spelling *ce* represents the sound /š/, which is also spelled *ci* and *ti*: *spacious, ambitious.*

Pattern: In words of the common language, when the sound is /šus/ the spelling is either *cious* or *tious*.

deous. Only one word ends *deous: hideous*, in contrast to the greater number ending *dious: invidious, perfidious, studious*, etc.

geous. In this ending, **ge** represents the sound /ǰ/. The following words must be learned as separate items to distinguish them from the greater number of words ending *gious: religious, prodigious*, etc.

advantageous   gorgeous   rampageous
courageous   outrageous   umbrageous
disadvantageous

neous. Several words pertaining to time end *neous:*

contemporaneous   simultaneous
instantaneous   spontaneous

Several words pertaining to likeness or difference end *neous:*

extraneous   heterogeneous
homogeneous   miscellaneous

teous. In some words ending *ty*, the sound /t/ is retained when *ous* is added. To preserve this sound, the final *y* is changed to *e* rather than to *i*.

beauty — beauteous   pity — piteous
duty — duteous   plenty — plenteous

also

courtesy — courteous

In *righteous*, the *te* represents the sound /č/.

er and *re*

The final sound usually represented by the spelling *er* is spelled *re* in a few words in American English. This usage contrasts with the British, in which *re* occurs in such spellings as *centre, meagre, theatre,* etc.

In New York City, the spelling *theatre* appears frequently but not predominantly. *The New York Times* uses *theater,* but some of its advertisers prefer *theatre.* Elsewhere in the country *theater* is the predominant usage.

The following words are regularly spelled *re* in American English:

acre	macabre	timbre (tone quality)
chancre	massacre	wiseacre
genre	mediocre	
lucre	ogre	

ify and *efy*

The regular verb ending is *ify,* which occurs in a large number of words. The ending *efy* appears only in the following words in the common language:

liquefy	rarefy
putrefy	stupefy

The spelling carries over into derivatives such as *liquefying, liquefied, stupefaction,* etc. But note *rarity.*

ise and *ize*

In American English, *ize* is the predominant ending, occurring in several hundred words. The ending *ise* occurs in the following words in the common language:

abscise	devise	incise
advertise	disguise	merchandise
advise	emprise	previse
apprise	enterprise	revise

chastise	excise	rise
circumcise	exercise	supervise
compromise	exorcise	surmise
comprise	franchise	surprise
demise	guise	televise
despise	improvise	wise

Note: The *ise* spelling also appears in all compound words built upon *wise: otherwise, likewise,* etc.

Although dictionaries also list the spellings *advertize, exorcize,* and *merchandize,* the predominant spellings are those listed above.

ity and *ety*

The basic pattern in American English is to use *ity* as a noun ending.

The ending *ety* appears in a limited number of words as the result of two processes:

1. *ty* is added to a few adjectives ending *e.*

entirety	nicety	subtlety
naivety	safety	surety

2. *ety* is added to word stems ending *i* in order to avoid two *i's* in succession.

anxiety	inebriety	propriety
contrariety	insobriety	satiety
dubiety	moiety	sobriety
gaiety	nimiety	society
impiety	notoriety	ubiety
impropriety	piety	variety

nse and *nce*

The regular ending in American English is *nce* rather than *nse.* The following list contains the words in common use that end *nse:*

35

condense	immense	prepense
defense	incense	pretense
dense	intense	recompense
dispense	license	response
expanse	manse	rinse
expense	nonsense	sense
frankincense	offense	suspense
		tense

The British spellings *defence, licence, offence,* and *pretence* are more consistent with the general pattern, but they do not appear in current American usage.

t and *d*

The regular ending of the past tense in the great majority of verbs is *ed.* This spelling is pronounced in three ways:

/id/ after *d* and *t:*   wan*ted,* fa*ded*
/d/:   *bothered, called, flowed*
/t/:   knock*ed,* hop*ed,* fish*ed*

The spelling *t* occurs in the past tense of a limited number of verbs.

1. In a few verbs ending *end:*

bend — bent   rend — rent   spend — spent
lend — lent   send — sent

But in an equal number of verbs ending *end,* the regular *ed* is found: *blended, ended, fended, mended, tended.*

2. In several verbs in which the long open sound in the present tense changes to the short checked sound in the past tense.

LO	SC	LO	SC
creep — crept		deal — dealt	
keep — kept		feel — felt	
sleep — slept		kneel — knelt	

36

sweep — swept
weep — wept

If the vowel sound does not differ in the past tense, the regular *ed* form occurs: *beeped, peeped, steeped, reeled,* etc.

3. In a few verbs in which there is no vowel change as between the present and past tenses.

Exceptions:

build — built   dwell — dwelt

XI. Doubling the Final Consonant

In One-Syllable Words

In a one-syllable word ending consonant-vowel-consonant (*c-v-c*), the vowel letter represents the short checked sound: m*a*p, r*i*p, r*u*b.

If a suffix beginning with *e, i,* or *y* is added to such words, the vowel sound changes.

$$SC \qquad LO$$
m*o*p + ing → m*o*ping
r*u*b + y   → r*u*by
str*i*p + ed → str*i*ped

To retain the short checked vowel sound, it is necessary to double the last consonant. A doubled consonant marks the short checked sound for the preceding vowel. See Section II.

Pattern: The final consonant of a one-syllable *c-v-c* word is doubled before a vowel suffix but not before a consonant suffix.

There is no change of vowel sound when a consonant suffix is added: hot + ly → hotly; big + ness → bigness. Hence, it is unnecessary to double the consonant.

The letters *w*, *x*, and *y* are never doubled:

slow + er → slower   play + ed → played
mix + ed → mixed

The doubling pattern carries over to words formed by adding a prefix to a one-syllable *c-v-c* word:

re + cap → recap → recap*p*ed
un + fit → unfit → unfi*tt*ed

The pattern also carries over to compounds in which the last element is a one-syllable *c-v-c* word:

out + fit → outfit → outfi*tt*ed
bow + leg → bowleg → bowle*gg*ed

Exception:

In American usage, the final *s* is not doubled when suffixes are added to *nonplus:* nonplused, nonplusing.

Doubling occurs in a few words which do not end *c-v-c:*

rail   + ery → rai*ll*ery
flame   + able → fla*mm*able
inflame + able → infla*mm*able; also, infla*mm*ation,
                 infla*mm*atory

In Longer Words

Doubling in longer words depends upon the location of the stress.

Doubling occurs only when the word ends *c-v-c* and only when a vowel suffix is added.

Pattern: If the last syllable of a *c-v-c* word is stressed, the final consonant is doubled before a vowel suffix, but not when a consonant suffix is added.

be	· gin′	+ er	→ begi*nn*er
re	· gret′	+ able	→ regre*tt*able
com	· mit′	+ ment	→ commi*t*ment
an	· nul′	+ ment	→ annu*l*ment

Exceptions: cha · grin′ : chagri*n*ed, chagri*n*ing
cro · chet′ : croche*t*ed, croche*t*ing
Also, words ending *fer*. See below.

For words in which the last syllable is not stressed, usage is less regular, but there is a clearly predominant pattern in American usage.

Pattern: If the last syllable of a *c-v-c* word is not stressed, the final consonant is not doubled.

ben′ e · fit + ed → benefi*t*ed
trav′ el + er → trave*l*er

Rebel and combat. These words may be used either as verbs or as nouns. In the noun form, the first syllable is stressed: *a re′ bel, the com′ bat.* In the verb form, the second syllable is stressed. Suffixes are added to the verb form of *rebel* and to the noun form of *combat.*

re · bel′ : rebe*ll*ed, rebe*ll*ion, rebe*ll*ious, etc.
com′ bat: comba*t*ed, comba*t*ant, etc.

Words ending *fer*. Current usage for these words is as follows:

confer: confe*rr*ed, confe*rr*ing, confe*rr*able, confe*rr*er
confe*rr*al
confe*r*ence (meeting), confe*rr*ence (bestowal)
confe*r*ee

defer:	deferred, deferring, deferrable, deferrer, deferral
	deference, deferent, deferential
prefer:	preferred, preferring, preferrer, preferredly
	preference, preferable, preferably, preferential
refer:	referred, referring, referrer, referral
	reference, referent, referable, referee, referential
transfer:	transferred, transferring, transferrer, transferral
	transference, transferal, transferable
	transferential, transferee
infer:	inferred, inferring, inferrer
	inference, inferable, inferential

Notes:

1. The *r* is doubled in all *fer* words before *ed, er,* and *ing.*

2. The *r* is not doubled in *fer* words before *ence, ent, ential,* or *ee.*

Words ending *ffer* follow the regular pattern. Since the first syllable in these words is stressed, there is no doubling.

$$of'fer \ + ing \ \rightarrow offering$$
$$suf'fer \ + ance \rightarrow sufferance$$

Exceptions:

In words with unstressed final syllables, the exceptions are of two sorts: **1.** Those words in which doubling occurs in all derivatives; **2.** those in which doubling occurs in only one derivative.

All derivatives

crys'tal	crystalline, crystallize, crystallizing, crystallization
met'al	metallic, metallurgy, metallize, bimetallic, bimetallism

mon'og · ram	monogrammed, monogramming, monogrammatic
pro'gram	programmed, programmer, programming, programmatic
ton'sil	tonsillar, tonsillitis, tonsillectomy

One derivative only

can'cel	cancellation
di'agram	diagrammatic
le'gion	legionnaire
med'al	medallion
prom'isor	promissory
ques'tion	questionnaire
tran'quil	tranquillity
wool	woolly

XII.   Final /l/

l or *ll*

In one-syllable words, two *l*'s are required if a single vowel letter comes immediately before final /l/. Otherwise, only one *l* appears.

> *Single vowel letter:* r*o*ll, c*a*ll, f*i*ll, p*u*ll
> *Two vowel letters:* s*ea*l, p*ee*l, g*oa*l
> *Consonant letter:* spra*w*l, sna*r*l

When *qu* occurs in these words, the sound is /kw/, and *u* is regarded as a consonant; hence: qui*ll*, squa*ll*, etc.

Words of more than one syllable usually end *l: equal, central,* etc. A number of words consist of a prefix added to a word or stem ending *ll*. When a prefix is added to a word or word stem, no other spelling change occurs. Hence, these words are not exceptions.

41

```
ap + pall   → appall        in + stall → install
en + roll   → enroll        in + still → instill
en + thrall → enthrall      di + still → distill
```

Exceptions: *atoll, idyll.*

Pattern: When a single vowel comes immediately before final /l/, one-syllable words are spelled *ll*; longer words are spelled *l*.

The Ending *al*

The ending *al* occurs in many nouns derived from adjectives. Often the form of the noun and the adjective is the same.

animal   capital   moral
cardinal   manual   principal

Other nouns ending *al* are derived from verbs.

betray*al*   deni*al*   rehears*al*
avow*al*   dismiss*al*   renew*al*

Primarily, however, *al* is an adjective ending, simply added to a noun or verb.

occasion*al*   education*al*
accident*al*   norm*al*

Vowels before final *al*. In a considerable number of adjectives another vowel letter appears before *al*. This letter often combines with the preceding consonant to spell the sounds /č/, /ǰ/, /š/, or /ž/.

act — act*u*al /č/   race — rac*i*al /š/
grade — grad*u*al /ǰ/   sense — sens*u*al /š/
part — part*i*al /š/   use — us*u*al /ž/
space — spat*i*al /š/

Usually, when *y* changes to *i* before *al,* the sound of *i* is retained.

industry — industr*i*al   bury — bur*i*al
ceremony — ceremon*i*al   try — tr*i*al

Predominantly, *i* is the vowel letter occurring before final *al.* The endings *eal* and *ial* sound alike, but *eal* occurs in only a few words in the common language. The following are those most likely to be encountered:

arbor*eal*   corpor*eal*   funer*eal*   lin*eal*
cer*eal*   lact*eal*   vener*eal*

The Endings *cal* and *cle*

The suffix *cal* is usually an adjective ending; *cle* is always a noun ending to which *s* may be added to form a plural.

A few exceptions occur because some words ending *cal* may be used either as noun or verb.

a radical   *but*   radical proposals
a chemical   *but*   chemical changes

XIII.   Vowels Before Final *r*

In an unstressed syllable, the vowel before final *r* represents the schwa sound /ə/. This sound may be spelled by any of the vowel letters.

sug′ar   fa′vor   me′ter   mar′tyr

ar

This spelling occurs in a number of commonly used words which must be remembered as separate items. For example:

altar (church)	dollar	scholar
beggar	familiar	similar
burglar	grammar	sugar
cellar	pillar	vinegar
collar	peculiar	

Pattern: In words ending **ul-r**, the letter *a* occurs before the *r*.

> **Exception:** ruler.

or

This ending occurs in a number of nouns, such as *valor, vigor, rancor,* and *honor,* which denote a general quality or condition. It also occurs in nearly 500 words with the specific meaning "one that is something or does something." Most of these words can be accounted for by the following pattern and guides.

Pattern: The suffix *or* is regularly added to verbs ending with the suffix *ate*.

> elevate + or → elevator   decorate + or → decorator

> **Exceptions:**

The exceptions are for the most part seldom-used words:

desecrater	inflater	placater
dissipater	locater	relater

Note: In words such as *hate, mate, date, bate,* and *debate* the ending *ate* is part of the word stem, not a suffix. Hence *hater, mater, debater,* etc., are not exceptions.

Guide 1: The suffix *or* is usually added to verbs ending *ct:*

> collect + or → collector
> direct   + or → director
> connect + or → connector

Exceptions:

The exceptions are for the most part seldom-used words:

abstracter	indicter	neglecter	respecter
distracter	inflicter	rejecter	

Guide 2: The suffix *or* is usually added to verbs ending *ess:*

conf*ess* + or → confessor   proc*ess* + or → processor
prof*ess* + or → professor

Exceptions: dresser, guesser, presser.

Guide 3: Words relating to rank or position, including titles of government officials and employees end *or:*

inferi*or*	juni*or*	ambassad*or*	counsel*or*
exteri*or*	jur*or*	execut*or*	

but not

higher	officer
lower	commissioner

er

In more than 2,000 words the agent suffix *er* occurs with the meaning "one who is something or does something." It is the predominant suffix bearing this meaning.

One-syllable words ending consonant-vowel-consonant (*c-v-c*) double the final consonant when vowel suffixes are added. With three exceptions, all those that add an agent ending, approximately 100, add *er.*

Pattern: The agent ending *er* is added to one-syllable *c-v-c* words.

Exceptions: warrior, bettor (one who bets), beggar.

45

XIV. Unpronounced and Doubled Consonants

In words such as *ripper* and *canned,* the doubled consonant is essential as a marker of the preceding vowel sound. Without it both sound and meaning would change: *riper, caned.* In these and similar words, the consonant is doubled. See Section XI.

In some longer words, a middle consonant is doubled, often for no apparent reason. The list of such words is almost indefinitely expansible. The following occur with enough frequency to be of general concern:

bata*ll*ion	emba*rrass*	para*ll*el	resu*rr*ect
cente*nn*ial	gu*tt*ural	pere*nn*ial	sate*ll*ite
colo*ss*al	mi*ll*enium	perso*nne*l	scinti*ll*ate
dia*rr*hea	misce*ll*aneous	po*ll*ution	sy*ll*abus
dile*mm*a	para*ff*in		sy*mm*etry

Notes:

1. The *n* in the ending *neous* is never doubled.
2. All derivatives of *tyrant* are spelled with a doubled *n:* tyra*nn*y, tyra*nn*ical, tyra*nn*ous, etc.

A related problem occurs with unpronounced consonants which may appear at any point in a word. Those occurring at the beginning cause least difficulty.

*g*naw	*k*nee	*p*salm	*w*ring
*g*narled	*k*nowledge	*p*sychology	*w*retch

At or near the end of some words, *b, g,* and *n* are not pronounced: bom*b*, autum*n*, sig*n*. But when suffixes are added, the sound of these letters is distinct: bom***bard***, autum-***nal***, ***sig***nal, etc. In general, this change occurs at syllable boundaries: *hym·nal, malig·nant,* etc.

In some words ending *sten* and *stle,* the *t* is unpronounced: glis*t*en, has*t*en, whis*t*le, etc.

In a few words *w* is unpronounced: *w*ho, *w*hole, ans*w*er, t*w*o, s*w*ord.

The letter *h* is unpronounced in a variety of words, chiefly in the following situations:

1. When separating two vowels, both of which are pronounced.

anni*h*ilate   ve*h*ement
ni*h*ilism   ve*h*icle

2. In the consonant combination *rh*.

*rh*eumatism   *rh*ubarb

3. Following the prefix *ex*.

ex*h*aust: ex*h*austion, ex*h*austible, ex*h*austive, etc.
ex*h*ibit: ex*h*ibition, ex*h*ibitor, etc.
ex*h*ilarate: ex*h*ilaration, ex*h*ilarative, etc.
ex*h*ort: ex*h*ortation, ex*h*ortative, etc.

4. In the middle of words borrowed from other languages.

diarr*h*ea   sacc*h*arine
hemmorr*h*age   sil*h*ouette

XV. Plurals

The plural of most English nouns is regularly formed by adding *s*. This includes the plural of names: *Springfields, Pedros, Kellys, Smiths, Centervilles.*

Pattern: The plural of words and names ending *s, ss, sh, x,* and *ch* is formed by adding *es*, which becomes an added syllable.

This pattern extends to one-syllable *c-v-c* words in which the last consonant is *s*.

$$yes + es \rightarrow yeses \qquad bus + es \rightarrow buses$$
$$gas + es \rightarrow gases \qquad plus + es \rightarrow pluses$$

In these words, the pattern for plurals overrides the doubling pattern. See Section XI.

Words Ending y

The plural of words ending y follows the regular pattern for adding suffixes.

Pattern: If preceded by a consonant letter, final y changes to i, and es is added to form the plural. If preceded by a vowel letter, y does not change, and s is added to form the plural.

$$coun\textit{ty} + es \rightarrow coun\textit{ties} \qquad surv\textit{ey} + s \rightarrow surv\textit{eys}$$
$$par\textit{ty} + es \rightarrow par\textit{ties} \qquad displ\textit{ay} + s \rightarrow displ\textit{ays}$$

This pattern does not apply to proper names, which are always formed by adding s: Kellys, Germanys, Shelbys, etc.

Words Ending with a Vowel

The plural of words ending a, e, i, and u is formed by adding s.

$$enigm\textit{a} + s \rightarrow enigma\textit{s} \qquad tax\textit{i} + s \rightarrow taxi\textit{s}$$
$$simil\textit{e} + s \rightarrow simile\textit{s} \qquad men\textit{u} + s \rightarrow menu\textit{s}$$

Words Ending o

When a vowel letter precedes final o, the plural is formed by adding s.

$$rad\textit{io} + s \rightarrow radio\textit{s} \qquad cam\textit{eo} + s \rightarrow cameo\textit{s}$$
$$stud\textit{io} + s \rightarrow studio\textit{s} \qquad rod\textit{eo} + s \rightarrow rodeo\textit{s}$$

When a consonant letter precedes final o, the plural is usually formed by adding s. This is true for all musical terms.

al*tos*	pia*nos*	tremo*los*
ban*jos*	concer*tos*	

48

For some words, the dictionaries show both *s* and *es* for the plural of nouns with a consonant preceding final *o*. In many instances, no indication is given as to which is the preferred spelling. Consensus of the dictionaries and of usage in current publications shows that *es* predominates in the following words and *s* predominates in all others:

bastinadoes	grottoes	noes (noun)
bravadoes	heroes	outgoes (noun)
bravoes (thugs)	hoboes	peccadilloes
cargoes	innuendoes	porticoes
desperadoes	jingoes	potatoes
dominoes (game)	lingoes	strappadoes
echoes	magnificoes	stuccoes
embargoes	mangoes	tornadoes
fiascoes	manifestoes	torpedoes
frescoes	mosquitoes	vertigoes
fungoes	mottoes	vetoes
goes (noun)	mulattoes	viragoes
	Negroes	volcanoes

Compound Words

Usually, the most important noun in a compound is made plural. This noun never occurs in a modifying phrase. Compounds consisting of a noun or verb plus an adverb follow no consistent pattern.

attorneys-general	lyings-in		build-ups
attorneys-at-law	goings-on	*but*	sit-ins
commanders-in-chief	passers-by		lean-tos
brothers-in-law	hangers-on		talking-tos

Numbers, Signs, and Letters

The plural is formed by adding *'s*.

5's   &'s   t's   three R's   ABC's

If the number is written out, the plural is formed by adding *s* or by changing *y* to *i* and adding *es: fours, twenties*. The plurals of decades are either written out: *twenties, seventies;* or written in figures without an apostrophe: *1980s.*

Words as Items

The plurals of words considered as words are formed by adding *s*, but for clarity *'s* is used in some constructions:

ins and outs	is's
ohs and ahs	the's
ups and downs	do's and don'ts

Words of Quantity

The plurals of words ending *ful* are formed by adding a final *s:* cupful*s*, roomful*s*.

When words such as *dozen, score,* and *hundred* occur in a modifier position before nouns, no *s* is added.

four score years	seven-year itch
several dozen women	
four hundred pages	

Words from Latin and Greek

The basic pattern in American English is to form the plural of Latin words by adding *s:*

podiums	plantariums
aquariums	deliriums

In some words the Latin plural has been absorbed into English:

Singular	*Plural*	*Singular*	*Plural*
addendum	— addenda	medium	— media
alga	— algae	minutia	— minutiae
alumnus	— alumni	stratum	— strata

datum — data   radius — radii
fungus — fungi

The plural of Greek words follows no consistent pattern. For some words, the Greek plural has been absorbed into English; for others, the plural is formed by adding *s:*

analysis — analyses   carcinoma — carcinomas
crisis — crises   gymnasium — gymnasiums
criterion — criteria   stadium — stadiums
phenomenon — phenomena   (building)

Words Ending *f*

There is no consistent plural pattern. In some words *f* changes to *v* and *es* is added. In others, the plural is formed by adding *s:*

leaf — leaves   reef — reefs
thief — thieves   dwarf — dwarfs
wolf — wolves   belief — beliefs

Change of Vowel Letter

In seven words the plural is formed by the change of the vowel letters:

foot — feet   mouse — mice
goose — geese   tooth — teeth
louse — lice   woman — women
man — men

XVI. Compound Words

Strictly speaking, the writing of compound words is a matter of punctuation rather than of spelling, but for most writers, the question of how to write a word is a matter of spelling whether the word is compound or not.

The parts of a compound word may be hyphenated (*heart-rending*), closed up (*heartbeat*), or written separately (*heart failure*). There is no regular pattern. Predominant usage varies almost from year to year. The trend is to close up the parts of a compound word as soon as it becomes securely established in the language. The family of Webster's dictionaries published by G. & C. Merriam Company has noted this trend in every major edition since 1890.

Since practice is irregular and the writing of a particular compound unpredictable, it is necessary to consult a reference when uncertainty arises. It may be observed that the dictionaries disagree more widely on the writing of compound words than on any other matter.

The main area of contention is in the use of hyphens. In general, there is less use of hyphens than formerly: many words once hyphenated are now closed up. There are, nonetheless, some compound words in which hyphens are required for clarity or firmly established by usage. The patterns which follow are predominant in current usage.

Compounds as Unit Modifiers

When a compound is used as a modifying unit directly before or after the word it modifies, the parts are joined by hyphens. A variety of grammatical elements may be combined to act as a unit modifier, but the same combination used as a complement or adverbial modifier is usually not a compound and is therefore not hyphenated.

It was an *across-the-board* salary cut. (adj. modifier)
The salary cut was *across the board*. (complement)
They played it *across the board*. (adv. modifier)
It is a *well-known* fact. (adj. modifier)
His disability was *well known*. (complement)

The following examples of unit modifiers are representative; others may be found in the main listing of this *Handbook*.

above-mentioned	daylight-saving time
age-old	ball-park
air-to-air	bell-bottom
all-important	black-and-blue
awe-struck	bleary-eyed
blow-by-blow	blue-green

Compounds as Nouns

Compounds consisting of noun + noun or noun + adjective are not usually hyphenated when used as nouns: *coffee break, coffeepot, cold cream, colorblind.*

Other grammatical combinations may be hyphenated when used as nouns, but there are many in which no hyphen occurs. As a consequence it is essential to use a reference in order to determine the predominant spelling. The following examples are representative:

blast-off	checkup
close-up	childbearing
cover-up	churchgoing
crack-up	clearing house
cross-reference	comeback

Compounds as Verbs

Many compounds used as verbs have been in the language a long time. In the general drift away from use of hyphens, they have come to be written solid: *to eavesdrop, to safeguard, to broadcast.* Verbs consisting of a verb + adverb are usually written as separate words:

to wind up the clock	to watch out for danger
to look up a record	to call on a friend

Those compounds of more recent origin used as verbs are generally hyphenated. They may consist of a variety of grammatical elements. The following examples are representative:

to chain-smoke   to cross-file
to dry-clean   to deep-fry
to crash-dive   to double-cross
to ad-lib   to double-space

Conventional Uses of Hyphens

The following uses of hyphens are conventional means of helping the reader to follow meaning and avoid misunderstanding:

1. Titles

    secretary-treasurer
    representative-at-large

2. Composite numbers and fractions

    twenty-one   one-half (*adj.* or *adv.*)
    twenty-first   a two-thirds majority

3. Avoidance of triple consonants

    bell-like   hull-less
    well-liked

4. Apostrophe in the first element

    bird's-eye   hound's-tooth
    cat's-paw   baby's-breath

5. Family relationships

    father-in-law   daughter-in-law
    great-grandmother   great-aunt

but

    granddad   stepson
    grandson   stepfather

Nonce Words and Invented Words

Nonce words are those created for a particular occasion or situation. If they are especially striking, they may persist and enter the language. Related to them are invented words, coined to express a new notion or device. If nonce words and invented words are compounds, they are usually hyphenated:

A-OK	degree-day	fail-safe
carry-back	do-it-yourself	rent-a-car
cease-fire	double-think	sit-in

but

space suit	space station	thruway

Prefixes

Usually prefixes are joined solid to the following element unless it begins with a capital in which case a hyphen is required.

unbalanced	nonresident	anticlimax
un-American	non-Aryan	anti-Nazi

For a full discussion of this subject, see Section VI, where the usage of hyphens with prefixes is presented.

XVII. Dictionary Spellings

For many words, the dictionaries show *variant* spellings; that is, two or more different spellings. In some instances there is no clear indication of which spelling occurs more frequently and is therefore preferred. Usually, however, a preference is shown. But for about 2,000 words in the common language, the dictionaries disagree as to which spelling is predominant.

This difference of opinion is in sharp contrast to the uniformity of spelling observed in current publications. To anyone acquainted with the long struggle to regularize English spelling, this uniformity is a remarkable achievement which should not be obscured by the diversity found in the dictionaries.

Two questions arise: 1. Why does this difference between the dictionaries and other current publications exist? 2. Why do the dictionaries disagree? The answers lie in the method and purpose of dictionary making.

A dictionary is a collection of usages, derived from perusal of printed materials by editors and their readers. If enough instances of a variant spelling occur in this reading, the editors include it in the dictionary. Necessarily, the editors of one dictionary do not read the same materials as the editors of another. They may easily disagree, therefore, as to the frequency with which a particular spelling occurs.

Most of the established dictionaries undergo frequent revision. Spellings change, as a result, from one edition of a dictionary to another.

Every dictionary has its own system of indicating frequency or preference of spellings. Occasionally, the editors find that two spellings occur with equal frequency. This is indicated by placing them together in alphabetic order, or with the word *or* between them. In these instances, the editors are unwilling or unable to indicate any preference.

When the frequency of usage does differ, the following devices are used to mark one spelling as preferable to the others that may be shown:

1. A spelling found in one dictionary may not occur at all in another, suggesting that the editors do not find it important enough to be considered.
2. The editors may state in the introduction to the work that the first of two or more spellings is preferred. On the other hand, two dictionaries specifically state that the first spelling is no more to be preferred than the second.
3. Limiting labels such as *archaic, poetic, obsolete,* or *British* may indicate that the spelling is not suitable for general American use.

4. If the word *Also* appears between two spellings, the second is less frequent, and the first is preferred.
5. If variant spellings are widely separated in the entry list, the definitions occur with the more frequent spelling. The others are marked *Var.* or *Same as.* . . .
6. If two spellings shown together are out of alphabetic order, the first is usually the preferred spelling.

The introductory pages of a dictionary contain an explanation of the methods used to indicate preference. This explanation must be read and understood if the work is to be used effectively for spelling reference.

In this *Handbook,* only one spelling is given for each of the 20,000 words in the Word List. This is the predominant American spelling so far as can be determined by consensus of the major dictionaries, style manuals, and the usage of current American periodicals, books, newspapers, and other publications.

The Listing

A

ab·a·cus, *plural*
  abacuses
ab·a·lo·ne
aban·don
abate
abate·ment
ab·bé (title)
ab·bey (monastery
  or church)
ab·bre·vi·ate
ABC's
ab·di·cate
ab·di·ca·tor
ab·do·men
ab·dom·i·nal
ab·duc·tor
ab·er·rance
ab·er·rant
ab·er·ra·tion
abet
abet·ment
abet·ted
abet·ting
abet·tor
abey·ance
abey·ant
ab·hor

ab·horred
ab·hor·rence
ab·hor·rent
ab·hor·ring
ab·jure
ab·jur·er
able-bod·ied
ab·lu·tion
ab·lu·tion·ary
ab·ne·gate
ab·ne·ga·tor
ab·nor·mal
ab·nor·mal·i·ty
ab·nor·mi·ty
abol·ish
ab·o·li·tion
ab·o·li·tion·ary
abom·i·na·ble
abom·i·nate
ab·o·rig·i·ne
abort
about-face
above·board
above·ground
above-men·tioned
above-named
ab·ra·ca·dab·ra

abrade
ab·ra·sion
ab·ra·sive
abridg·a·ble
abridg·er
abridg·ing
abridg·ment
ab·ro·gate
ab·ro·ga·tor
ab·scess
ab·scise
ab·scis·sa, *plural*
  abscissas
ab·scond
ab·scond·er
ab·sence
ab·sen·tee
ab·sen·tee·ism
ab·sent-mind·ed
ab·sent with·out
  leave
ab·sinthe
ab·solve
ab·solv·er
ab·sorb
ab·sorb·able
ab·sor·ben·cy

Note: The word divisions in this handbook are for purposes of typing or preparing copy; they are not
    intended as guides to pronunciation.

ab·sor·bent
ab·sorb·er
ab·sorp·tion
ab·stain
ab·stain·er
ab·ste·mi·ous
ab·sten·tion
ab·sti·nence
ab·sti·nent
ab·stract·er
ab·strac·tion
ab·surd
ab·sur·di·ty
abun·dance
abun·dant
abuse
abu·sive
abut
abut·ment
abut·tal
abut·ted
abut·ter
abut·ting
abys·mal
abyss
ac·a·dem·ic
ac·a·de·mi·cian
acad·e·my
a cap·pel·la
ac·cede
ac·ced·ence
ac·cel·er·ate
ac·cel·er·a·tor
ac·cent
ac·cen·tu·ate
ac·cept (receive;
   see except)
ac·cept·able

ac·cep·tance
ac·cept·er
ac·cep·tor
   (finance)
ac·cess (admit-
   tance, increase;
   see excess)
ac·ces·si·ble
ac·ces·sion
ac·ces·so·ry
ac·ci·dence
ac·ci·dent
ac·claim
ac·claim·er
ac·cla·ma·tion
   (approval)
ac·cli·mate
ac·cli·ma·tion
   (adjustment)
ac·cli·ma·tize
ac·co·lade
ac·com·mo·date
ac·com·mo·da·tion
ac·com·mo·da·tor
ac·com·pa·ny
ac·com·pa·ni·ment
ac·com·pa·nist
ac·com·plice
ac·com·plish
ac·com·plish·able
ac·cord
ac·cor·dance
ac·cor·dant
ac·cor·di·on
ac·cost
ac·count
ac·count·able
ac·count·an·cy

ac·count·ant
ac·cou·ter
ac·cou·ter·ment
ac·cred·it
ac·cre·tion
ac·cru·al
ac·crue
ac·crued
ac·crue·ment
ac·cru·ing
ac·cu·mu·late
ac·cu·mu·la·tor
ac·cu·ra·cy
ac·cu·rate
ac·curs·ed
ac·cus·al
ac·cu·sa·to·ry
ac·cus·er
ac·cus·tom
ace-high
ace in the hole
acerb
ac·er·bate
acer·bi·ty
ace·tic (acid)
acet·y·lene
achieve
achiev·able
achieve·ment
achiev·er
acid·ic
acid·i·fy
acid·i·ty
ac·i·do·sis
acid·u·lous
ac·knowl·edge·able
ac·knowl·edg·ment
ac·me

ac·ne
acous·tics
ac·quaint
ac·quaint·ance
ac·qui·esce
ac·qui·es·cence
ac·qui·es·cent
ac·quir·able
ac·quire
ac·quire·ment
ac·qui·si·tion
ac·quis·i·tive
ac·quit
ac·quit·tal
ac·quit·tance
ac·quit·ted
ac·quit·ting
acre
acre·age
ac·rid
ac·ri·mo·ni·ous
ac·ri·mo·ny
ac·ro·bat
ac·ro·nym
ac·ro·pho·bia
acrop·o·lis
across-the-board
  (adj)
acros·tic
acryl·ic
ac·tion·able
ac·ti·vate
ac·ti·va·tion
ac·ti·va·tor
act of God
act of war
ac·tor
ac·tu·al

ac·tu·al·i·ty
ac·tu·al·ize
ac·tu·al·ly
ac·tu·ar·i·al
ac·tu·ary
ac·tu·ate
ac·tu·a·tor
acu·ity
acu·men
acu·punc·ture
ad·age
ada·gio, *plural*
  adagios
ad·a·mant
adapt·able
adapt·er
add·able
ad·den·dum, *plural*
  addenda
ad·dict
ad·di·tive
ad·dle
ad·dle·brained
ad·dress
ad·dress·ee
ad·dress·er
ad·duce
ad·duc·er
ad·duc·i·ble
ad·e·noi·dal
ad·e·noids
adept
ad·e·qua·cy
ad·e·quate
ad·her·ence
ad·her·ent
ad·he·sive
ad hoc

adieu, *plural* adieus
ad in·fi·ni·tum
ad in·ter·im
ad·i·pose
ad·ja·cen·cy
ad·ja·cent
ad·join
ad·journ
ad·judge
ad·ju·di·cate
ad·ju·di·ca·tor
ad·junct
ad·ju·ra·tion
ad·jure
ad·jur·er
ad·just
ad·just·able
ad·just·er
ad·ju·tan·cy
ad·ju·tant
ad-lib (*verb, noun,*
  adj)
ad lib (*adv*)
ad-libbed
ad-lib·bing
ad·min·is·ter
ad·min·is·tra·ble
ad·min·is·tra·tor
ad·mi·ra·ble
ad·mi·ral
ad·mi·ral·ty
ad·mir·er
ad·mis·si·ble
ad·mis·sion
ad·mit·ta·ble
ad·mit·tance
ad·mit·ted
ad·mit·ting

ad·mo·ni·tion
ad·mon·i·tor
ad·mon·i·to·ry
ad nau·se·am
ado·be
ad·o·les·cence
ad·o·les·cent
adopt·able
adop·ter
adop·tion
ador·able
ad·o·ra·tion
adorn
ad·re·nal
adroit
ad·sci·ti·tious
ad·sorb
ad·sorb·able
ad·sor·bent
ad·sorp·tion
ad·u·late
ad·u·la·tor
ad·u·la·to·ry
adul·ter·ant
adul·ter·ate
adul·ter·a·tor
adul·ter·er
adul·ter·ess
  (woman)
adul·ter·ous
  (pertaining to or
  guilty of)
adul·tery
ad va·lo·rem
ad·vanced stand·ing
ad·vance·ment
ad·van·ta·geous
ad·ven·ti·tious

ad·ven·tur·er
ad·ven·ture·some
ad·ven·tur·ess
  (woman)
ad·ven·tur·ous
  (daring)
ad·ver·sary
ad·verse
ad·ver·si·ty
ad·vert (refer)
ad·ver·tence
ad·ver·tent
ad·ver·tise
ad·ver·tise·ment
ad·ver·tis·er
ad·vice (opinion
  given)
ad·vis·able
ad·vise (to give
  advice)
ad·vise·ment
ad·vis·er
ad·vi·so·ry
ad·vo·ca·cy
ad·vo·cate
ad·vo·ca·tor
adz
ae·gis
aer·ate
aer·a·tor
aer·i·al (TV, radio;
  see areal)
aer·i·al·ist
ae·rie
aero·bat·ics
aero·dy·nam·ics
aero·med·i·cine
aero·nau·tics

aero·sol
aero·space
aes·thete
aes·thet·ic
afeard
af·fa·ble
af·fair
af·fect (*verb* to
  influence or
  pretend, *noun*
  feeling or
  stimulus; *see*
  effect)
af·fec·ta·tion
af·fec·tion
af·fec·tive (relating
  to emotion)
af·fer·ent
af·fi·ance
af·fi·da·vit
af·fil·i·ate
af·fin·i·ty
af·firm
af·firm·able
af·fir·ma·tive
af·firm·er
af·fix
af·fixed
af·fix·ing
af·fla·tus
af·flict
af·flic·tion
af·flu·ence
af·flu·ent
af·ford
af·for·es·ta·tion
af·fran·chise
af·fright

af·front
afore·men·tioned
afore·said
afraid
Af·ro-Amer·i·can
Af·ro-As·ian
af·ter (Compound
   words beginning
   with *after* are
   written solid
   without a hyphen
   or word break:
   aftercare.)
af·ter·ward
agape
ag·ate
ag·ate·ware
age·less
age·long
agen·cy
agen·da, *plural*
   agendas
age-old
ag·er·a·tum
ag·glom·er·ate
ag·glu·ti·nate
ag·gran·dize
ag·gran·di·zer
ag·gra·vate
ag·gra·va·tion
ag·gra·va·tor
ag·gre·gate
ag·gres·sion
ag·gres·sive
ag·gres·sor
ag·grieve
aghast
ag·ile

ag·ile·ly
agil·i·ty
ag·ing
ag·i·tate
ag·i·ta·tor
aglit·ter
aglow
ag·nos·tic
agog
à go·go
ag·o·nize
ag·o·ny
agrar·i·an
agree·able
agreed
agree·ing
agron·o·my
ague
agu·ish
aide (assistant)
aide-de-camp, *plural*
   aides-de-camp
aide-mé·moire
ai·grette
air base
air·borne
air brake
air·brush
air coach
air-con·di·tion
   (*verb*)
air-con·di·tioned
air con·di·tion·er
air con·di·tion·ing
air-cool (*verb*)
air-cooled
air·craft
air·crew

air cush·ion
air·drop
air·dropped
air·drop·ping
air ex·press
air·field
air·flow
air·foil
air force
air freight
air gun
air·i·er
air·i·ly
air·i·ness
air·lane
air·lift
air·line
air·mail (*noun* and
   verb)
air·man
air mass
air-mind·ed
air·plane
air·port
air raid
air ri·fle
air shaft
air·sick
air·space
air·speed
air·strip
air·tight
air-to-air (*adj*)
air-to-sur·face (*adj*)
air·wave
air·way
air·wor·thy
aisle

akim·bo
al·a·bas·ter
a la carte
alac·ri·ty
à la king
a la mode
alarm clock
al·ba·tross
al·be·it
al·bi·no, *plural*
  albinos
al·bum
al·bu·men (egg)
al·bu·min
  (biochemistry)
al·che·my
al·co·hol
al·cove
al·der·man
alert
al·fal·fa
al·fres·co
al·ga, *plural* algae
al·ge·bra·ic
alias, *plural* aliases
al·i·bi, *plural* alibis
al·i·bied
al·i·bi·ing
alien
alien·able
alien·a·tor
alien·or
align
align·ment
al·i·men·ta·ry
  (food)
al·i·mo·ny

al·ka·li, *plural*
  alkalis
all-Amer·i·can
all-around (*adj*)
al·lay
al·layed
al·lay·er
al·lay·ing
all clear (*noun*)
al·le·ga·tion
al·lege
al·lege·a·ble
al·leged
al·le·giance
al·leg·ing
al·le·gor·i·cal
al·le·go·rist
al·le·go·rize
al·le·go·ry
al·ler·gic
al·ler·gy
al·le·vi·ate
al·ley, *plural* alleys
al·ley cat
al·ley·way
all-fired
All Fools' Day
all fours
al·li·ance
al·lied
al·lies
al·li·ga·tor
all-im·por·tant
all-in·clu·sive
al·lit·er·a·tion
al·lo·ca·ble
al·lo·cate

al·lo·cat·ed
al·lo·cat·ing
al·lo·ca·tion
al·lot
al·lot·ment
al·lot·ted
al·lot·ting
all-out (*adj*)
all out (*adv*)
all·over (*adj*)
all over (*adv*)
al·low·able
al·low·ance
al·loy, *plural* alloys
al·loyed
al·loy·ing
all-pur·pose
all right
  (satisfactory)
all-round
All Saints' Day
All Souls' Day
all·spice
all-star (*adj*)
all-time
all told
al·lude (refer)
al·lure
al·lure·ment
al·lu·sion
  (reference)
al·lu·sive
al·ly
al·ly·ing
al·ma ma·ter
al·ma·nac
al·might·i·ness

Al·mighty (God)
al·mighty
al·mond
al·mo·ner
al·oe, *plural* aloes
along·shore
along·side
al·pha·bet·ic
al·pha·bet·ize
al·pha·nu·mer·ic
al·ready
    (previously)
al·so-ran
al·tar (center of
    worship)
al·tar boy
al·tarpiece
al·tar rail
al·ter (change)
al·ter·able
al·ter·ant
al·ter·ca·tion
al·ter·nate
al·ter·na·tor
al·though
al·tim·e·ter
al·ti·tude
al·to, *plural* altos
al·to·geth·er
    (completely, on
    the whole)
al·tru·ism
alu·mi·num
alum·na (*fem*),
    plural alumnae
alum·nus (*masc* or
fem), *plural* alumni

A.M. (before noon)
amal·gam
amal·gam·a·tor
am·a·ryl·lis
amass
amass·er
am·a·teur
am·a·to·ry
amaze
amazed
amaze·ment
amaz·ing
am·bas·sa·dor
am·bas·sa·do·ri·al
am·ber
am·ber·gris
am·bi·ance
am·bi·dex·trous
am·bi·ent
am·bi·gu·ity
am·big·u·ous
am·bit
am·bi·tion
am·bi·tous
am·biv·a·lence
am·biv·a·lent
am·ble
am·bler
am·bu·lance
am·bu·lant
am·bu·la·to·ry
am·bus·cade
ame·lio·rate
ame·lio·ra·tor
amen·a·ble
amend (to change;
    see emend)

amend·able
amen·da·to·ry
amend·er
amen·i·ty
Amer·i·ca·na
Amer·i·can·ize
am·e·thyst
ami·a·ble
am·i·ca·ble
amiss
am·mo·nia
am·mu·ni·tion
am·ne·sia
am·nes·ty
amoe·ba, *plural*
    amoebas
amok (*noun*)
am·o·rous
amor·phous
am·or·tiz·able
am·or·tize
am·phib·i·an
am·phib·i·ous
am·phi·the·a·ter
am·pho·ra, *plural*
    amphoras
am·ple (sufficient)
am·pli·fied
am·pli·fy
am·pli·fy·ing
am·pli·tude
am·ply
am·pul (container)
am·pu·tate
am·pu·ta·tion
am·pu·ta·tor
am·pu·tee

am·trac
amuck (*adj* and *adv*)
am·u·let
amus·er
anach·ro·nism
ana·gram
ana·gram·mat·ic
ana·grammed
an·al·ge·sic
an·a·log com·pu·ter
anal·o·gize
anal·o·gous
an·a·logue
anal·o·gy
anal·y·sis, *plural*
    analyses
an·a·lyst
an·a·lyt·ic
an·a·lyze
an·a·lyz·er
an·a·lyz·ing
an·ar·chist
an·ar·chy
anath·e·ma
anat·o·my
an·ces·tor
an·ces·tral
an·ces·try
an·chor
an·chor man
an·cho·vy
an·cient
an·cil·lary
and·iron
an·ec·dote
an·e·cho·ic

ane·mia
ane·mic
anem·o·ne
an·es·the·sia
an·es·thet·ic
an·es·the·tist
an·es·the·tize
an·eu·rysm
an·gel food cake
an·gel·ic
An·ge·lus
an·gi·na
an·gle iron
an·gler
an·gle·worm
An·gli·cism
An·gli·cize
An·glo-Amer·i·can
An·glo-Cath·o·lic
An·glo-Nor·man
An·glo·phile
An·glo·phobe
An·glo-Sax·on
an·gri·er
an·gri·ly
an·guish
an·gu·lar
an·i·line
an·i·mad·ver·sion
an·i·mad·vert
an·i·mate
an·i·ma·tor
an·i·mos·i·ty
an·i·mus
anise
an·kle·bone

an·nal·ist
an·nals
an·neal
an·nex
an·nex·a·tion
an·nexed
an·nex·ing
an·ni·hi·late
an·ni·hi·la·tor
an·ni·ver·sa·ry
an·no·tate
an·no·ta·tor
an·nounce
an·nounce·ment
an·nounc·er
an·noy·ance
an·noyed
an·noy·er
an·noy·ing
an·nu·al
an·nu·i·tant
an·nu·i·ty
an·nul
an·nu·lar
an·nulled
an·nul·ling
an·nul·ment
an·nun·ci·ate
an·nun·ci·a·tor
an·o·dyne
anoint
anom·a·lous
anom·a·ly
an·o·mie
an·o·nym
an·o·nym·i·ty

anon·y·mous
an·swer·able
an·tag·o·nism
an·tag·o·nist
an·tag·o·nize
ant·arc·tic
Ant·arc·ti·ca
an·te (stake)
an·te·bel·lum
an·te·cede
an·te·ced·ence
an·te·ced·ent
an·te·cham·ber
an·ted (*verb*)
an·te·date
an·te·di·lu·vi·an
an·te·ing (*verb*)
an·te·lope
an·te·me·ri·di·an
an·te me·ri·di·em
  (A.M.)
an·ten·na (radio),
  plural antennas
  (biology), *plural*
  antennae
an·te·ri·or
an·te·room
an·them
an·ther
ant·hill
an·thol·o·gist
an·thol·o·gize
an·thol·o·gy
an·thra·cite
an·thro·poid
an·thro·pol·o·gy

an·ti (Words
  beginning with the
  prefix *anti* are
  written solid:
  antibody, unless
  the second
  element begins
  with a capital
  letter: *anti-*
  American or as
  otherwise shown
  below.)
an·ti·air·craft
an·ti-bal·lis·tic
  mis·sile
an·ti·bi·ot·ic
an·tic, *plural* antics
an·tic·i·pate
an·tic·i·pa·tor
an·tic·i·pa·to·ry
an·ticked
an·tick·ing
an·ti·cli·mac·tic
an·ti·cli·max
an·ti·dote
an·ti·gen
an·ti-he·ro
an·ti·his·ta·mine
an·ti-ic·er
an·ti-
  in·tel·lec·tu·al
an·ti·ma·cas·sar
an·ti·pas·to
an·tip·a·thet·ic
an·tip·a·thy
an·tiph·o·nal

an·tiph·o·ny
an·ti·quary
an·ti·quate
an·tique
an·tiq·ui·ty
an·ti-Se·mit·ic
an·ti·sep·tic
an·ti·se·rum
an·tith·e·sis
an·ti·thet·ic
an·ti·tox·in
an·ti·viv·i·sec·tion
an·vil
anx·i·ety
anx·ious
any·more
any·way
any·wise
A-OK
apart·heid
ap·a·thet·ic
ap·a·thy
aper·i·tif
ap·er·ture
apex, *plural* apexes
apha·sia
aphid
aph·o·rism
aph·ro·dis·i·ac
api·ary
apiece
aplomb
apoc·a·lypse
apoc·ry·phal
apo·gee
apol·o·get·ic

apol·o·gize
apol·o·gy
ap·o·plec·tic
ap·o·plexy
apos·ta·sy
apos·tate
apos·tle (emissary,
    advocate; see
    epistle)
ap·os·tol·ic
apos·tro·phe
apoth·e·cary
ap·pall
ap·palled
ap·pal·ling
ap·pa·nage
ap·pa·ra·tus (*sing*
    and *plural*)
ap·par·el
ap·par·eled
ap·par·el·ing
ap·par·ent
ap·pa·ri·tion
ap·peal
ap·peal·able
ap·pealed
ap·peal·ing
ap·pear
ap·pear·ance
ap·peas·able
ap·pease
ap·pease·ment
ap·peas·er
ap·pel·lant
ap·pel·late
ap·pel·la·tion
ap·pel·lee

ap·pend
ap·pend·age
ap·pen·dant
ap·pen·dec·to·my
ap·pen·di·ci·tis
ap·pen·dix, *plural*
    appendixes
ap·per·cep·tion
ap·per·tain
ap·pe·ten·cy
ap·pe·tite
ap·pe·tiz·er
ap·pe·tiz·ing
ap·plaud
ap·plaud·er
ap·plause
ap·ple·cart
ap·ple green
ap·ple·jack
ap·ple-pie or·der
ap·ple pol·ish·er
ap·ple·sauce
ap·pli·ance
ap·pli·ca·ble
ap·pli·cant
ap·pli·ca·tor
ap·plied
ap·pli·er
ap·pli·qué
ap·pli·quéd
ap·pli·qué·ing
ap·pli·qués
ap·point
ap·point·ee
ap·point·er
ap·point·ive
ap·point·ment

ap·poin·tor (law)
ap·por·tion
ap·por·tion·ment
ap·pos·a·ble
ap·pose
ap·po·site
ap·po·si·tion
ap·pos·i·tive
ap·prais·a·ble
ap·prais·al
ap·prais·er
ap·pre·cia·ble
ap·pre·ci·ate
ap·pre·cia·tive
ap·pre·ci·a·tor
ap·pre·hend
ap·pre·hen·si·ble
ap·pre·hen·sion
ap·pre·hen·sive
ap·pren·tice·ship
ap·prise (inform)
ap·proach
ap·proach·able
ap·pro·ba·tion
ap·pro·ba·to·ry
ap·pro·pri·a·ble
ap·pro·pri·ate
ap·pro·pri·a·tive
ap·pro·pri·a·tor
ap·prov·able
ap·prov·al
ap·prove
ap·prov·er
ap·prov·ing
ap·prox·i·mal
ap·prox·i·mate
ap·pur·te·nance

ap·pur·te·nant
apri·cot
April fool
April Fools' Day
a pri·o·ri
ap·ro·pos
apse
ap·ti·tude
aq·ua·cade
aq·ua·ma·rine
aq·ua·plane
aquar·i·um, *plural*
    aquariums
aquat·ic (*adj*)
aquat·ics (*noun*)
aq·ua·tint
aq·ue·duct
aque·ous
aq·ui·line
Ar·a·bic nu·mer·al
ar·a·besque
ar·a·ble
ar·bi·ter
ar·bi·tra·ble
ar·bi·trage
ar·bit·ra·ment
ar·bi·trary
ar·bi·trate
ar·bi·tra·tor
ar·bor
ar·bo·re·al
ar·bo·re·tum
ar·bu·tus
ar·chae·ol·o·gist
ar·chae·ol·o·gy
ar·cha·ic
ar·cha·ism

arch·an·gel
arch·di·o·cese
arch·duke
arch·en·e·my
arch·ery
ar·che·type
ar·chi·pel·a·go,
    plural archi-
    pelagos
ar·chi·tect
ar·chi·tec·ture
ar·chi·val
ar·chive
ar·chi·vist
arch·way
arcked (arc)
arcking
arc·tic
Arc·tic Cir·cle
Arc·tic Ocean
ar·den·cy
ar·dent
ar·dor
ar·du·ous
ar·ea code
ar·e·al (area; *see*
    aerial)
ar·ea·way
are·na
ar·go·sy
ar·got
ar·gu·able
ar·gue
ar·gued
ar·gu·fy
ar·gu·ing
ar·gu·ment

ar·gyle
ar·id
arid·i·ty
ar·is·toc·ra·cy
ar·is·to·crat
arith·me·ti·cian
ar·ma·da
ar·ma·ment
ar·ma·ture
arm·chair
armed forces
arm·ful, *plural*
    armfuls
arm·hole
ar·mi·stice
ar·mor
ar·mor·er
ar·mory
arm·pit
arm·rest
ar·my ant
Ar·my of the Unit·ed
    States
ar·my worm
aro·ma
ar·o·mat·ic
arous·al
arouse
ar·raign
ar·range·ment
ar·rang·er
ar·rant (out-and-
    out; *see* errant)
ar·ray
ar·ray·al
ar·rayed
ar·ray·ing

ar·rear·age
ar·rears
ar·rest
ar·rest·er
ar·riv·al
ar·ro·gance
ar·ro·gant
ar·ro·gate
ar·row·head
ar·row·root
ar·royo, *plural*
  arroyos
ar·se·nal
ar·se·nic
ar·son
ar·te·ri·al
ar·tery
ar·te·sian well
ar·thri·tis
ar·ti·choke
ar·ti·cle
ar·tic·u·lar
ar·tic·u·late
ar·tic·u·la·tor
ar·ti·fact
ar·ti·fice
ar·ti·fi·cer
ar·ti·fi·cial
ar·til·lery
ar·ti·san
ar·tist·ry
asa·fet·i·da
as·bes·tos
as·cend
as·cend·able
as·cend·ance
as·cen·dan·cy
as·cen·dant

as·cend·er
as·cen·sion
as·cent (rise)
as·cer·tain
as·cer·tain·able
as·cet·ic
as·cet·i·cism
as·crib·able
as·cribe
as·crip·tion
asep·tic
ash·can
ash·tray
as·i·nine
as·i·nin·i·ty
askance
askew
as·par·a·gus
as·per·i·ty
as·per·sion
as·phalt
as·phyx·i·ate
as·phyx·i·a·tor
as·pic
as·pir·ant
as·pi·rate
as·pi·ra·tion
as·pi·ra·tor
as·pi·rin
as·sail
as·sail·able
as·sail·ant
as·sail·er
as·sas·sin
as·sas·si·nate
as·sault
as·say (analysis)
as·say·er

as·sem·blage
as·sem·ble
as·sem·bler
as·sem·bly line
as·sem·bly·man
as·sem·bly plant
as·sent (agreement)
as·sent·er
as·sert·er
as·ser·tion
as·sert·ive
as·sess
as·sess·able
as·sess·ment
as·ses·sor
as·sev·er·ate
as·si·du·ity
as·sid·u·ous
as·sign
as·sign·able
as·sig·na·tion
as·sign·ee
as·sign·er
as·sign·or (law)
as·sim·i·la·ble
as·sim·i·late
as·sis·tance
as·sis·tant
as·size
as·so·ci·ate
as·so·ci·a·tion
as·so·ci·a·tive
as·so·nance
as·sort
as·sort·ed
as·sort·ment
as·suage
as·suage·ment

as·sum·able
as·sume
as·sump·tion
as·sur·ance
as·sure (to give
    confidence, make
    certain)
as·sured
as·sur·er
as·ter
as·ter·isk
as·ter·oid
asth·ma
as·tig·ma·tism
as·ton·ish
as·tound
astrad·dle
as·tra·khan
as·trin·gen·cy
as·trin·gent
as·tro·dome
as·trol·o·ger
as·trol·o·gy
as·tro·naut
as·tro·nau·tics
as·tron·o·mer
as·tro·nom·i·cal
as·tron·o·my
as·tute
asun·der
asy·lum
asym·met·ric
at·a·vism
atax·ia
athe·ism
ath·lete
ath·let·ic
at-home (*noun*)

athwart
at·mo·sphere
atoll
at·om
at·om bomb
at·om·ize
at·om·iz·er
atone·ment
atro·cious
atroc·i·ty
at·ro·phy
at·tach·able
at·ta·ché
at·ta·ché case
at·tacked
at·tack·ing
at·tain
at·tain·able
at·tain·der
at·tar
at·tempt
at·tend
at·ten·dance
at·ten·dant
at·ten·tion
at·ten·u·ate
at·ten·u·a·tor
at·test
at·tes·ta·tion
at·test·er
at·tire
at·ti·tude
at·ti·tu·di·nize
at·tor·ney
at·tor·ney at law
at·tor·neys gen·er·al
at·tract
at·tract·able

at·trac·tor
at·trib·ut·able
at·trib·ute
at·trib·ut·er
at·trib·u·tive
at·tri·tion
at·tune
atyp·i·cal
au·burn
auc·tion·eer
au·da·cious
au·dac·i·ty
au·di·ble
au·di·ence
au·dio·vi·su·al
au·dit
au·dit·ed
au·dit·ing
au·di·tion
au·di·tor
au·di·to·ri·um
au·di·to·ry
au·ger (tool)
aught (anything
    whatever; *see*
    ought)
aug·ment·er
au gra·tin
au·gur (foretell)
au·gu·ry
au·gust
aunt·ie
au·ra
au·ral (hearing)
au re·voir
au·ri·cle (heart; *see*
    oracle)
au·ric·u·lar

au·ro·ra bo·
re·al·is
aus·pice, *plural*
auspices
aus·pi·cious
aus·tere
aus·ter·i·ty
au·then·tic
au·then·ti·cate
au·then·ti·ca·tor
au·then·tic·i·ty
au·thor
au·thor·i·tar·i·an
au·thor·i·ta·tive
au·thor·i·ty
au·tho·ri·za·tion
au·tho·rize
au·tho·riz·er
au·to (Words
beginning with the
combining form
auto are written
solid: *autocrat*.)
au·to·bi·og·
ra·pher
au·to·bio·graph·
i·cal
au·to·bi·og·ra·phy
au·to·clave
au·toc·ra·cy
au·to-da-fé, *plural*
autos-da-fé

au·to·gi·ro
au·to·graph
au·to·hyp·no·sis
au·to·mate
au·to·mat·ic
au·to·ma·tion
au·tom·a·ton,
plural automatons
au·to·nom·ic
au·ton·o·mous
au·ton·o·my
au·top·sy
au·tumn
au·tum·nal
aux·il·ia·ry
avail·able
av·a·lanche
avant-garde
av·a·rice
av·a·ri·cious
aveng·er
av·e·nue
aver
aver·ment
averred
aver·ring
averse
aver·sion
avert (turn away)
avert·i·ble
avi·ary
avi·a·tor

av·id
avid·ity
av·o·ca·do, *plural*
avocados
avoid·able
avoid·ance
av·oir·du·pois
avow
avow·al
avow·ed·ly
avun·cu·lar
award
aware
awed
awe·less
awe·some
awe-strick·en
awe-struck
aw·ful
aw·ing
awk·ward
awn·ing
AWOL
awry
ax
ax·i·om
ax·is, *plural* axes
ax·le
aye, *plural* ayes
azal·ea
az·ure

B

bab·ble
bab·bler
ba·boon
ba·by·ish
ba·by's breath
ba·by-sit (*verb*)
ba·by-sit·ter
bac·ca·lau·re·ate
bach·e·lor
back (Compound
   words beginning
   with *back* are
   written solid:
   backbencher,
   except as
   otherwise shown
   below.)
back·break·ing
back·court
back·gam·mon
back·logged
back·log·ging
back num·ber
back or·der (*noun*)
back-or·der (*verb*)
back·ped·aled
back·ped·al·ing
back road
back seat

back-seat driv·er
back talk (*noun*)
back-talk (*verb*)
back to back (*adv*)
back-to-back (*adj*)
back·up (*noun*)
back-up (*adj*)
back·ward
bac·te·ri·um,
   plural bacteria
bad blood
bad·i·nage
bad·lands
Bad Lands
   (S. Dakota)
bad·min·ton
bad-tem·pered
baf·fle
baf·fle·ment
baf·fler
bag·a·telle
ba·gel
bag·ful, *plural*
   bagfuls
bag·gage
bagged
bag·gi·er
bag·ging
bag·gy

bag·pipe
bag·pip·er
bail·able
bail·er (one that
   bails)
bai·liff
bai·li·wick
bail·or (law)
bait·ed (used bait;
   see bated)
baize
bak·ery
bal·ance·a·ble
bal·anc·er
bal·ance sheet
bal·ance wheel
bal·co·ny
bald·faced
bald·head
bald·pate
bale·ful
bal·er (machine)
balk
balky
bal·lad (song or
   poem)
bal·lade (verse
   form, musical
   composition)

bal·lad·eer
bal·lad·ry
ball and chain
ball-and-sock·et
    joint
bal·last
ball bear·ing
bal·le·ri·na
bal·let
ball game
bal·lis·tic
bal·loon
bal·lot
bal·lot box
bal·lot·ed
bal·lot·er
bal·lot·ing
ball park (*noun*)
ball-park (*adj*)
ball·play·er
ball-point pen
ball·room
bal·ly·hoo
bal·ly·hooed
bal·ly·hoo·er
bal·ly·hoo·ing
balm·i·er
balm·i·ness
balmy
bal·sam
bal·us·ter
bal·us·trade
bam·boo, *plural*
    bamboos
bam·boo·zle
bam·boo·zler
ba·nal

ba·nana
ban·dan·na
band·box
ban·died
band·mas·ter
ban·do·leer
band saw
band shell
band·stand
band·wag·on
ban·dy
ban·dy·ing
bane·ful
ban·gle
ban·ish
ban·is·ter
ban·jo, *plural*
    banjos
ban·jo·ist
bank·able
bank ac·count
bank·book
bank hol·i·day
bank note
bank·roll
bank·rupt
bank·rupt·cy
banned
ban·ning
banns (church
    notice)
ban·quet (meal)
ban·quet·ed
ban·quet·er
ban·quet·ing
ban·quette (seat)
ban·tam

ban·ter
bap·tism
bap·tis·tery
bap·tize
bar·bar·ian
bar·bar·ic
bar·ba·rism
bar·bar·i·ty
bar·ba·rize
bar·ba·rous
bar·be·cue
bar·be·cued
bar·be·cu·ing
bar·bell
bar·ca·role
bare·back
bare·faced
bare·foot
bare·hand·ed
bare·head·ed
bare·leg·ged
bar·gain
bar·gain·er
bari·tone
bar·keep·er
bar·ley
bar·maid
bar·man
bar mitz·vah
bar·na·cle
barn·storm
barn·storm·er
barn·yard
ba·rom·e·ter
baro·met·ric
bar·on (peer)
bar·on·et·cy

ba·ro·ni·al
ba·roque
bar·rack
bar·ra·cu·da
bar·rage
bar·ra·try
barred
bar·rel
bar·rel-chest·ed
bar·reled
bar·rel·ful, *plural*
  barrelfuls
bar·rel·house
bar·rel·ing
bar·rel or·gan
bar·ren
  (unproductive)
bar·ren·ness
bar·rette (clasp)
bar·ri·cade
bar·ri·er
bar·ring
bar·ris·ter
bar·room
bar·row
bar·tend·er
bar·ter
bar·ter·er
bas·al
base·board
base·born
base·burn·er
base hit
base·less
base line
base·man
base pay

base run·ner
ba·sil
ba·sil·i·ca
ba·sin
ba·sis, *plural* bases
bas·ket·ball
bas·ket·ry
bas·ket weave
bas-re·lief
bass (fish, deep
  voice)
bass clef
bass drum
bass fid·dle
bas·soon
bass viol
bass·wood
bas·tard
bas·tard·ize
bas·tille
bas·ti·na·do, *plural*
  bastinadoes
bas·tion
ba·teau, *plural*
  bateaux
bat·ed (lessened;
  see baited)
ba·thos
ba·tik
bat mitz·vah
ba·ton
bat·tal·ion
bat·ted
bat·ten
bat·ter
bat·tery
bat·ti·er

bat·ting
bat·tle-ax
bat·tle·field
bat·tle roy·al,
  plural battles
  royal
bat·tle·ship
bat·ty
bau·ble (trinket)
bawd·i·er
bawdy
bawl (cry)
bay·ber·ry
bay leaf
bay·o·net
bay·o·net·ed
bay·o·net·ing
bay·ou, *plural*
  bayous
ba·zaar (market)
BB gun
beach·comb·er
beach·head
beach wag·on
bea·gle
beak·er
bear·able
bear·er
be·a·tif·ic
be·at·i·fy
be·at·i·tude
beau, *plural* beaus
beau geste, *plural*
  beaux gestes
beau·te·ous
beau·ti·cian
beau·ti·fied

beau·ti·fy
beau·ti·fy·ing
beau·ty shop
bea·ver
be·calm
beak·on
bed (Compound
   words beginning
   with *bed* are
   written solid:
   bedpan, except as
   otherwise shown
   below.)
be·daz·zle
bed·ded
bed·der
bed·ding
be·dev·iled
be·dev·il·ing
bed jack·et
bed·lam
bed lin·en
bed·ou·in
be·drag·gled
bed rest
bed·rid·den
bed-wet·ting
beech (tree)
beefs (complaints)
beef·steak
bee·hive
bee·keep·er
bee·line
bee·tle
bee·tling
beeves (meat)
be·fit
be·fit·ted

be·fit·ting
be·fog
be·fogged
be·fog·ging
be·fore·hand
be·fud·dle
be·get
be·get·ting
beg·gar
beg·gar·ing
beg·gar·ly
beg·gary
begged
beg·ging
be·gin·ner
be·gin·ning
be·got·ten
be·guile
be·guile·ment
be·guil·er
be·guil·ing
be·guine
be·hav·ior
be·hind·hand
be·hold·en
be·hoove
be·hooved
be·hoov·ing
be·jew·el
be·jew·eled
be·jew·el·ing
be·lay
be·layed
be·lay·ing
bel can·to
bel·dam
be·lea·guer
be·lea·guered

bel·fry
be·lie
be·lied
be·lief
be·li·er
be·liev·able
be·lieve
be·liev·er
be·lit·tle
be·lit·tle·ment
be·lit·tler
be·lit·tling
bell-bot·tom (*adj*)
bell buoy
belles-let·tres
bel·le·tris·tic
bel·li·cose
bel·lig·er·ence
bel·lig·er·ent
bell·weth·er
bel·ly·ache
bel·ly·band
bel·ly·ful
bel·ly-land (*verb*)
bel·ly land·ing
bel·ly laugh
be·ly·ing
bench mark
bench war·rant
ben·e·dict
ben·e·dic·tion
ben·e·dic·to·ry
ben·e·fac·tor
ben·e·fice
be·nef·i·cence
be·nef·i·cent
ben·e·fi·cial
ben·e·fi·ci·ary

ben·e·fit
ben·e·fit·ed
ben·e·fit·ing
be·nev·o·lence
be·nev·o·lent
be·nign
be·nig·nant
be·nig·ni·ty
be·queath
be·queath·al
be·quest
be·rate
be·reave
be·reave·ment
be·ret (cap)
ber·serk
berth (ship's space, bunk)
be·seech
be·set·ment
be·set·ting
be·siege
be·sieg·er
be·sought (*past of* beseech)
bes·tial
bes·ti·al·i·ty
bes·ti·ary
be·stir
be·stirred
be·stir·ring
best man
be·stow·al
best sell·er
best-sell·ing (*adj*)
be·tel
beth·el
be·tray·al

be·trayed
be·tray·er
be·tray·ing
be·troth·al
be·trothed
bet·ting
bet·tor (one who bets)
be·tween·times
bev·el
bev·eled
bev·el·ing
bev·er·age
be·wil·der
be·wil·dered
bi·an·nu·al
bi·as, *plural* biases
bi·ased
bi·as·ing
Bib·li·cal
bib·li·og·ra·pher
bib·li·og·ra·phy
bib·lio·phile
bib·u·lous
bi·cam·er·al
bi·car·bon·ate
bi·cen·te·na·ry
bi·cen·ten·ni·al
bi·ceps (*sing* and *plural*)
bick·er
bi·col·ored
bi·cy·cle
bi·cy·clist
bid·da·ble
bid·den
bid·der
bid·ding

bi·en·ni·al
bi·en·ni·um, *plural* bienniums
bier (platform for coffin)
bi·fo·cal
bi·fur·cate
big·a·mist
big·a·mous
big·a·my
big·ger
big·gest
big·gish
big·head
big·head·ed
big·heart·ed
bight (bay, curve, loop)
big-league (*adj*)
big league (*noun*)
big leagu·er
big·ot
big·ot·ry
big-tick·et (*adj*)
big top
big·wig
bi·jou, *plural* bijoux
bi·ki·ni
bi·lat·er·al
bi·lin·gual
bil·ious
bilk
bill·a·ble
bill·board
bil·let
bil·let-doux, *plural* billets-doux
bill·fold

bill·head
bil·liards
bil·lion
bil·lion·aire
bill of fare
bill of goods
bill of health
bill of lad·ing
bill of rights
bill of sale
bil·low
bi·met·al
bi·me·tal·lic
bi·met·al·lism
bi·month·ly
bi·na·ry
bin·au·ral
bind·er
bind·ery
bin·na·cle
binned
bin·ning
bin·oc·u·lar
bi·no·mi·al
bio (Words
   beginning with
   the combining
   form *bio* are
   written solid:
   biography.)
bi·og·ra·pher
bi·ol·o·gy
bi·op·sy
bi·par·ti·san
bi·par·tite
bi·ped
bird·bath
bird·brain

bird·call
bird dog (*noun*)
bird·dog (*verb*)
bird·house
bird's-eye (*noun*
   and *adj*)
bird·ie·ing
bird·watch (*noun*)
bird watch·er
bird watch·ing
birl (logspinning)
birth cer·tif·i·cate
birth·mark
birth·place
birth·rate
birth·right
birth·stone
bis·cuit
bi·sec·tor
bish·op·ric
bi·son
bisque
bit·ing
bit·ten
bit·ter end
bit·ter-end·er
bit·ter·root
bit·ter·sweet
bi·tu·men
bi·tu·mi·nous
bi·valve
biv·ouac
biv·ouacked
biv·ouack·ing
bi·week·ly
bi·year·ly
bi·zarre (odd)
blabbed

blab·ber
blab·ber·mouth
blab·bing
black-and-blue (*adj*)
black and white
   (*noun*)
black-and-white
   (*adj*)
black·ball (*noun*
   and *verb*)
black·ber·ry
black·bird
black·board
black book
black eye
black-eyed (*adj*)
black·guard
black·head
black·jack
black·list
black mag·ic
black·mail
black mark
black mar·ket
   (*noun*)
black-mar·ket
   (*verb*)
black mar·ket·eer
black out (*verb*)
black·out (*noun*)
black pow·er
black·smith
black tie (*noun*)
black-tie (*adj*)
black wid·ow
blad·der
blam·able
blame·ful

blame·wor·thy
blanc·mange
blan·dish·er
blank check
blan·ket stitch
blar·ney
bla·sé
blas·pheme
blas·phe·mous
blas·phe·my
blast off (*verb*)
blast-off (*noun*)
bla·tan·cy
bla·tant
blath·er
blat·ted
blat·ting
blaz·er
bla·zon
bla·zon·er
bla·zon·ry
bleach·er
bleak
bleary-eyed
blem·ish
bless·ed (*adj*)
blight
blind al·ley
blind date
blind·fold
blind·man's buff
blind spot
blipped
blip·ping
blithe
blithe·some
bliz·zard
bloat (swell)

blobbed
blob·bing
bloc (alliance)
block·ade-run·ner
block and tack·le
block·bust·er
block·bust·ing
block·head
block·house
block let·ter
blond (*masc* or *fem*)
blonde (*fem* only)
blood bank
blood bath
blood broth·er
blood cell
blood count
blood·cur·dling
blood group
blood·guilt
blood·hound
blood·i·er
blood·let·ting
blood mon·ey
blood poi·son·ing
blood pres·sure
blood-red
blood·shed
blood·shot
blood·stain
blood·stream
blood·suck·er
blood test
blood·thirsty
blood-type (*verb*)
blood type (*noun*)
blos·som
blot·ted

blot·ter
blot·ting
blow-by-blow (*adj*)
blow·gun
blow·hard
blow out (*verb*)
blow·out (*noun*)
blow·torch
blow up (*verb*)
blow·up (*noun*)
blow·zy
blub·ber
blud·geon
blue ba·by
blue·ber·ry
blue·bird
blue blood (*noun*)
blue book
blue cheese
blue chip (*noun*)
blue-chip (*adj*)
blue-col·lar (*adj*)
blue·fish
blue flag (iris)
blue·grass
blue jay
blue jeans
blue law
blue·nose
blue-pen·cil (*verb*)
blue-pen·ciled
blue-pen·cil·ing
blue·point (oyster)
blue·print
blue-rib·bon (*adj*)
blue-sky (*adj*
   worthless)
blue·stock·ing

blu·ing (*noun* and
  verb)
blu·ish
blurb
blurred
blur·ri·ness
blur·ring
blur·ry
blurt
blus·ter·er
blus·tery
board foot
board·ing·house
board·ing school
board room
board·walk
boat hook
boat·house
boat·load
boat·man
boat train
bobbed
bob·ber
bob·bin
bob·bing
bob·ble (up and
  down, error)
bob·by pin
bob·by socks
bob·by sox·er
bod·ice
bod·i·less
bod·i·ly
body·guard
bo·gey (golf)
bo·gey·man
bogged
bog·gi·er

bog·gi·ness
bog·ging
bog·gle
bog·gling
bog·gy
bo·gus
bo·gy (evil spirit)
boil·er·mak·er
boil·er·plate
boil·ing point
bois·ter·ous
bold·face (*noun*)
bold-faced (*adj*)
boll wee·vil
bo·lo·gna (sausage)
bol·ster
bo·lus, *plural*
  boluses
bom·bar·dier
bom·bast
bomb·shell
bona fide
bo·nan·za
bond·hold·er
bond pa·per
bone·black
bone chi·na
bone-dry
bone·fish
bone meal
bon·ho·mie
bon·i·er (bony)
bo·ni·to, *plural*
  bonitos
bon mot, *plural*
  bons mots
bon·net
bon·ni·er (bonny)

bo·nus, *plural*
  bonuses
bon vi·vant, *plural*
  bons vivants
bony
boo·boo
boo·hoo
boo·hooed
boo·hoo·ing
book (Compound
  words beginning
  book are written
  solid: *bookcase,*
  except as
  otherwise shown
  below.)
book club
book end
book jack·et
book learn·ing
book match·es
book re·view
book val·ue
boom·er·ang
boom town
boon·dog·gle
boor
boot camp
boo·tee (shoe)
boot·jack
boot·legged
loot·leg·ger
boot·leg·ging
boo·ty (loot)
bor·del·lo
bor·der·line (*noun*
  and *adj*)
bore·dom

born (birthed)
borne
bor·ough (town)
bo's'n
bo·som
bo·somed
bot·a·nist
bot·a·nize
bot·a·ny
bot·tle·ful, *plural*
bottlefuls
bot·tle·neck
bou·doir
bou·gain·vil·lea
bouil·lon (soup)
boul·der
bou·le·vard
bou·le·var·dier
bound·a·ry
bound·er
boun·te·ous
boun·ti·ful
bou·quet
bour·geois
bour·geoi·sie
bou·ton·niere
bowd·ler·ize
bow·el (intestine)
bow·er
bow·ery
bow·front
bow·knot
bow·leg
bow·leg·ged
bowl·ing (game)
bow·string
bow tie
bow win·dow

box·car
box kite
box lunch
box of·fice (*noun*)
box-of·fice (*adj*)
box score
box seat
box spring
boy·cott
boy·cott·ed
boy·cott·er
boy·cott·ing
boy·friend
brad·ded
brad·ding
brag·ga·do·cio
brag·gart
bragged
brag·ger
brag·ging
Braille (writing
system)
brain·child
brain·pow·er
brain·storm
brain trust
brain·wash
brain·wash·ing
brain wave
brand-new
brass hat
bras·siere
brass knuck·les
brass tacks
brat·ti·ness
brat·tish
brat·tish·ness
brat·ty

bra·va·do, *plural*
bravadoes
brav·ery
bra·voes (assassins)
bra·vos (shouts)
brawl
bra·zier (for coals)
bread and but·ter
(*noun*)
bread-and-but·ter
(*adj*)
bread·bas·ket
bread·win·ner
break·able
break·away
break·down (*noun*)
break-even (*adj*)
break·front
break·neck (*adj*)
break·out (*noun*)
break·through
(*noun*)
break·up (*noun*)
break·wa·ter
breast·bone
breast-fed
breast-feed (*verb*)
breast·stroke
breast·work
breath·able
breath·tak·ing
bre·vet·cy
bre·vet·ted
bre·vet·ting
bre·vi·ary
brew·er
brew·ery
brib·able

brib·ery
brick·bat
brick·lay·er
brick red (*noun*)
brick-red (*adj*)
brick·work
brick·yard
brid·al (wedding)
bride·groom
brides·maid
bridge·able
bridge·head
bridge·work
bri·dle (for horses)
bri·dle path
brief
bri·er
bri·er·root
bri·er·wood
brig·a·dier
brig·and
bril·liance
bril·lian·cy
bril·liant
brim·ful
brimmed
brim·ming
brin·dle
briny
bri·oche
bri·quette
bri·quet·ted
bri·quet·ting
bris·ket
bris·tle
bris·tling
bris·tly
Bri·tan·nic

brit·tle
broad·ax
broad bean
broad·cast·er
broad·cloth
broad gauge (*noun*)
broad-gauged (*adj*)
broad jump
broad-leaved (*adj*)
broad·loom
broad-mind·ed
broad·side
bro·cade
broc·co·li
bro·chette
bro·chure
brogue
bro·ken-down
bro·ken·heart·ed
bron·chi·al
bron·co, *plural*
   broncos
broth·el
broth·ers-in-law
brou·ha·ha
brown bread
brown·ie
brown·out (*noun*)
brown·stone
brown study
brown sug·ar
browse
bru·net (*masc* and
   fem)
bru·nette (*fem* only)
brusque
bru·tal·ize
brut·ish

bub·bler
buc·ca·neer
buck·a·roo
buck·et bri·gade
buck·et·fuls
buck·et seat
buck·et shop
buck fe·ver
buck·le
buck·ler
buck-pass·er
buck-pass·ing
   (*noun*)
buck·ram
bu·col·ic
bud·ded
bud·der
bud·ding
bud·get
bud·get·ary
bud·get·er
buf·fa·lo, *plural*
   buffaloes
buf·fa·loed
buf·fa·lo·ing
buff·er
buf·fet
buf·foon
buf·foon·ery
bug·a·boo, *plural*
   bugaboos
bug·bear
bugged
bug·ger
bug·gi·er
bug·gies
bug·ging
bug·gy

bu·gler
build-up (*noun*)
built-in (*adj*)
built-up (*adj*)
bul·bar
bul·bous
bulgy
bull·doze
bull·doz·er
bul·le·tin
bull·fight
bull·head·ed
bull·horn
bul·lion (metal)
bull·neck
bull·necked
bull·pen
bull·ring
bull-roar·er
bull ses·sion
bull's-eye
bull ter·ri·er
bull·whip
bul·rush
bul·wark
bum·ble
bum·ble·bee
bum·bling
bummed
bum·ming
bump·kin
bump·tious
bun·co, *plural*
   buncos
bun·coed
bun·co·ing
bun·ga·low
bun·gle

bun·gler
bun·ion
bun·kum
buoy
buoy·an·cy
buoy·ant
bur (seed case,
   dental drill)
bur·ble
bu·reau, *plural*
   bureaus
bu·reau·cra·cy
bu·reau·crat
bu·rette
bur·geon
bur·gess
bur·gher
burg·lar
bur·glar·i·ous
bur·glar·ize
bur·gla·ry
bur·i·al
bur·ied
burl (knot)
bur·lesque
bur·ley (tobacco)
bur·ly (muscular)
bur·nish
burr (sound, metal
   edge)
burred
bur·ring
bur·ro (donkey),
   plural burros
bur·row (hole)
bur·sar
bur·sa·ry
bur·si·tis

bury
bury·ing
bused
bus·es (*noun* and
   verb)
bush·el
bush·el·bas·ket
bush·eled
bush·el·er
bush·el·ing
bush league (*noun*)
bush-league (*adj*)
bush leagu·er
bush·whack·er
bus·ied
bus·i·er
bus·i·ly
busi·ness
busi·ness·like
busi·ness·man
bus·ing
bus·tle
busy·body
busy·ness (being
   busy)
busy-work
butch·ery
butt (base, target,
   to push)
butte (hill)
but·ter·ball
but·ter bean
but·ter·cup
but·ter·fat
but·ter·fin·gered
but·ter·fly
but·ter knife
but·ter·milk

85

but·ter·nut

but·ter·scotch

but·tery

but·tock

but·ton-down (*adj*)

but·ton·hole

but·ton·hook

but·tress

bux·om

buz·zard

buz·zer

by and by (*adv*)

by-and-by (*noun*)

by and large

bye, *plural* byes

by-elec·tion

by·gone, *plural* bygones

by·law

by-line

by·pass (*noun*)

by·passed (*verb*)

by·past (*adj*)

by·path

by·play

by-prod·uct

by·road

by·stand·er

by·street

by·way

by·word

C

ca·bal (intrigue)
ca·ba·la
cab·al·ist
ca·balled
ca·bal·ling
ca·bana
cab·a·ret
cab·driv·er
cab·in class
cab·i·net·mak·er
cab·i·net·work
ca·ble·gram
ca·ble stitch
ca·boo·dle
ca·boose
ca·cao
cache
ca·chet
cack·le
cack·ler
ca·coph·o·ny
cac·tus, *plural*
  cactuses
ca·dav·er
ca·dav·er·ous
cad·die (golf)
cad·died
cad·dy·ing

cad·dy (container)
ca·dence
ca·den·za
cadg·er
cad·re
Cae·sar·e·an
  sec·tion
caf·e·te·ria
caf·feine
ca·gey
ca·gi·er
ca·gi·ly
ca·gi·ness
ca·hoots
cais·son
ca·jole
ca·jol·er
ca·jol·ery
cal·a·bash
ca·lam·i·tous
ca·lam·i·ty
cal·ci·fied
cal·ci·fy
cal·ci·fy·ing
cal·ci·mine
cal·cu·la·ble
cal·cu·late
cal·cu·la·tor

cal·cu·lus, *plural*
  calculi
cal·dron
cal·en·dar (time
  system or
  schedule)
cal·en·der (pass
  between rollers)
calf, *plural* calves
calf·skin
cal·i·ber
cal·i·brate
cal·i·bra·tor
cal·i·co, *plural*
  calicos
cal·i·per
cal·is·then·ic
  (*adj*)
cal·is·then·ics
  (*noun sing* and
  plural)
calk (shoe
  attachment)
call·able
call·boy
cal·lig·ra·pher
cal·lig·ra·phy
call let·ters

call loan
cal·low
cal·lous (*adj*
  hardened)
call-up (*noun*)
cal·lus (*noun* hard
  skin area)
ca·lo·ric
cal·o·rie
ca·lum·ni·ate
ca·lum·ni·a·tor
ca·lum·ni·ous
cal·um·ny
Cal·vin·ism
ca·ma·ra·de·rie
cam·bric
ca·mel·lia
cam·el's hair (*noun*)
cam·el's-hair (*adj*)
cam·eo, *plural*
  cameos
cam·era
cam·era-shy
cam·ou·flage
cam·paign
cam·paign·er
cam·pa·ni·le
camp·fire
camp·ground
cam·phor
camp meet·ing
camp·site
cam·shift
ca·nal·boat
ca·nal·ize
can·a·pé
ca·nard
ca·nary (bird)

can·cel
can·celed
can·cel·er
can·cel·ing
can·cel·la·tion
can·cer
can·cer·ous
can·di·da·cy
can·di·date
can·dle-foot
can·dle·light
can·dle·pow·er
can·dle·stick
can·dor
ca·nine
can·is·ter
can·ker
can·ker sore
can·ker·worm
canned
can·nel coal
can·ner
can·nery
can·ni·bal
can·ni·bal·ize
can·ni·er
can·ni·ly
can·ni·ness
can·ning
can·non (gun)
can·non·ade
can·non·ball
can·non·eer
can·ny
ca·noe, *plural*
  canoes
ca·noed
ca·noe·ing

ca·noe·ist
can·on (rule, clergy)
ca·non·i·cal
can·on·ize
can·on law
can·o·py
can·ta·loupe
can·tan·ker·ous
can·ta·ta
can·teen
can·ter (horse's
  pace)
can·ti·cle (hymn)
can·ti·le·ver
can·to, *plural*
  cantos
can·ton
can·tor (singer)
can·vas (cloth)
can·vass (to
  examine or poll)
can·vassed
can·vass·er
can·vass·ing
can·yon
ca·pa·bil·i·ty
ca·pa·ble
ca·pa·cious
ca·pac·i·tor
ca·pac·i·ty
ca·par·i·son
ca·per
cap·il·lary
cap·i·tal (*adj*
  serious,
  important; *noun*
  stock of goods,
  money, city)

cap·i·tal·ism
cap·i·tal·ize
cap·i·tol
(building)
Cap·i·tol (in
Washington,
D.C.)
ca·pit·u·late
ca·pon
ca·pon·ize
capped
cap·per
cap·ping
ca·price
ca·pri·cious
cap·size
cap·su·lar
cap·sule
cap·sul·ize
cap·tain·cy
cap·tion
cap·tious
cap·ti·vate
cap·ti·va·tor
cap·tiv·i·ty
cap·tor
cap·ture
ca·ra·bao
car·a·cul (fur)
ca·rafe
car·a·mel
car·a·mel·ize
car·at (weight)
car·a·van
car·a·van·sa·ry
car·a·vel
car·a·way
car·bine (firearm)

car·bi·neer
car·bon (element)
car·bon black
car·bon copy
car·bon·ize
car·bon pa·per
car·bun·cle
car·bu·re·tor
car·cass
car·cin·o·gen
car·ci·no·ma,
    plural carcinomas
card·board
car·di·ac
car·di·gan
car·di·nal
car·dio·gram
ca·reen
ca·reer
ca·reer·ist
care·free
ca·ress
car·et (∧)
care·tak·er
care·worn
car·go, *plural*
    cargoes
car·i·ca·ture
car·ies (tooth
    decay)
car·il·lon
car·load
car·mine (color)
car·nage
car·nal
car·ni·val
car·ni·vore
car·niv·o·rous

car·ol
car·oled
car·ol·er
car·ol·ing
car·om
car·omed
car·om·ing
ca·rot·id
ca·rous·al (party)
ca·rouse
car·pen·try
car·pet·bag·ger
car pool
car·port
car·rel
car·riage
car·ri·er
car·ri·on
car·rot (vegetable)
car·rou·sel (merry-
    go-round)
car·ry·all
car·ry·ings-on
car·ry-over (*noun*)
car·sick
car·tel
car·ti·lage
car·tog·ra·pher
car·tog·ra·phy
car·ton (box)
car·toon (drawing)
car·tridge
car·wash
case·book
case·hard·en
case·hard·ened
case his·to·ry
case knife

case law
case·load
case·ment
case study
case·work
cash-and-car·ry
cash·book
cash·box
cash·ier
cash·mere
cash reg·is·ter
ca·si·no (building),
    plural casinos
cas·ket
cas·se·role
cas·sette
cas·si·no (game)
cas·sock
cast·away
caste (social class)
cast·er (one that
    casts, container,
    wheel)
cas·ti·gate
cas·ti·ga·tor
cast iron (*noun*)
cast-iron (*adj*)
cas·tle
cast·off (*noun* and
    adj)
cas·tor oil
ca·su·al
ca·su·al·ty
ca·su·ist
ca·su·ist·ry
cat·a·clysm
cat·a·clys·mic
cat·a·comb

cat·a·lep·sy
cat·a·log
cat·a·loged
cat·a·log·er
cat·a·log·ing
cat·a·lyst
cat·a·lyze
cat·a·pult
cat·a·ract
ca·tarrh
ca·tas·tro·phe
cat·bird
cat·boat
cat·call
catch·all
catch-as-catch-can
catch·ment
catch phrase
catch·word
cat·e·chism
cat·e·chize
cat·e·gor·i·cal
cat·e·go·rize
cat·e·go·ry
ca·ter
ca·ter-cor·nered
ca·ter·er
cat·er·pil·lar
cat·er·waul
cat·fish
ca·thar·sis
ca·thar·tic
ca·the·dral
cath·e·ter
cath·e·ter·ize
cath·o·lic
    (universal)
Cath·o·lic (church)

Ca·thol·i·cism
cat·napped
cat·nap·ping
cat-o'-nine-tails
cat's cra·dle
cat's-paw
cat·tail
cat·tle (*plural* only)
cat·ty
cau·cus, *plural*
    caucuses
cau·cused
cau·cus·ing
cau·li·flow·er
caulk (*verb* to stop
    up)
caulk·er
caus·al
cau·sal·i·ty
cau·sa·tion
cause·way
caus·tic
cau·ter·ize
cau·tery
cau·tion
cau·tion·ary
cau·tious
cav·al·cade
cav·a·lier
cav·al·ry
ca·ve·at
ca·ve·at emp·tor
cave dwell·er
cave-in (*noun*)
cave man
cav·ern
cav·ern·ous
cav·i·ar

cav·il
cav·iled
cav·il·er
cav·il·ing
cav·i·ty
ca·vort
cay·enne
cease-fire (*noun*)
ce·dar
cede (give up)
ceil·ing
cel·e·brant
cel·e·brate
cel·e·bra·tor
ce·leb·ri·ty
ce·ler·i·ty
cel·ery
ce·les·ta
ce·les·tial
cel·i·ba·cy
cel·i·bate
cel·lar
cel·la·ret
cel·list
cel·lo, *plural* cellos
cel·lo·phane
cel·lu·lar
cel·lu·loid
cel·lu·lose
ce·ment
cem·e·tery
cen·o·taph
cen·ser (vessel for
    incense)
cen·sor
cen·so·ri·ous
cen·sor·ship
cen·sur·able

cen·sure
cen·sus
cen·taur
cen·te·nar·i·an
cen·te·na·ry
cen·ten·ni·al
cen·ter·board
cen·ter field
cen·ter field·er
cen·ter of grav·i·ty
cen·ter·piece
cen·ti·grade
cen·ti·gram
cen·ti·me·ter
cen·ti·pede
cen·tral·ism
cen·tral·i·ty
cen·tral·ize
cen·trif·u·gal
cen·tri·fuge
cen·trip·e·tal
ce·phal·ic
ce·ram·ic
ce·re·al (grain)
ce·re·bral
cer·e·brate
cer·e·mo·ni·al
cer·e·mo·ni·ous
cer·e·mo·ny
cer·tain
cer·ti·fi·able
cer·tif·i·cate
cer·ti·fi·ca·tion
cer·ti·fied check
cer·ti·fied mail
cer·ti·fied pub·lic
    ac·count·ant
cer·ti·fy

cer·ti·fy·ing
cer·ti·tude
cer·vi·cal
cer·vix
ces·sa·tion
ces·sion (a yielding)
cess·pool
cha-cha
cha-chaed
cha-cha·ing
chafe (irritate)
chaff (seed cover,
    light talk)
chaf·fer
chaf·ing dish
cha·grin
cha·grined
cha·grin·ing
chain gang
chain let·ter
chain-re·act (*verb*)
chain re·ac·tion
chain saw
chain-smoke
chain smok·er
chain stitch
chain store
chair·manned
chair·man·ning
chaise longue,
    plural chaise
    longues
cha·let
chal·ice
chalk·board
chalk talk
chal·lenge·able
chal·leng·er

cham·ber
cham·bered
cham·ber·maid
cham·ber mu·sic
cham·ber of
  com·merce
cha·me·leon
cham·ois
cham·oised
cham·ois·ing
cham·pagne
chan·cel
chan·cel·lery
chan·cel·lor
chan·cery
chanc·i·er
chanc·ing
chan·cre
chancy
chan·de·lier
chan·dlery
change·able
change·less
change·ling
change·over
chan·nel
chan·neled
chan·nel·ing
chan·nel·ize
chan·teuse
chan·tey
chan·ti·cleer
chan·try
cha·os
cha·ot·ic
chap·ar·ral
chap·el

chap·er·on, *plural*
  chaperons
chap·er·oned
chap·er·on·ing
chap·lain
char
char·ac·ter
char·ac·ter·is·tic
char·ac·ter·ize
cha·rade
charge·able
charge ac·count
charge-a-plate
charge plate
char·i·ly
char·i·ness
char·i·ot
char·i·o·teer
cha·ris·ma
char·is·mat·ic
char·i·ta·ble
char·i·ty
char·la·tan
char·ley horse
char·nel
charred
char·ring
char·treuse
chary (careful)
chasm
chas·sis (*sing* and
  plural)
chaste
chas·ten
chas·tened
chas·ten·ing
chas·tise

chas·tise·ment
chas·tis·er
chas·ti·ty
châ·teau, *plural*
  châteaus
chat·ted
chat·tel
chat·ter
chat·ter·er
chat·ter·ing
chat·ting
chauf·feur
chauf·feured
chauf·feur·ing
chau·vin·ism
cheap·skate
check·book
check·er·board
check list
check mark
check·mate
check·off (*noun*)
check·out (*noun*)
check·point
check·rein
check·room
check·up (*noun*)
ched·dar
cheek·bone
cheek·i·est
cheek·i·ly
cheek·i·ness
cheeky
cheery
cheer·i·est
cheer·i·ly
cheese·burg·er

cheese·cake
cheese·cloth
cheesy
chef
chef-d'oeu·vre,
   plural chefs-
   d'oeuvre
chem·i·cal
che·mise
chem·is·try
che·nille
cher·ry·stone
cher·ub
cher·vil
chess·board
chess·man
che·va·lier
chev·i·ot
chev·ron
chew·able
chew·i·er
chew·ing gum
chic
chi·ca·nery
chi·chi
chick·en feed
chick·en hawk
chick·en-heart·ed
chick·en-liv·ered
chick·en pox
chick·en wire
chic·o·ry
chic·quer (more
   chic)
chic·quest
chide
chid·ed

chief jus·tice
Chief Jus·tice
   (U.S.)
chief of staff
chief of state
chief·tain
chif·fon
chif·fo·nier
chig·ger
chil·blain
child·bear·ing
child·bed
child·bed fe·ver
child·birth
child la·bor
child·like
child's play
chili, *plural* chilies
chili con car·ne
chili sauce
chill·i·er
chilly
chi·me·ra
chi·mer·i·cal
chim·ney cor·ner
chim·ney pot
chim·ney sweep
chim·pan·zee
Chi·na·town
chi·na·ware
chin·chil·la
Chi·nese cab·bage
Chi·nese chest·nut
Chi·nese lan·tern
Chi·nese puz·zle
Chi·nese wall
Chi·nese white

chinned
chin·ning
chintz·i·er
chintzy
chip·munk
chipped
chip·per
chip·ping
chi·rop·o·dist
chi·rop·o·dy
chi·ro·prac·tic
chi·ro·prac·tor
chis·el
chis·eled
chis·el·er
chis·el·ing
chit·chat
chit·ter·lings
chiv·al·ric
chiv·al·rous
chiv·al·ry
chiv·vy
chlo·rine
chlo·ro·phyll
chock-full
choc·o·late
choir·boy
choir loft
choir·mas·ter
choky
cho·ler
chol·era
cho·ler·ic
choos·i·er
choosy
chop·house
chopped

chop·per

chop·pi·er

chop·ping

chop·py

chop·sticks

chop su·ey

cho·ral (pertaining to chorus or choir)

cho·rale (hymn, musical composition)

chord (music and math)

chore

cho·re·og·ra·pher

cho·re·og·ra·phy

cho·ris·ter

chor·tle

chor·tler

cho·rus

chow·chow (pickles)

chow·der

chow mein

chris·ten

Chris·ten·dom

Chris·tain era

Chris·tian·ize

Chris·tian Sci·ence

Christ·mas Eve

Christ·mas·tide

Christ·mas tree

chro·mat·ic

chrome

chrome green

chrome red

chrome steel

chrome yel·low

chro·mo·some

chron·ic

chron·i·cal·ly

chron·i·cle

chron·o·log·i·cal

chro·nol·o·gy

chro·nom·e·ter

chrys·a·lis

chry·san·the·mum

chrys·o·prase

chub·bi·er

chub·bi·ness

chub·by

chuck·hole

chuck·le

chuck wag·on

chugged

chug·ging

chummed

chum·ming

chum·my

church·go·er

church·go·ing

church·man

church·war·den

church·yard

churl·ish

churn

chute

chute-the-chute

chut·ney

ci·ca·da

cic·a·trix

ci·ce·ro·ne, *plural* cicerones

ci·der

cig·a·rette

cin·der

cin·e·ma

cin·er·ar·i·um

cin·er·a·tor

cin·na·mon

ci·pher (zero or code)

cir·clet

cir·cuit

cir·cuit break·er

cir·cu·itous

cir·cuit·ry

cir·cu·ity

cir·cu·lar

cir·cu·lar·ize

cir·cu·late

cir·cu·la·tion

cir·cu·la·to·ry

cir·cum·cise

cir·cum·ci·sion

cir·cum·fer·ence

cir·cum·lo·cu·tion

cir·cum·nav·i·gate

cir·cum·scribe

cir·cum·scrip·tion

cir·cum·spect

cir·cum·stance

cir·cum·stan·tial

cir·cum·vent

cir·cus

cir·rho·sis

cis·tern

cit·able (cite)

cit·a·del

ci·ta·tion

cit·i·fied

cit·i·zen·ry

cit·ron

cit·rus
city ed·i·tor
city fa·ther
city hall
city man·ag·er
city-state
civ·et
civ·ic
civ·il de·fense
ci·vil·ian
ci·vil·i·ty
civ·i·li·za·tion
civ·i·lize
civ·il law
civ·il ser·vice
claim·able
claim·ant
claim·er
clair·voy·ance
clair·voy·ant
clam·bake
clam·ber
clam·ber·er
clammed
clam·mi·er
clam·mi·ly
clam·mi·ness
clam·ming
clam·my
clam·or
clam·or·ous
clamp·down (*noun*)
clam·shell
clan·des·tine
clan·gor
clan·gor·ous
clan·nish
clap·board

clapped
clap·per
clap·ping
clap·trap
claque
clar·et
clar·i·fy
clar·i·net
clar·i·net·tist
clar·i·on
clar·i·ty
class book
class-con·scious
class con·scious·
 ness
class day
clas·si·cal
clas·si·cist
clas·si·fi·able
clas·si·fi·ca·tion
clas·si·fied
clas·si·fi·er
clas·si·fy
clas·si·fy·ing
class·mate
class·room
class strug·gle
clat·ter
claus·al
claus·tro·pho·bia
clav·i·chord
clav·i·cle
cla·vier
clay·ey
clean·able
clean-cut
clean·hand·ed
clean-limbed

clean·li·ness
cleanse
cleans·er
clean-shav·en
clean·up (*noun*)
clear·ance
clear-cut
clear-eyed
clear·head·ed
clear·ing house
clear-sight·ed
cleat
cleav·able
cleav·age
cleave
cleaved
cleav·er
clef
cleft pal·ate
cle·ma·tis
clem·en·cy
clem·ent
clench
clere·sto·ry
cler·gy·man
cler·ic
cler·i·cal
cler·i·cal col·lar
cler·i·sy
cli·ché
cli·ent
cli·ent·age
cli·en·tele
cliff dwell·er
cliff·hang·er
cliff·hang·ing
cli·mac·ter·ic
cli·mac·tic

cli·mat·ic
cli·max
climb·able
climb·er
clinch·er
cling·ing
clin·ic
clin·i·cal
cli·ni·cian
clink·er
clip·board
clipped
clip·per
clip·ping
clip·sheet
clique
cliqu·ish
clo·aca
cloak-and-dag·ger
  (adj)
cloak·room
cloche (hat)
clock·wise
clock·work
clod·dish
clod·hop·per
clog dance
clogged
clog·ging
cloi·son·né
clois·ter
clois·tral
clone (asexual
  generation)
close call
closed cir·cuit
  (noun)
closed-cir·cuit (adj)

closed cor·po·ra·
  tion
closed-end
close·down (noun
  and adj)
closed sea·son
closed shop
close·fist·ed
close-fit·ting
close-grained
close-hauled
close·mouthed
close or·der (noun)
close-or·der (adj)
close·out (noun)
close quar·ters
close shave
clos·et
close-up (noun and
  adj)
clo·sure
clothe (verb)
clothed
clothes·horse
clothes·line
clothes·pin
clothes·press
clothes tree
cloth·ier
cloth·ing
clo·ture
cloud·burst
cloud-capped
cloud cham·ber
cloud·land
cloud nine
clo·ver·leaf
club·ba·ble

clubbed
club·bi·er
club·bing
club·by
club car
club·foot
club·house
club·room
club steak
club·wom·an
clue (noun and
  verb signal)
clued (verb)
clu·ing
clum·si·ly
clum·si·ness
clum·sy
clus·ter
clut·ter
clut·tery
coach·man
co·ac·tion
co·ad·ju·tant
co·ad·ju·tor
co·ag·u·lant
co·ag·u·late
coal car
co·alesce
co·alesced
co·ales·cence
co·ales·cent
co·alesc·ing
coal field
coal gas
co·a·li·tion
coal oil
coal tar
coarse (rough)

coarse-grained
coast·al
coast·er
coast·er brake
coast guard
coast·guards·man
coast·line
coast·ward
coat of arms
coat·tail
co·au·thor
coax
coaxed
coax·er
co·ax·i·al
coax·ing
co·balt blue
cob·bler
cob·ble·stone
co·bel·lig·er·ent
co·bra
cob·web
cob·webbed
cob·web·by
co·caine
coc·cyx
cock·ade
cock-a-doo·dle-doo
cock-and bull
  sto·ry
cocked hat
cock·er·el
cock·er span·iel
cock·eye
cock·eyed
cock·fight
cock·i·er
cock·i·ly

cock·i·ness
cock·le
cock·le·bur
cock·le·shell
cock·ney, *plural*
  cockneys
cock·pit
cock·roach
cocks·comb
cock·sure
cock·tail
co·coa
co·co·nut
co·coon
cod·dle
cod·dling
co·de·fen·dant
co·deine
cod·ger
cod·i·cil
cod·i·fi·ca·tion
cod·i·fied
cod·i·fi·er
cod·i·fy
cod·i·fy·ing
cod-liv·er oil
co·ed
co·ed·u·ca·tion
co·ef·fi·cient
co·equal
co·equal·i·ty
co·erce
co·erc·er
co·er·ci·ble
co·er·cion
co·er·cive
co·eval
co·ex·ec·u·tor

co·ex·ist
co·ex·is·tence
co·ex·is·tent
co·ex·ten·sive
cof·fee break
cof·fee·cake
cof·fee·house
cof·fee klatch
cof·fee mill
cof·fee·pot
cof·fee shop
cof·fee ta·ble
cof·fer
cof·fer·dam
co·gency
co·gent
cog·i·tate
cog·i·ta·tor
co·gnac
cog·nate
cog·ni·tion
cog·ni·za·ble
cog·ni·zance
cog·ni·zant
cog·no·men
co·gno·scen·te,
  plural
  cognoscenti
cog rail·way
cog·wheel
co·hab·it
co·hab·i·tant
co·heir
co·here
co·her·ence
co·her·ent
co·he·sion
co·he·sive

co·hort, *plural*
 cohorts
coif
coiffed
coif·fing
coif·feur (*masc*
 hairdresser)
coif·fure
 (arrangement)
coin·age
co·in·cide
co·in·ci·dence
co·in·ci·dent
co·in·ci·den·tal
co·in·sur·ance
co·in·sure
co·in·sur·er
col·an·der (utensil)
cold-blood·ed
cold cream
cold cuts
cold frame
cold front
cold·heart·ed
cold pack
cold shoul·der
 (*noun*)
cold-shoul·der
 (*verb*)
cold snap
cold sore
cold stor·age
cold sweat
cold war
cold wave
cole·slaw
col·ic
col·icky

col·i·se·um
co·li·tis
col·lab·o·rate
col·lab·o·ra·tion
col·lab·o·ra·tor
col·lage
col·lapse
col·laps·ible
col·lar
col·lar·bone
col·lar but·ton
col·late
col·lat·er·al
col·la·tion
col·la·tor
col·league
col·lect·ible
col·lec·tion
col·lec·tive
col·lec·tiv·ism
col·lec·tiv·ize
col·lec·tor
col·le·gial
col·le·gian
col·le·giate
col·lide
col·lier
col·liery
col·li·sion
col·lo·ca·tion
col·loid
col·lo·qui·al
col·lo·qui·um,
 plural
 colloquiums
col·lo·quy, *plural*
 colloquies
col·lude

col·lu·sion
co·logne
co·lon
col·o·nel
col·o·nel·cy
co·lo·nial
col·o·nist
col·o·nize
col·o·niz·er
col·on·nade
col·o·ny
col·o·phon
col·or·able
col·or·ant
col·or·a·tion
col·or·a·tu·ra
col·or·blind
col·or blind·ness
co·los·sal
co·los·sus
col·umn
co·lum·nar
col·um·nist
co·ma
 (unconsciousness)
co·mak·er
co·ma·tose
com·bat
com·bat·ant
com·bat·ed
com·bat·ing
com·bat·ive
comb·er
com·bin·able
comb·ings
com·bo, *plural*
 combos
com·bus·ti·ble

com·bus·tion
com·bus·tor
come·back (*noun*)
co·me·di·an (*masc*)
co·me·di·enne
   (*fem*)
come·down (*noun*)
come-hith·er (*adj*)
come·li·ness
come·ly
co·mes·ti·ble
com·et
come·up·pance
com·fort·able
com·fort·er
com·i·cal
com·ic book
com·ic strip
com·i·ty
com·man·dant
com·man·deer
com·man·der in
   chief
com·mand·ery
com·man·do, *plural*
   commandos
com·mem·o·rate
com·mem·o·ra·tor
com·mem·o·ra·
   to·ry
com·mence
com·mence·ment
com·mend
com·mend·able
com·men·da·tion
com·men·da·to·ry
com·men·su·ra·ble
com·men·su·rate

com·men·tary
com·men·ta·tor
com·merce
com·mer·cial
com·mer·cial·ism
com·mer·cial·ize
com·min·gle
com·mis·er·ate
com·mis·sar
com·mis·sar·i·at
com·mis·sary
com·mis·sion
com·mis·sion·er
com·mit
com·mit·ment
com·mit·ta·ble
com·mit·tal
com·mit·ted
com·mit·tee
com·mit·tee·man
com·mit·tee of the
   whole
com·mit·ting
com·mix
com·mix·ture
com·mode
com·mo·di·ous
com·mod·i·ty
com·mo·dore
com·mon·al·i·ty
com·mon·al·ty
com·mon·er
com·mon law
com·mon-law
   mar·riage
com·mon·place
com·mon sense
com·mon·weal

com·mon·wealth
com·mo·tion
com·mu·nal
com·mune
com·mu·ni·ca·ble
com·mu·ni·cant
com·mu·ni·ca·tor
com·mu·nion
com·mu·ni·qué
com·mu·nism
com·mu·ni·ty
com·mu·nize
com·mut·able
com·mu·ta·tion
com·mu·ta·tor
com·mute
com·mut·er
com·pact·er (*noun*
   and *adj*)
com·pan·ion·able
com·pan·ion·ate
com·pan·ion·ship
com·pan·ion·way
com·pa·ra·ble
com·par·a·tive
com·par·a·tor
com·par·i·son
com·part·men·tal·
   ize
com·pass
com·pas·sion
com·pas·sion·ate
com·pat·i·ble
com·peer
com·pel
com·pel·la·ble
com·pelled
com·pel·ling

com·pen·di·ous
com·pen·di·um,
  plural
  compendiums
com·pen·sa·ble
com·pen·sate
com·pen·sa·tor
com·pen·sa·to·ry
com·pete
com·pe·tence
com·pe·ten·cy
com·pe·tent
com·pe·ti·tion
com·pet·i·tive
com·pet·i·tor
com·pi·la·tion
com·pil·er
com·pla·cence
com·pla·cen·cy
com·pla·cent
  (smug)
com·plain·ant
com·plai·sance
com·plai·sant
  (affable)
com·ple·ment
  (completing)
com·ple·men·tal
com·ple·men·ta·ry
com·ple·tion
com·plex·ion
com·plex·ioned
com·plex·i·ty
com·pli·ance
com·pli·ant
com·pli·ca·cy
com·pli·cate
com·pli·ca·tion

com·plic·i·ty
com·plied
com·pli·ment (to
  express esteem)
com·pli·men·ta·ry
com·ply
com·ply·ing
com·po·nent
com·pos·er
com·pos·ite
com·po·si·tion
com·pos·i·tor
com·pos men·tis
com·po·sure
com·pote
com·pound·able
com·pre·hend
com·pre·hend·ible
com·pre·hen·si·ble
com·pre·hen·sion
com·press
com·press·ible
com·pres·sion
com·pres·sor
com·pris·al
com·prise
com·pro·mise
com·pro·mis·er
comp·trol·ler
  (auditor)
com·pul·sion
com·pul·so·ry
com·punc·tion
com·pur·ga·tor
com·put·able
com·pu·ta·tion
com·put·er
com·put·er·ize

com·rade
com·rade·ly
com·rade·ship
co·na·tive
con·cat·e·na·tion
con·cave
con·ceal
con·cede
con·ceit
con·ceiv·able
con·ceive
con·ceiv·er
con·cen·trate
con·cen·tra·tor
con·cen·tric
con·cept
con·cep·tion
con·cep·tu·al
con·cep·tu·al·ize
con·cern
con·cert
con·cert·mas·ter
con·cer·to, *plural*
  concertos
con·ces·sion
con·ces·sion·aire
con·ces·sion·ary
con·cierge
con·cil·i·ar
con·cil·i·ate
con·cil·i·a·tion
con·cil·i·a·tor
con·cil·i·a·to·ry
con·cise
con·clave
con·clu·sion
con·coc·tion
con·com·i·tance

con·com·i·tant
con·cor·dance
con·cor·dant
con·cor·dat
con·course
con·cu·bine
con·cu·pis·cence
con·cu·pis·cent
con·cur
con·curred
con·cur·rence
con·cur·rent
con·cur·ring
con·cus·sion
con·demn
con·dem·na·ble
con·dem·na·tion
con·dem·na·to·ry
con·demn·er
con·dens·able
con·dense
con·dens·er
con·de·scend
con·de·scen·dence
con·de·scen·sion
con·dign
con·di·ment
con·di·tion·er
con·do·la·to·ry
con·dole
con·do·lence
con·dol·er
con·dom
con·do·min·i·um
con·duce
con·du·cive
con·duc·tance
con·duct·ible

con·duc·tor
con·duit
con·fec·tion·ary
  (adj)
con·fec·tion·er
con·fec·tion·ery
  (noun candies,
  shop)
con·fed·er·a·cy
con·fed·er·ate
con·fer
con·fer·ee
con·fer·ence
  (meeting and
  bestowal)
con·fer·ment
con·fer·ra·ble
con·fer·ral
con·ferred
con·fer·rer
con·fer·ring
con·fess
con·fess·ed·ly
con·fes·sion
con·fes·sion·al
con·fes·sor
con·fet·ti
con·fi·dant (masc
  one trusted)
con·fi·dante (fem)
con·fi·dence
con·fi·dent
con·fi·den·tial
con·fid·ing
con·fig·u·ra·tion
con·fin·a·ble
con·fine·ment
con·firm·able

con·fir·ma·to·ry
con·fis·cate
can·fis·ca·tor
con·fis·ca·to·ry
con·fla·gra·tion
con·flu·ence
con·flu·ent
con·form·able
con·form·al
con·form·ance
con·form·er
con·form·ist
con·for·mi·ty
con·frere
con·fu·sion
con·fute
con·fut·er
con·geal
con·geal·a·ble
con·gen·ial
con·gen·i·tal
con·ge·ries (sing
  and plural)
con·ges·tion
con·glom·er·ate
con·grat·u·la·tor
con·grat·u·la·to·ry
con·gre·gate
con·gre·ga·tor
con·gress
Con·gress (U.S.)
con·gres·sion·al
con·gress·man
con·gru·ence
con·gru·ent
con·gru·ity
con·gru·ous
con·ic

101

con·i·cal
co·ni·fer
con·jec·tur·a·ble
con·jec·tur·al
con·jec·ture
con·jec·tur·er
con·ju·gal
con·ju·gate
con·ju·ga·tor
con·junc·tion
con·junc·ti·va
con·junc·tive
con·junc·ti·vi·tis
con·jur·er
con·nec·tion
con·nec·tor
conned
con·ning
con·nip·tion
con·niv·ance
con·nive
con·niv·er
con·nois·seur
con·no·ta·tion
con·note
con·nu·bi·al
con·quer·or
con·quis·ta·dor
con·san·guin·e·ous
con·san·guin·i·ty
con·science
con·science-strick·
  en
con·sci·en·tious
con·scious
con·script
con·se·crate
con·se·cra·tion

con·se·cra·tor
con·sec·u·tive
con·sen·su·al
con·sen·sus
con·sent·er
con·sen·tient
con·se·quence
con·se·quent
con·se·quen·tial
con·ser·van·cy
con·ser·va·tion
con·ser·va·tive
con·ser·va·tor
con·ser·va·to·ry
con·sid·er·able
con·sid·er·ate
con·sign·able
con·sign·ee
con·sign·ment
con·sign·or
con·sis·tence
con·sis·ten·cy
con·sis·tent
con·sis·to·ry
con·sol·a·ble
con·so·la·tion
con·so·la·to·ry
con·sole
con·soled
con·sol·i·da·tion
con·sol·i·da·tor
con·sol·ing
con·som·mé
con·so·nance
con·so·nant
con·sor·tium
con·spec·tus
con·spic·u·ous

con·spir·a·cy
con·spir·a·tor
con·sta·ble
con·stab·u·lar
con·stab·u·lary
con·stan·cy
con·stel·la·tion
con·ster·nate
con·ster·na·tion
con·sti·pa·tion
con·stit·u·en·cy
con·stit·u·ent
con·sti·tute
con·sti·tu·tion·al
con·strain
con·straint
con·stric·tor
con·stru·able
con·struc·tion
con·struc·tive
con·struc·tor
con·strue
con·strued
con·stru·ing
con·sul
  (government
  official)
con·sul·ar
con·suls gen·er·al
con·sul·tant
con·sul·ta·tion
con·sul·ta·tive
con·sult·er
con·sul·tor (priest)
con·sum·able
con·sum·er
con·sum·mate
con·sum·ma·tion

con·sum·ma·tor
con·sum·ma·to·ry
con·sump·tion
con·tac·tor
con·ta·gion
con·ta·gious
con·tain·able
con·tain·er
con·tam·i·nant
con·tam·i·nate
con·tam·i·na·tor
con·temn
con·tem·ner
con·tem·plate
con·tem·pla·tor
con·tem·po·ra·ne·ity
con·tem·po·ra·ne·ous
con·tem·po·rary
con·tempt
con·tempt·ible
con·temp·tu·ous
con·tend·er
con·ten·tion
con·ten·tious
con·ter·mi·nous
con·test·able
con·tes·tant
con·tex·tu·al
con·ti·gu·ity
con·tig·u·ous
con·ti·nence
con·ti·nent
con·tin·gence
con·tin·gen·cy
con·tin·gent
con·tin·u·al

con·tin·u·ance
con·tin·u·ant
con·tin·u·a·tion
con·tin·u·a·tor
con·tin·ue
con·ti·nu·ity
con·tin·u·ous
con·tin·u·um
con·tort
con·tor·tion·ist
con·tour
con·tra·band
con·tra·cep·tion
con·tract·ible
con·trac·tile
con·trac·tor
con·trac·tu·al
con·tra·dict·able
con·tra·dic·tor
con·tra·dic·to·ry
con·tral·to,
    plural contraltos
con·tra·ri·ety
con·tra·ri·wise
con·trary
con·trast·able
con·tra·vene
con·tre·temps
con·trib·u·tor
con·trib·u·to·ry
con·trite
con·triv·a·ble
con·tri·vance
con·triv·er
con·trol
con·trol·la·ble
con·trolled
con·trol·ler

con·trol·ling
con·tro·ver·sial
con·tro·ver·sy
con·tro·vert
con·tro·vert·er
con·tro·vert·ible
con·tu·ma·cious
con·tu·ma·cy
con·tu·me·li·ous
con·tu·me·ly
con·tu·sion
co·nun·drum
con·va·lesce
con·va·lesced
con·va·les·cence
con·va·les·cent
con·va·lesc·ing
con·vec·tion
con·vec·tor
con·ven·er
con·ve·nience
con·ve·nient
con·ven·tion·al
con·ven·tion·eer
con·verge
con·ver·gence
con·ver·gent
con·vers·able
con·ver·sance
con·ver·sant
con·verse
con·vert·er
con·vert·ible
con·vex
con·vex·i·ty
con·vey
con·vey·ance
con·veyed

con·vey·or
con·vey·ing
con·vinc·er
con·vin·ci·ble
con·viv·ial
con·vo·ca·tion
con·voke
con·vo·lut·ed
con·vo·lu·tion
con·voyed
con·voy·ing
con·vulse
con·vul·sion
coo
cooed
coo·ing
cook·book
cook·ery
cook·ie
cook·out
cook·stove
cool·ant
cool·er
cool-head·ed
coo·lie
co-op
coop·er (barrel
  maker)
co·op·er·ate
co·op·er·a·tion
co·op·er·a·tive
co-opt
co-op·ta·tion
co-op·tion
co·or·di·nate
co·or·di·na·tion
co·or·di·na·tor

co·pa·cet·ic
co·part·ner
cope·stone
cop·ied
cop·i·er
co·pi·lot
co·pi·ous
copped
cop·pery
cop·ping
copy·book
copy·cat
copy desk
copy·ing
copy·ist
copy·read·er
copy·right
copy·right·able
copy·right·er
  (holder of
  copyright)
co·quet (*verb*)
co·quet·ry
co·quette (*noun
  fem*)
co·quet·ted
co·quet·ting
co·quet·tish
cor·al pink
cor·al reef
cor·al snake
cor·beled
cor·bel·ing (*noun
  and verb*)
cor·dial
cor·dial·i·ty
cor·don

cor·do·van
cor·du·roy
cord·wood
cor·er
co·re·spon·dent
  (divorce case)
cor·mo·rant
corn bor·er
corn bread
corn·cob
corn·crib
cor·ner·back
cor·ner·stone
cor·ner·wise
cor·net·tist
corn·field
corn·flakes
corn·flow·er
corn·husk
cor·nice
corn·meal
corn pone
corn silk
corn·stalk
corn·starch
corn syr·up
cor·nu·co·pia
corn whis·key
cor·ol·lary
co·ro·na, *plural*
  coronas
cor·o·nary
cor·o·na·tion
cor·o·ner
cor·po·ral (of the
  body, officer)
cor·po·rate

cor·po·re·al
(physical,
tangible)
corps (group)
corpse (dead body)
corps·man
cor·pu·lence
cor·pu·lent
cor·pus
cor·pus·cle
cor·ral (enclosure)
cor·ralled
cor·ral·ling
cor·rect·able
cor·rec·ti·tude
cor·rec·tor
cor·re·late
cor·re·la·tion
cor·rel·a·tive
cor·re·spond
cor·re·spon·dence
cor·re·spon·dent
(writer)
cor·ri·dor
cor·ri·gi·ble
cor·rob·o·rate
cor·rob·o·ra·tor
cor·rob·o·ra·to·ry
cor·rode
cor·rod·ible
cor·ro·sion
cor·ru·gate
cor·rupt
cor·rupt·er
cor·rupt·ible
cor·rup·tion
cor·sage

cor·sair
corse·let
(underwear)
cor·se·tiere
cor·tege
cor·tex, *plural*
cortices
cor·ti·cal
cor·ti·sone
cor·us·cate
cor·us·ca·tion
cor·vette
co·sign
co·sig·na·to·ry
co·sign·er
cos·met·ic
cos·me·ti·cian
cos·mic
cos·mo·naut
cos·mo·pol·i·tan
cos·mos
co·spon·sor
co·star
co·starred
co·star·ring
cost-plus
cos·tum·er
co·ten·ant
co·te·rie
cot·tage cheese
cot·tag·er
cot·ton bat·ting
cot·ton can·dy
cot·ton flan·nel
cot·ton gin
cot·ton pick·er
cot·ton·seed

cot·ton·tail
cot·ton·wood
cou·gar
cou·lee (stream,
ravine)
coun·cil (group)
coun·cil·man
coun·cil·or
(member of
group)
coun·sel (*noun*
advice)
coun·sel (*verb* to
give advice)
coun·seled
coun·sel·ing
coun·sel·or (one
who gives advice)
count·able
count·down
count·te·nance
coun·ter
(Compound
words beginning
with the
combining form
counter are
written solid:
counteract.)
coun·ter·at·tack
coun·ter·bal·ance
coun·ter·feit
coun·ter·pane
(bedspread)
coun·tri·fied
coun·try-dance
coun·try·man

coun·try mu·sic
coun·try·side
coup (sudden
   successful move)
coup de grace
coup d'état, *plural*
   coups d'état
coupe (auto)
cou·ple
cou·pled
cou·pler
cou·pling
cou·pon
cou·ra·geous
cou·ri·er
cour·te·ous
cour·te·san
cour·te·sy
court·house
cour·ti·er
court-mar·tial,
   plural courts-
   martial
court-mar·tialed
court-mar·tial·
   ing
court·room
court·ship
court·yard
cous·in (relative)
cou·ture (women's
   clothing business)
cou·tu·ri·er (male
   engaged in
   women's clothing
   business)
cou·tu·ri·ere (*fem*)
co·var·i·ant

cov·e·nant
cov·e·nant·er
cov·er·age
cov·er·all
cov·er charge
cov·er crop
cov·er girl
cov·ert
cov·er-up (*noun*)
cov·et
cov·et·ous
cov·ey
cow·ard
cow·ard·ice
cow·bird
cow·boy
cow·catch·er
cowed
cow·er
cow·hand
cow·hide
cow·ing
cowl (hood)
cow·lick
co-work·er
cow po·ny
cow·punch·er
cox·comb
cox·comb·ry
cox·swain
coy·ly
coy·ote
coz·en (cheat)
co·zi·er
co·zi·ly
co·zi·ness
co·zy
crab·bed (*adj*)

crabbed (*verb*)
crab·bed·ly
crab·bed·ness
crab·ber
crab·bi·er
crab·bing
crab·by
crab·cake
crab·grass
crab·meat
crack·brain
crack·down (*noun*)
crack·er-bar·rel
   (*adj*)
crack·er·jack
crack·le
crack·ling
crack·pot
crack-up (*noun*)
cra·dle
cra·dle·song
crafts·man·ship
craft union
crag·ged
crag·gi·er
crag·gi·ness
crag·gy
crammed
cram·mer
cram·ming
cram·pon
cra·ni·al
cra·ni·um, *plural*
   cramiums
crank·case
crank·shaft
cran·ny
crape myr·tle

crap·shoot·er
crap·u·lence
crap·u·lent
crap·u·lous
crash dive (*noun*)
crash-dive (*verb*)
crash hel·met
crash-land (*verb*)
crash land·ing
 (*noun*)
crass
cra·ter
cra·vat
cra·ven
cray·fish
cray·on
cra·zy quilt
creak (sound)
cream cheese
cream-col·ored
cream·er
cream·ery
cream puff
cream sauce
cre·ate
cre·a·tion
cre·a·tor
crea·ture
cre·dence
cre·den·tial
cre·den·za
cred·i·ble
cred·it·able
cred·i·tor
cre·do
cre·du·li·ty
cred·u·lous
creed·al

cre·ma·tor
cre·ma·to·ry
cren·el·at·ed
cren·el·a·tion
cre·ole
crepe (thin,
 wrinkled material)
crepe pa·per
crepe rub·ber
crepe su·zette,
 plural crepes
 suzette
cre·pus·cule
cre·scen·do, *plural*
 crescendos
cres·cent
crest·fall·en
cre·tin (idiot)
cre·tin·ism
cre·tonne (cloth)
cre·vasse (deep
 crack as in a dike
 or glacier)
crev·ice
 (narrow opening)
crew cut
crew·el·work
crew neck
crib·bage
cribbed
crib·ber
crib·bing
cri·er
crim·i·nal
crim·son
cringe
cring·er
cring·ing

crin·kle
crin·kly
crin·o·line
crip·ple
cri·sis, *plural* crises
crisp·i·er
crisp·i·ness
criss·cross
cri·te·ri·on, *plural*
 criteria
crit·i·cal
crit·i·cism
crit·i·ciz·able
crit·i·cize
cri·tique
cro·chet
cro·cheted
cro·chet·er
cro·chet·ing
crock·ery
croc·o·dile
cro·cus, *plural*
 crocuses
crois·sant
cro·ny
cro·ny·ism
croon·er
crop-dust
crop-eared
cropped
crop·per
crop·pie
crop·ping
cro·quet (game)
cro·quette (food)
cro·sier
cross·able
cross·bar

cross·beam
cross·bones
cross·bow
cross·bred
cross·breed
cross-coun·try
  (*adj* and *adv*)
cross·cur·rent
cross·cut
cross-ex·am·i·na·
  tion
cross-ex·am·ine
cross-eyed
cross-fer·til·ize
cross-file
cross fire
cross-grained
cross hair
cross·hatch
cross-in·dex
cross-leg·ged
cross·over
cross·patch
cross-pol·li·nate
cross-pur·pose
cross-ques·tion
cross-re·fer
cross-ref·er·ence
cross-re·ferred
cross-re·fer·ring
cross·road
cross·ruff
cross sec·tion
cross-stitch
cross-town (*adj*)
cross·walk
cross·way
cross·wind

cross·wise
cross·word puz·zle
crotch·ety
croup
  (inflammation)
crou·pi·er
crou·ton
crow's-foot, *plural*
  crow's-feet
crow's-nest
cru·cial
cru·ci·ble
cru·ci·fied
cru·ci·fix
cru·ci·fix·ion
cru·ci·form
cru·ci·fy
cru·ci·fy·ing
cru·di·ty
cru·el
cru·el·er
cru·el·est
cru·et
cruis·er
crul·ler
crum·ble
crum·bly
crum·ple
crup·per
crux, *plural* cruxes
cry·ba·by
cry·ing
crypt
cryp·tic
cryp·to·gram
crys·tal
crys·tal-clear
crys·tal gaz·er

crys·tal·line
crys·tal·lize
cub·bish
cub·bish·ness
cub·by·hole
cu·bi·cal (like a
  cube)
cu·bi·cle (small
  space)
cub·ism
cuck·old
cuck·oo
cuck·oo clock
cu·cum·ber
cud·dle
cud·dly
cud·gel
cud·geled
cud·gel·ing
cued
cu·ing
cui·rass
cui·sine
cul-de-sac, *plural*
  cul-de-sacs
cu·li·nary
cul·mi·nant
cul·mi·nate
cul·pa·ble
cul·prit
cul·ti·va·ble
cul·ti·va·tor
cul·tur·al
cul·vert
cum·ber·some
cum·brance
cum·brous
cu·mu·la·tive

cu·mu·lous (adj)
cu·mu·lus (noun)
cu·ne·i·form
cun·ning
cup·bear·er
cup·board
cup·cake
cup·ful, plural
   cupfuls
cu·pid·i·ty
cu·po·la
cu·po·laed
cupped
cup·ping
cur·able
cu·ra·cy
cu·ra·re
cu·rate
cu·ra·tor
curb·stone
cur·dle
cure-all
cur·few
cu·ria
cu·rio, plural curios
cu·ri·os·i·ty
cu·ri·ous
curli·cue
cur·mud·geon
cur·rant (fruit)
cur·ren·cy
cur·rent (at present,
   a flow)
cur·ric·u·lar
cur·ric·u·lum,
   plural curricula
cur·ric·u·lum
   vi·tae

cur·ried
cur·ri·er
cur·rish
cur·ry·comb
cur·ry·ing
cur·ry pow·der
cursed (past of
   curse)
curs·ed (adj)
cur·sive
cur·so·ri·ly
cur·so·ry
cur·tail
cur·tain
cur·tain call
cur·tain rais·er
curt·sy (noun and
   verb)
cur·va·ceous
cur·va·ture
cur·vi·lin·ear
curvy
cus·tard
cus·to·di·al
cus·to·di·an
cus·to·dy
cus·tom
cus·tom·ar·i·ly
cus·tom·ary
cus·tom-built
cus·tom·house
cus·tom·ize
cus·tom-made
cut-and-dried
cu·ta·ne·ous
cut·away
cut·back (noun)
cut glass (noun)

cut-glass (adj)
cu·ti·cle
cut-in (noun and
   adj)
cut·lass
cut·lery
cut·off (noun and
   adj)
cut·out (noun)
cut·over (adj)
cut·purse
cut-rate (adj)
cut·ter
cut·throat
cut·ting
cut·up (noun)
cut·work (noun)
cut·worm
cy·a·nide
cy·ber·net·ics
cy·cla·men
cy·clic
cy·clist
cy·clone
cy·clo·pe·dia
cy·clo·ra·ma
cy·clo·tron
cyl·in·der
cy·lin·dri·cal
cym·bal (music)
cyn·ic
cyn·i·cal
cyn·i·cism
cy·no·sure
cy·press
cyst
czar

D

dabbed
dab·ber
dab·bing
dab·ble
dab·bler
dab·bling
dachs·hund
da·do, *plural*
  dadoes
daf·fo·dil
da·guerre·o·type
dahl·ia
dail·ly
dai·qui·ri
dairy cat·tle
dairy farm
dairy·ing
dairy·maid
dairy·man
dai·sy
dal·li·ance
dal·lied
dal·li·er
dal·ly·ing
dam·age·a·ble
dam·ag·ing
dam·ask
dammed

dam·ming
dam·na·ble
dam·na·to·ry
damned·est
damn·ing
damp-dry
damp·en·er
damp·er
damp·ing-off
  (*noun*)
damp off (*verb*)
dam·sel
dan·de·li·on
dan·der
dan·dle
dan·druff
dan·druffy
dan·gle
dan·gler
dap·per
dap·ple
dare·dev·il
dark horse
dark lan·tern
dark·room
das·tard·ly
da·ta (*sing* and
  plural)

dat·able
date·line
  (newspaper)
date line (180th
  meridian)
da·tum, *plural*
  data
daub·ery
daugh·ter-in-law,
  plural daughters-
  in-law
daunt
daw·dle
day·bed
day·book
day·break
day-care cen·ter
day·dream
day la·bor·er
day let·ter
day·light
day·light-sav·ing
  time
day·long (*adj* and
  adv)
day nur·sery
day school
day·time

110

day-to-day (*adj*)
daz·zle
daz·zler
dea·con
de·ac·ti·vate
dead·beat
dead cen·ter
dead end (*noun*)
dead-end (*adj*)
dead·eye
dead·fall
dead hand
dead·head
dead heat
dead let·ter
dead lift
dead·line
dead·lock
dead march
dead·pan (*adj* and
   adv)
dead reck·on·ing
dead set
dead weight
dead·wood
deaf-and-dumb (*adj*)
deaf-mute
dean·ery
dearth
deary
death·bed
death bell
death·blow
death cham·ber
death mask
death rate
death's-head
death trap

death war·rant
death·watch
de·ba·cle
de·bar
de·barred
de·bar·ring
de·bat·able
de·bat·er
de·bauch·ee
de·bauch·ery
de·ben·ture
de·bil·i·tate
de·bil·i·ty
deb·o·nair
de·brief
de·bris
debt·or
de·but
deb·u·tant (anyone
   making first
   appearance)
deb·u·tante (young
   woman making
   first appearance
   in society)
dec·a·dence
dec·a·dent
Deca·logue
de·cant·er
de·cap·i·tate
de·cayed
de·cay·ing
de·cease
de·ce·dent
   (deceased)
de·ceit
de·ceiv·able
de·ceive

de·ceiv·er
de·cel·er·ate
de·cen·cy
de·cen·ni·al
de·cen·ni·um,
   plural decen-
   niums
de·cen·tral·ize
de·cep·tion
deci·bel
de·cid·able
de·cid·u·ous
dec·i·mal
dec·i·mate
de·ci·pher
de·ci·pher·able
de·ci·sion
de·ci·sive
deck chair
deck·hand
deck·house
deck·le-edged (*adj*)
de·claim
de·claim·er
de·cla·ma·tion
de·clam·a·to·ry
de·clar·able
de·clar·a·to·ry
de·clar·er
de·clas·si·fy
de·cliv·i·ty
dé·col·le·tage
dé·col·le·té
de·con·trol
de·con·trolled
de·con·trol·ling
dec·o·rate
dec·o·ra·tor

dec·o·rous
de·co·rum
de·coyed
de·coy·ing
de·cree
de·cree·ing
dec·re·ment
de·crep·it
de·cre·tal
de·cri·al
de·cried
de·cri·er
de·cry·ing
ded·i·cate
ded·i·ca·tor
ded·i·ca·to·ry
de·duce
de·duc·ible
de·duct·ible
de-em·pha·sis
de-em·pha·size
deep-chest·ed
deep-dish pie
deep-dyed
Deep·freeze
  (trademark)
deep freez·er
deep-fried
deep-fry
deep-fry·ing
deep-laid
deep-root·ed
deep-sea (adj)
deep-seat·ed
deep space
de-es·ca·late
de fac·to

de·fal·cate
de·fal·ca·tor
de·fam·a·to·ry
de·fam·er
de·fault·er
de·fea·sance
de·fea·si·ble
de·fec·tor
de·fend·able
de·fen·dant
de·fen·es·tra·tion
de·fense
de·fen·si·ble
de·fen·sive
de·fer
def·er·ence
def·er·ent
def·er·en·tial
de·fer·ment
de·fer·ra·ble
de·fer·ral
de·ferred
de·fer·ring
de·fi·ance
de·fi·ant
de·fi·cien·cy
de·fi·cient
def·i·cit
de·fi·er
de·fin·able
de·fin·er
def·i·nite
de·fin·i·tive
de·fla·tion·ary
de·flec·tion
de·flec·tor
de·fo·li·ant

de·fo·li·ate
de·fo·li·a·tor
de·for·mi·ty
de·fray·able
de·fray·al
de·frayed
de·fray·ing
de·funct
de·fuse
de·gen·er·a·cy
de·gen·er·ate
de·grad·able
deg·ra·da·tion
de·gree-day
de·hu·man·ize
de·hu·mid·i·fied
de·hu·mid·i·fi·er
de·hu·mid·i·fy
de·hu·mid·i·fy·ing
de·ice
de·ic·er
de·i·fy
deign
de·ism
de·i·ty
de·layed
de·lay·er
de·lay·ing
de·lec·ta·ble
de·lec·ta·tion
del·e·ga·ble
del·e·ga·cy
del·e·gate
de·lete
del·e·te·ri·ous
de·lib·er·a·tor
del·i·ca·cy

del·i·ca·tes·sen
de·li·cious
de·lin·eate
de·lin·ea·tor
de·lin·quen·cy
de·lin·quent
del·i·ques·cence
de·lir·i·ous
de·lir·i·um, *plural*
  deliriums
de·liv·er·able
de·liv·er·ance
de·liv·er·er
de·lud·er
del·uge
de·lu·sion
de·lu·so·ry
de·luxe
dem·a·gog·ic
dem·a·gogue
dem·a·gogu·ery
dem·a·gogy
de·mand·able
de·mar·cate
de·mar·ca·tion
de·mean
de·mean·or
demi·god
de·mil·i·ta·rize
de·mise
de·mit
de·mit·ted
de·mit·ting
demi·urge
demi·ur·gic
de·mo·bi·lize
de·moc·ra·tize

de·mog·ra·pher
de·mog·ra·phy
de·mo·li·tion
de·mon
de·mon·e·tize
de·mo·ni·ac
de·mon·ic
de·mon·stra·ble
dem·on·stra·tor
de·mor·al·ize
de·mount·able
de·mur
de·mur·rage
de·mur·ral
de·murred
de·mur·rer
de·mur·ring
de·nat·u·ral·ize
de·na·tur·ant
den·e·ga·tion
  (denial)
den·gue
de·ni·able
de·ni·al
den·i·grate
den·im
den·i·zen
de·nom·i·na·tor
de·noue·ment
de·nounce
de·nounc·er
dense
den·si·ty
den·tal
den·ti·frice
den·tin
den·tist·ry

de·ny·ing
de·odor·ant
de·odor·ize
de·odor·iz·er
de·part·men·
  tal·ize
de·pend·able
de·pen·dence
de·pen·den·cy
de·pen·dent
de·per·son·al·ize
de·pic·tor
dep·i·late
dep·i·la·tor
de·pil·a·to·ry
de·plet·able
de·plete
de·ple·tion
de·plor·able
de·ploy
de·ployed
de·ploy·ing
de·ploy·ment
de·pon·ent
de·pop·u·late
de·pop·u·la·tor
de·port·able
de·pos·al
de·po·si·tion
de·pos·i·tor
de·pos·i·to·ry
de·pot
de·prav·i·ty
de·pre·cate
de·pre·ca·tor
dep·re·ca·to·ry
de·pre·cia·ble

de·pre·ci·ate
de·pre·ci·a·tor
de·pre·cia·to·ry
dep·re·date
dep·re·da·tion
de·pres·sant
de·press·ible
de·pres·sor
de·pri·va·tion
dep·u·ta·tion
de·pute
dep·u·tize
dep·u·ty
der·e·lict
der·e·lic·tion
de ri·gueur
de·ri·sion
de·ri·so·ry
de·riv·able
de·riv·a·tive
der·o·gate
de·rog·a·to·ry
der·rick
der·ring-do
der·rin·ger
de·scend
de·scen·dant
  (noun)
de·scen·dent (adj)
de·scend·er
de·scend·ible
de·scent
de·scrib·able
de·scried
de·scry
de·scry·ing
des·e·crate
des·e·crat·er

de·seg·re·ga·tion
de·sen·si·tize
de·sen·si·tiz·er
de·sert (noun
  barren area,
  deserved reward;
  adj barren; verb
  leave)
de·sert·er
des·ic·cate
des·ic·ca·tor
de·sid·er·a·tion
des·ig·na·tor
des·ig·nee
de·sign·er
de·sir·able
de·sir·ous
de·sis·tance
des·o·late
des·o·lat·or
de·spair
des·per·a·do,
  plural desper-
  adoes
des·per·ate
de·spi·ca·ble
de·spise
de·spoil·er
de·spo·li·a·tion
de·spon·dence
de·spon·den·cy
de·spon·dent
des·pot
des·sert (food)
des·sert·spoon
des·sert wine
des·ti·ny
des·ti·tute

de·stroyed
de·stroy·er
de·stroy·ing
de·struc·ti·ble
de·struc·tive
de·struc·tor
de·sue·tude
des·ul·to·ry
de·tach·able
de·tect·able
de·tec·tor
dé·tente
de·ter
de·ter·gent
de·te·ri·o·rate
de·te·ri·o·ra·tion
de·ter·ment
de·ter·min·able
de·ter·mi·na·cy
de·ter·mi·nant
de·ter·mi·na·tor
de·ter·min·er
de·ter·min·ism
de·terred
de·ter·rence
de·ter·rent
de·ter·ring
de·test·able
det·o·na·tor
de·tour
de·trac·tor
det·ri·ment
deuce
de·val·u·a·tion
de·val·ue
de·val·u·ing
dev·as·tate
dev·as·ta·tor

de·vel·op
de·vel·op·able
de·vel·op·er
de·vel·op·ment
de·vi·ance
de·vi·ant
de·vi·ate
de·vi·a·tor
de·vice (scheme,
  plan, mechanism)
dev·il
dev·iled
dev·il·ing
dev·il-may-care
  (*adj*)
dev·il's food cake
dev·il·try
de·vi·ous
de·vis·able
de·vise (invent)
de·vi·see (law)
de·vis·er
de·vi·sor (law)
de·vi·tal·ize
de·void
dev·o·tee
de·vour·er
de·vout
dew·ber·ry
dew·drop
dew·fall
dew·i·er
dew·i·ness
dew·lap
dew point
dew worm
dewy-eyed
dex·ter·i·ty

dex·ter·ous
di·a·be·tes
di·a·bol·ic
di·a·crit·ic
di·a·dem
di·ag·nos·able
di·ag·no·sis, *plural*
  diagnoses
di·ag·nos·tic
di·ag·nos·ti·cian
di·ag·o·nal
di·a·gram
di·a·gramed
di·a·gram·ing
di·a·gram·mat·ic
di·al
di·a·lect
di·aled
di·al·er
di·a·logue
di·al tone
di·am·e·ter
di·a·met·ric
di·a·mond
di·a·per
di·aph·a·nous
di·a· phragm
di·a·rist
di·ar·rhea
di·a·ry
di·a·tribe
di·chot·o·my
dick·ey
dic·ta·tor
dic·tion·ary
dic·tum, *plural*
  dicta
di·dac·tic

did·dle
di·do, *plural* didos
die (cube), *plural*
  dice
die (tool), *plural*
  dies
die·back
die cast·ing
dis-hard (*noun* and
  adj)
die·sel
di·e·tary
di·et·er
di·e·tet·ic
di·e·ti·tian
dif·fer·ence
dif·fer·ent
dif·fer·en·tia,
  plural differentiae
dif·fer·en·tial
dif·fer·en·ti·ate
dif·fi·dence
dif·fi·dent
dif·fract
dif·fuse (to spread)
dif·fus·er
dif·fus·ible
di·gest·er
di·gest·ible
dig·ger
dig·ging
dig·it
dig·i·tal
dig·ni·fied
dig·ni·fy
dig·ni·fy·ing
dig·ni·tary
dig·ni·ty

di·gress
di·gres·sion
dike
di·lap·i·date
di·lap·i·da·tor
di·lat·able
di·la·ta·tion
di·la·tion
di·la·tor
dil·a·to·ry
di·lem·ma
dil·et·tante, *plural*
dilettantes
dil·et·tant·ish
dil·et·tant·ism
dil·i·gence
dil·i·gent
dil·ly·dal·lied
dil·ly·dal·ly
dil·ly·dal·ly·ing
di·lute
di·lut·er
di·men·sion
di·min·ish·able
di·min·u·en·do,
plural
diminuendos
dim·i·nu·tion
di·min·u·tive
dimmed
dim·mer
dim·mest
dim·ming
dim·ness
dim·out
dim·wit·ted
din·ghy (boat)

din·gi·est
din·gy (dirty)
din·key (*noun*)
din·ky (*adj*)
dinned
din·ning
di·no·saur
di·oc·e·san
di·o·cese, *plural*
dioceses
di·o·ra·ma
diph·the·ria
di·plo·ma, *plural*
diplomas
di·plo·ma·cy
di·plo·mate
(medical
specialist)
dipped
dip·per
dip·per·ful, *plural*
dipperfuls
dip·ping
dip·stick
di·rec·tor
di·rec·to·ry
dire·ful
dirge (lament)
di·ri·gi·ble
dirn·dl
dirt-cheap
dirt farm·er
dis·abil·i·ty
dis·able
dis·able·ment
dis·abuse
dis·ac·cord

dis·ad·van·tage
dis·ad·van·
ta·geous
dis·af·fect
dis·af·fec·tion
dis·af·firm
dis·agree
dis·agree·able
dis·agree·ing
dis·agree·ment
dis·al·low
dis·al·low·ance
dis·ap·pear
dis·ap·pear·ance
dis·ap·point
dis·ap·pro·ba·tion
dis·ap·prov·al
dis·ap·prove
dis·ar·ma·ment
dis·ar·range
dis·ar·ray
dis·as·sem·ble
dis·as·so·ci·ate
dis·as·ter
dis·as·trous
dis·avow
dis·avow·al
dis·bar·ment
dis·barred
dis·bar·ring
dis·be·lief
dis·be·lieve
dis·burs·a·ble
dis·burse (to pay;
see disperse)
dis·burse·ment
dis·burs·er

disc (phonograph
   record; *see* disk)
dis·cern
dis·cern·er
dis·cern·ible
dis·ci·ple
dis·ci·plin·ary
dis·ci·pline
dis·claim·er
dis·clo·sure
dis·cog·ra·pher
dis·cog·ra·phy
dis·col·or
dis·com·bob·u·late
dis·com·fit
dis·com·fit·ed
dis·com·fit·ing
dis·com·fi·ture
dis·com·mode
dis·con·cert
dis·con·so·late
dis·con·tin·u·ance
dis·con·tin·ue
dis·con·tin·u·ing
dis·con·tin·u·ous
dis·cor·dance
dis·cor·dant
dis·co·theque
dis·coun·te·nance
dis·cour·age
dis·cour·age·ment
dis·course
dis·cour·te·ous
dis·cour·te·sy
dis·cov·er·able
dis·cov·er·er
dis·cred·it·able

dis·creet (prudent)
dis·crep·an·cy
dis·crep·ant
dis·crete (separate,
   distinct)
dis·cre·tion
dis·cre·tion·ary
dis·crim·i·na·ble
dis·crim·i·nant
dis·crim·i·na·tor
dis·crim·i·na·to·ry
dis·cur·sion
dis·cur·sive
dis·cus (sport
   event)
dis·cuss (talk)
dis·cus·sant
dis·cuss·ible
dis·dain
dis·dain·ful
dis·em·bark
dis·em·bar·ka·tion
dis·em·bod·ied
dis·em·bod·y·ing
dis·em·bow·eled
dis·em·bow·el·ing
dis·em·bow·el·
   ment
dis·en·chant
dis·en·fran·chise
dis·en·fran·chis·
   ing
dis·en·tan·gle
dis·en·thrall
dis·en·thrall·ment
dis·fa·vor
dis·fran·chise

dis·fran·chise·ment
dis·fran·chis·ing
dis·gorge
dis·grun·tle
dis·guise
dis·gust
dis·ha·bille
dis·heart·en
di·shev·el
di·shev·eled
di·shev·el·ing
di·shev·el·ment
dis·hon·or
dis·hon·or·able
dish·rag
dish tow·el
dish·wash·er
dish·wa·ter
dis·il·lu·sion
dis·in·fec·tant
dis·in·gen·u·ous
dis·in·her·i·tance
dis·in·te·grate
dis·in·te·gra·tor
dis·in·ter
dis·in·ter·ment
dis·in·terred
dis·in·ter·ring
disk (all meanings
   except phono-
   graph record;
   see disc)
disk·like
disk wheel
dis·lik·able
dis·lodg·ment
dis·mal

dis·man·tle
dis·miss
dis·miss·al
dis·miss·i·ble
dis·o·be·di·ence
dis·o·be·di·ent
dis·o·bey
dis·o·beyed
dis·o·bey·ing
dis·or·ga·nize
dis·par·age
dis·par·age·ment
dis·par·ag·er
dis·pa·rate (unlike)
dis·par·i·ty
dis·pas·sion·ate
dis·patch
dis·patch·er
dis·pel
dis·pelled
dis·pel·ling
dis·pens·able
dis·pen·sa·ry
dis·pense
dis·pens·er
dis·pers·al
dis·perse (to
    scatter; *see*
    disburse)
dis·pers·ible
dis·per·sion
dis·pir·it
dis·place·able
dis·plea·sure
dis·pos·able
dis·pos·al

dis·pos·er
dis·po·si·tion
dis·pos·sess
dis·pos·ses·sor
dis·pro·por·tion
dis·prov·able
dis·pu·ta·ble
dis·pu·tant
dis·pu·ta·tious
dis·put·er
dis·qui·et
dis·qui·etude
dis·qui·si·tion
dis·rep·u·ta·ble
dis·re·spect·ful
dis·rupt
dis·rupt·er
dis·rup·tion
dis·sat·is·fac·to·ry
dis·sat·is·fy
dis·sect
dis·sec·tor
dis·sem·blance
dis·sem·ble
dis·sem·bler
dis·sem·i·nate
dis·sem·i·na·tor
dis·sen·sion
dis·sent
dis·sent·er
dis·ser·ta·tion
dis·ser·vice
dis·sev·er
dis·sev·er·ance
dis·si·dence
dis·si·dent

dis·sim·i·lar
dis·sim·u·late
dis·sim·u·la·tor
dis·si·pate
dis·si·pat·er
dis·so·ci·ate
dis·sol·u·ble
dis·so·lute
dis·solv·able
dis·solve
dis·sol·vent
dis·so·nance
dis·so·nant
dis·suade
dis·suad·er
dis·sua·sion
dis·sua·sive
dis·taff
dis·tance
dis·tant
dis·tend
dis·ten·si·ble
dis·ten·tion
dis·till
dis·til·late
dis·til·la·tion
dis·tilled
dis·till·er
dis·till·ery
dis·till·ing
dis·tinc·tion
dis·tin·guish·able
dis·tract·er
dis·tract·ible
dis·trai·nor
dis·traught

dis·tress
dis·trib·u·tor
dis·turb·ance
dis·turb·er
dit·to, *plural* dittos
di·ur·nal
di·va·gate
di·va·ga·tion
di·van
dive-bomb
di·ver·gence
di·ver·gent
di·vers (various,
  several)
di·verse (unlike)
di·ver·si·fied
di·ver·si·fy
di·ver·si·fy·ing
di·ver·sion·ary
di·ver·si·ty
di·vert
di·vert·er
di·vest
di·vest·i·ture
di·vid·able
div·i·dend
di·vid·er
div·i·na·tion
di·vin·er
di·vin·i·ty
di·vis·i·ble
di·vi·sor
di·vor·cé (*masc*)
di·vor·cée (*fem*)
div·ot
di·vul·gence

do·able
do·cent
doc·ile
do·cil·i·ty
dock·age
dock·et
dock·side
doc·tor·al
doc·tri·naire
doc·u·men·ta·ry
dod·der
do·do, *plural* dodos
doe (animal, *plural*
  does; *see* dough)
do·er
dog bis·cuit
dog·bite
dog·cart
dog·catch·er
dog col·lar
dog days
dog-ear
dog-eat-dog (*adj*)
dog·fight
dog·ged (*adj*)
dogged (*verb*)
dog·ged·ly
dog·ged·ness
dog·ger·el
dog·ging
dog·gish
dog·go
dog·gy
dog·house
do·gie (stray calf)
dog·leg

dog·leg·ged
dog·leg·ging
dog·ma, *plural*
  dogmas
dog·mat·ic
dog·ma·tize
do-good (*adj*)
do-good·er
dog·trot
dog·watch
dog·wood
doi·ly
do-it-your·self
dol·drums
dole
dol·lar
dol·lop
do·lor
do·lor·ous
do·main
do·mes·tic·i·ty
do·mi·cile
do·mi·cil·i·ary
dom·i·nance
dom·i·nant
dom·i·na·tor
dom·i·neer
do·min·ion
dom·i·no (game),
  plural dominoes
do·na·tor
don·key, *plural*
  donkeys
donned
don·ning
don·nish

do·nor
do-noth·ing (*noun* and *adj*)
door (Compound words beginning *door* are written solid: *doorjamb,* except as otherwise shown below.)
do-or-die (*adj*)
door prize
door-to-door
dope·ster
dop·ey
dop·i·er
dor·man·cy
dor·mant
dor·mer
dor·mi·to·ry
dos·age
do's and don'ts
dos·sier
dot·age
dot·ard
dot·ted
dot·ti·er
dot·ting
dot·tle
dot·ty
dou·ble-bar·reled
dou·ble bass
dou·ble boil·er
dou·ble-breast·ed
dou·ble-check (*noun* and *verb*)
dou·ble chin

dou·ble cross (*noun*)
dou·ble-cross (*verb*)
dou·ble-cross·er
dou·ble date (*noun*)
dou·ble-date (*verb*)
dou·ble-deal·er
dou·ble-deal·ing
dou·ble-deck·er
dou·ble-edged
dou·ble en·ten·dre
dou·ble en·try
dou·ble-faced
dou·ble fea·ture
dou·ble-head·er
dou·ble-joint·ed
dou·ble neg·a·tive
dou·ble-park
dou·ble play
dou·ble-quick
dou·ble-space (*verb*)
dou·ble stand·ard
dou·ble-stop (*verb*)
dou·ble take
dou·ble-talk
dou·ble·think
dou·ble time (*noun*)
dou·ble-time (*verb*)
doubt·able
doubt·er
doubt·ful
dough (flour mixture; *see* doe)
dough·nut
dough·ty

dour
douse (to make wet; *see* dowse)
dove·cote
dove·tail
dow·a·ger
dow·dy
dow·el
dow·eled
dow·el·ing
dow·er
down (Compound words beginning with *down* are written solid: *downhill,* except as otherwise shown below.)
down-bow
down-east (*adj*)
down·heart·ed
down pay·ment
down-to-earth (*adj*)
down·trod·den
down un·der (Australia)
down·ward
dow·ry
dowse (search for water; *see* douse)
dox·ol·o·gy
drab·ber
drab·best
draft board
draft·ee
draft·i·er
drafts·man

drafty
dragged
drag·ging
drag·gle
drag·gle·tail
drag·gling
drag·gy
drag·line
drag·net
drag·on (monster)
dra·goon (soldier, to force)
drain·age
drain·pipe
dram·a·tize
drap·er
drap·ery
dras·tic
draw·back
draw·bar
draw·bridge
draw·er
draw·ing board
draw·ing card
drawl (speech)
draw po·ker
draw·string
dray
dray·age
dread·nought
dream·boat
dream·land
dream world
dreary
dredg·er
dredg·ing
dress cir·cle

dress·i·ly
dress·ing-down
dress·ing gown
dress·ing room
dress·ing ta·ble
dress·mak·er
dress pa·rade
dress re·hears·al
dress suit
drib·ble
drib·bled
drib·bler
drib·bling
drib·let
dried
dried-up (*adj*)
dri·er (*adj* more dry; *see* dryer)
dri·er (*noun* drying agent)
dries
dri·est
drift·er
drift·weed
drift·wood
drill·mas·ter
drill press
drink·able
drip-dried
drip-dry
drip-dry·ing
drip grind
dripped
drip·per
drip·pi·er
drip·ping
drip·py

drive-in
driv·el
driv·eled
driv·el·er
driv·el·ing
drive shaft
drive·way
driz·zle
driz·zly
droll (amusing)
droll·ery
drom·e·dary
drool (salivate)
drop cloth
drop-forge (*verb*)
drop forg·ing (*noun* product)
drop kick (*noun*)
drop-kick (*verb*)
drop-kick·er
drop leaf (*noun*)
drop-leaf (*adj*)
drop·light
drop-off (*noun*)
drop·out
dropped
drop·per
drop·ping
drop shot
drop·si·cal
drop·sy
dross (waste matter)
drought
drowned
drown·ing
drowse
drows·i·er

drows·i·ly
drowsy
drubbed
drub·ber
drub·bing
drudg·ery
drugged
drug·ging
drug·gist
drug·store
drum·beat
drum·fire
drum·head
drum ma·jor
drum ma·jor·ette
(fem)
drummed
drum·mer
drum·ming
drum·stick
drunk·ard
drunk·o·me·ter
dry·as·dust (adj
and noun)
dry cell
dry-clean
dry clean·er
dry clean·ing
dry dock (noun)
dry-dock (verb)
dry·er (machine;
see drier)
dry-eyed
dry farm (noun)
dry-farm (verb)
dry farm·er
dry fly
dry goods

dry·ing
dry·ly
dry·ness
dry rot
dry run
dry-shod
dry wall (noun)
dry-wall (adj)
dry wash
du·al (two parts)
du·al-pur·pose
dubbed
dub·ber
dub·bing
du·bi·ety
du·bi·ous
duc·tile
dud·geon
du·el (combat)
du·eled
du·el·er
du·el·ing
du·el·ist
du·en·na
du·et
duf·fel bag
dul·cet
dull·ard
dulled
dull·ness
dul·ly (manner)
du·ly (in due
course)
dumb·bell
dumb show
dumb·strick·en
dumb·struck
dumb wait·er

dum·found
dun·ga·ree, plural
dungarees
dun·geon
dunned
dun·ning
duo, plural duos
du·plex
du·pli·ca·ble
du·pli·cate
du·pli·ca·tor
du·plic·i·ty
du·ra·ble
du·rance
du·ra·tion
du·ress
dust·bin
dust bowl
dust jack·et
dust·pan
dust·proof
dust storm
Dutch cour·age
Dutch door
Dutch·man
Dutch treat
Dutch un·cle
du·te·ous
du·ti·able
du·ti·ful
du·ty-free
dwarf, plural dwarfs
dwelled
dwell·er
dwell·ing place
dwin·dle
dye (color)
dyed (colored)

dyed-in-the-wool
dye·ing (coloring)
dy·er
dye·stuff
dy·ing (die)
dy·nam·ic

dy·na·mite
dy·na·mo, *plural*
  dynamos
dy·nas·ty
dys·en·tery

dys·func·tion
dys·lex·ia
dys·pep·sia
dys·pep·tic
dys·tro·phy

E

ea·ger
ea·gle
ea·gle-eyed
ear (Compound
    words beginning
    with *ear* are
    written solid:
    earful.)
earl (noble)
ear·nest
earth (Compound
    words beginning
    with *earth* are
    written solid:
    earthman, except
    as otherwise
    shown below.)
earth·i·ness
earth sci·ence
earth·ward
ea·sel
ease·ment
eas·i·er
eas·i·ly
eas·i·ness
east (direction)
East (section of the
    country or the
    world)

east·bound
east by north
east by south
east·er·ly
east·ern
East·ern·er
east·ern·most
East·ern Stand·ard
    Time
east-north·east
east-south·east
east·ward
easy·chair
easy·go·ing
easy mark
easy street
eat·able
eaves (overhang)
eaves·drop
eaves·dropped
eaves·drop·per
eaves·drop·ping
ebb tide
eb·o·ny
ebul·lience
ebul·lient
ec·cen·tric
ec·cen·tric·i·ty
ec·cle·si·as·tic

ech·e·lon
echo, *plural* echoes
ech·oed
echo·ic
echo·ing
éclair
éclat
ec·lec·tic
eclipse
eclip·tic
ecol·o·gy
eco·nom·ic
econ·o·mize
econ·o·my
ec·sta·sy
ec·stat·ic
ec·to·plasm
ec·u·men·i·cal
ec·ze·ma
ed·dy
ede·ma
edge·wise
edg·i·er
edg·i·ly
edg·i·ness
edg·ing
edgy
ed·i·ble
ed·i·fi·ca·tion

ed·i·fice
ed·i·fied
ed·i·fy
ed·i·fy·ing
ed·i·tor
ed·i·to·ri·al·ize
ed·i·tor in chief
ed·u·ca·ble
ed·u·ca·tor
educe
educ·ible
ee·rie
ee·ri·er
ee·ri·ly
ee·ri·ness
ef·face
ef·face·able
ef·fect (*noun* result, *verb* to bring about; *see* affect)
ef·fec·tor
ef·fec·tu·al
ef·fec·tu·ate
ef·fem·i·na·cy
ef·fem·i·nate
ef·fer·vesce
ef·fer·ves·cence
ef·fer·ves·cent
ef·fete
ef·fi·ca·cious
ef·fi·ca·cy
ef·fi·cien·cy
ef·fi·cient
ef·fi·gy
ef·flo·resce
ef·flo·res·cence
ef·flu·ence (flowing out; *see* affluence)

ef·flu·ent
ef·flu·vi·um
ef·fron·tery
ef·ful·gence
ef·ful·gent
ef·fu·sion
egal·i·tar·i·an
egg·beat·er
egg·nog
egg·plant
egg roll
egg·shell
ego·cen·tric
ego·ism (ethical doctrine)
ego·tism (self-importance)
egre·gious
egress
ei·der·down
eight ball
eighth
eight·i·eth
eighty-first, etc.
eighty-one, etc.
ejac·u·late
ejac·u·la·tor
ejac·u·la·to·ry
eject·able
ejec·tor
eke out
eked out
ek·ing out
elab·o·rate
elab·o·ra·tor
élan
elapse
elas·tic

elas·tic·i·ty
elat·ed
ela·tion
el·bow grease
el·bow·room
elec·tion·eer
elec·tor
elec·tor·ate
elec·tri·cian
elec·tri·fied
elec·tri·fy
elec·tri·fy·ing
elec·tu·ary
el·ee·mos·y·nary
el·e·gance
el·e·gant
ele·gi·ac
el·e·gize
el·e·gy
el·e·men·tal
el·e·men·ta·ry
el·e·phant
el·e·phan·ti·a·sis
el·e·va·tor
elf, *plural* elves
elic·it (draw out)
elic·i·tor
elide
el·i·gi·ble
elim·i·nate
elim·i·na·tor
elim·i·na·to·ry
eli·sion
elite
elix·ir
el·lipse
el·lip·sis, *plural* ellipses

125

el·lip·ti·cal
el·o·quence
el·o·quent
elu·ci·date
elu·ci·da·tor
elude
elu·sive (hard to
   grasp; *see* illusive)
ema·ci·ate
em·a·nate (come
   out from)
eman·ci·pate
eman·ci·pa·tor
eman·ci·pa·to·ry
emas·cu·late
emas·cu·la·tor
em·balm
em·balm·er
em·bar·go, *plural*
   embargoes
em·bark
em·bar·ka·tion
em·bar·rass
em·bas·sy
em·bed
em·bed·ded
em·bed·ding
em·bed·ment
em·bel·lish
em·ber
em·bez·zle
em·bez·zler
em·bit·ter
em·bla·zon
em·blem
em·bod·ied
em·bod·i·ment
em·body

em·body·ing
em·bo·lism
em·bo·lus
em·boss
em·bow·eled
em·brace
em·brace·able
em·broi·dery
em·broil
em·bryo
em·bry·ol·o·gy
em·bry·on·ic
em·cee
em·ceed
em·cee·ing
emend (to correct a
   text); *see* amend)
emen·da·tor
emen·da·to·ry
em·er·ald
em·er·ald green
emer·gence
emer·gen·cy
emer·gent
emer·i·tus
em·ery
em·e·sis
emet·ic
em·i·grant
em·i·grate (to leave;
   see immigrate)
em·i·nence (high
   rank)
em·i·nen·cy
em·i·nent
   (outstanding; *see*
   immanent and
   imminent)

em·is·sary
emis·sion
emit
emit·ted
emit·ter
emit·ting
emol·lient (making
   soft)
emol·u·ment
   (compensation)
emo·tion·al·ize
em·pa·thy
em·per·or
em·pha·sis
em·pha·size
em·phat·ic
em·pir·ic
em·pir·i·cal
em·pir·i·cism
em·place
em·place·ment
em·ploy
em·ploy·able
em·ploy·ee
em·ploy·er
em·po·ri·um,
   plural emporiums
em·prise
emp·ti·ly
emp·ti·ness
emp·ty-hand·ed
emp·ty-head·ed
em·py·re·an
em·u·late
em·u·la·tor
emul·si·fied
emul·si·fi·er
emul·si·fy

emul·si·fy·ing
en·ac·tor
enam·el
enam·eled
enam·el·er
enam·el·ing
en·am·or
en·case
en·case·ment
en·chain
en·chant·er
en·clave
en·close
en·clo·sure
en·co·mi·um,
   plural encomiums
en·com·pass
en·core
en·coun·ter
en·croach
en·cum·ber
en·cum·brance
en·cy·clo·pe·dia
en·cy·clo·pe·dic
en·cy·clo·pe·dist
en·cyst (to enclose)
end-all
en·dan·ger
en·dear
en·deav·or
en·dem·ic
en·dive
en·do·crine
en·dors·able
en·dorse
en·dor·see
en·dorse·ment
en·dors·er

en·dow
end·pa·per
end prod·uct
end run
end ta·ble
en·due
en·dued
en·du·ing
en·dur·able
en·dur·ance
end·ways
en·e·ma
en·er·gize
en·er·vate
en·er·va·tor
en·fee·ble
en·fold
en·force
en·force·able
en·force·ment
en·forc·er
en·fran·chise
en·fran·chise·ment
en·fran·chis·ing
en·gen·der
en·gi·neer
en·gorge
en·graft
en·gross
en·gulf
en·hance
en·hance·ment
enig·ma
en·join
en·joy·able
en·joyed
en·joy·ing
en·lace

en·large
en·large·ment
en·light·en
en·light·ened
en·light·en·ing
en·light·en·ment
en·liv·en
en·mi·ty
en·no·ble
en·no·bler
en·nui
enor·mi·ty
en·plane
en·rich
en·roll
en·rolled
en·roll·ee
en·roll·ing
en·roll·ment
en·sconce
en·sem·ble
en·sheathe
en·shrine
en·snare
en·snare·ment
en·sue
en·su·ing
en·sure (to make
   sure, guarantee;
   see insure)
en·tail
en·tan·gle·ment
en·tente
en·ter·prise
en·thrall
en·thrall·ment
en·throne
en·throne·ment

en·thuse
en·thu·si·asm
en·tice
en·tice·ment
en·tic·ing
en·tire·ty
en·ti·tle
en·ti·tle·ment
en·ti·ty
en·tomb
en·tomb·ment
en·trance
en·trant
en·trap·ment
en·trapped
en·trap·ping
en·treat
en·tre·chat
en·trée
en·trench
en·trench·ment
en·tre·pre·neur
en·tro·py
en·trust
en·trust·ment
en·twine
en·twine·ment
en·twist
enu·mer·a·ble
enu·mer·ate
enu·mer·a·tor
enun·ci·ate
enun·ci·a·tor
en·vel·op (*verb*)
en·ve·lope (*noun* container)
en·vel·oped
en·vel·op·ing

en·ven·om
en·vi·able
en·vied
en·vi·er
en·vi·ous
en·vi·ron·ment
en·vi·rons
en·vis·age
en·vi·sion
en·voy
en·vy·ing
en·wrap
en·wreathe
en·zyme
eon
ep·au·let
ephem·era, *plural* ephemeras
ephem·er·al
ep·ic (poem; *see* epoch)
ep·i·cal
ep·i·cure
ep·i·cu·re·an
ep·i·dem·ic
ep·i·der·mis
ep·i·gram
ep·i·gram·mat·ic
ep·i·graph
ep·i·lep·sy
ep·i·lep·tic
ep·i·logue
epis·co·pa·cy
epis·co·pal
ep·i·sode
ep·i·sod·ic
epis·tle (letter; *see* apostle)

epis·to·lary
ep·i·taph
ep·i·thet
epit·o·me
epit·o·mize
ep·och (period of time; *see* epic)
ep·och·al
ep·o·nym
ep·oxy
equa·ble
equaled
equal·ing
equal·i·tar·i·an
equal·i·ty
equal·ize
equal·iz·er
equal·ly
equa·nim·i·ty
equat·able (equate; *see* equitable)
equa·tor
equa·to·ri·al
eques·tri·an (*noun* and *adj*)
eques·tri·enne (*fem*)
equi·dis·tant
equi·lib·ri·um, *plural* equilib-riums
equi·nox
equip
eq·ui·page
equip·ment
equi·poise
equipped
equip·ping

eq·ui·ta·ble (fair,
    just; *see*
    equatable)
eq·ui·ty
equiv·a·lence
equiv·a·lent
equiv·o·cal
equiv·o·cate
equiv·o·ca·tor
erad·i·ca·ble
erad·i·cate
erad·i·ca·tor
eras·able
eras·er
era·sure
erec·tor
er·mine
erne (bird; *see* urn)
erod·ible
erog·e·nous
erose
ero·si·ble
erot·ic
erot·i·cism
er·ran·cy
er·rant (straying;
    see arrant)
er·rat·ic
er·ra·tum, *plural*
    errata
er·ro·ne·ous
er·ror
er·u·dite
erup·tion
es·ca·late
es·ca·la·tor
es·cal·lop
es·cap·able

es·ca·pade
es·ca·pist
es·car·got
es·ca·role
es·chew
es·cutch·eon
Es·ki·mo, *plural*
    Eskimos
esoph·a·gus
es·o·ter·ic
es·pal·ier
es·pe·cial
es·pi·al
es·pied
es·pi·o·nage
es·pla·nade
es·pous·al
es·pouse
es·py
es·py·ing
es·sence
es·sen·tial
es·teem
es·ti·ma·ble
es·ti·ma·tor
es·ti·vate
es·top
es·topped
es·top·pel
es·top·ping
es·tu·ary
et cet·era
et·cet·eras (extras)
eter·nal
eter·ni·ty
ether
ethe·re·al
ethe·re·al·ize

eth·i·cal
eth·nic
eth·yl
eti·ol·o·gy
et·i·quette
étude
et·y·mol·o·gy
eu·chre
eu·chred
eu·chring
eu·gen·ic
eu·lo·gize
eu·lo·gy
eu·nuch
eu·phe·mism
eu·pho·ny
eu·pho·ria
eu·phu·ism
eu·tha·na·sia
eu·then·ics
evac·u·a·tor
evac·u·ee
evad·able
eval·u·a·tor
ev·a·nesce
ev·a·nes·cent
evan·gel
evan·gel·ic
evan·gel·ize
evap·o·rate
evap·o·ra·tor
eva·sion
even·tem·pered
even·tu·al
even·tu·al·i·ty
even·tu·ate
ev·er·last·ing
ever·si·ble

ev·i·dence
ev·i·dent
ev·i·den·tial
evil·do·er
evil·do·ing
evil eye
evil·mind·ed
evince
evinc·ible
evis·cer·ate
evo·ca·tion
evoke
evo·lu·tion
evo·lu·tion·ary
evolve
ewe (sheep)
ew·er (pitcher)
ex (As a prefix
   meaning
   "former," *ex* is
   joined to the
   following element
   with a hyphen:
   ex-wife.)
ex·act
ex·ac·ti·tude
ex·ac·tor (*noun*)
ex·ag·ger·ate
ex·ag·ger·a·tor
ex·alt
ex·al·ta·tion
ex·am·in·able
ex·am·in·er
ex·as·per·ate
ex·ca·va·tor
ex·aceed
ex·cel

ex·celled
ex·cel·lence
ex·cel·len·cy
ex·cel·ling
ex·cel·si·or
ex·cept (other than;
   see accept)
ex·cep·tion·able
ex·cerpt
ex·cess (surplus;
   see access)
ex·ces·sive
ex·change·able
ex·che·quer
ex·cis·able
ex·cise
ex·cit·able
ex·cit·ant
ex·ci·ta·tion
ex·cit·er
ex·claim
ex·cla·ma·tion
ex·clam·a·to·ry
ex·clud·able
ex·clu·sive
ex·com·mu·ni·cate
ex·com·mu·ni·ca·
   tor
ex·co·ri·ate
ex·cre·ment
ex·cres·cence
ex·cres·cent
ex·cre·ta
ex·cre·to·ry
ex·cru·ci·at·ing
ex·cul·pate
ex·cul·pa·to·ry

ex·cur·sion
ex·cus·able
ex·e·cra·ble
ex·e·crate
ex·e·cra·tor
ex·e·cra·to·ry
ex·e·cu·tion·er
ex·ec·u·tor
ex·ec·u·to·ry
ex·e·ge·sis
ex·em·plar
ex·em·pla·ry
ex·em·pli·fied
ex·em·pli·fy
ex·em·pli·fy·ing
ex·empt·i·ble
ex·emp·tion
ex·er·cis·able
ex·er·cise
   (*see* exorcise)
ex·ert
ex·fo·li·ate
ex·hal·ant
ex·ha·la·tion
ex·haust
ex·haust·ible
ex·haus·tive
ex·hib·it
ex·hib·i·tor
ex·hib·i·to·ry
ex·hil·a·rant
ex·hil·a·rate
ex·hort
ex·hor·ta·to·ry
ex·hu·ma·tion
ex·hume
ex·i·gen·cy

ex·i·gent
ex·i·gi·ble
ex·ig·u·ous
ex·is·tence
ex·is·tent
ex·on·er·ate
ex·on·er·a·tor
ex·o·ra·ble
ex·or·bi·tance
ex·or·bi·tant
ex·or·cise (to
    expel; see
    exercise)
ex·or·di·um, *plural*
    exordiums
ex·ot·ic
ex·pand·able
ex·panse
ex·pan·si·ble
ex·pan·sion·ary
ex·pa·ti·ate
ex·pa·tri·ate
ex·pect·able
ex·pec·tan·cy
ex·pec·tant
ex·pec·to·rant
ex·pe·di·en·cy
ex·pe·di·ent
ex·pe·dite
ex·pe·dit·er
ex·pe·di·tion
ex·pe·di·tion·ary
ex·pe·di·tious
ex·pel
ex·pel·la·ble
ex·pel·lant
ex·pelled

ex·pel·ling
ex·pend·able
ex·pen·di·ture
ex·pense
ex·pe·ri·ence
ex·per·i·ment·er
ex·per·tise
ex·pi·a·ble
ex·pi·ate
ex·pi·a·tor
ex·pi·a·to·ry
ex·pi·ry
ex·plain·able
ex·plan·a·to·ry
ex·ple·tive
ex·pli·ca·ble
ex·pli·cate
ex·pli·ca·tor
ex·pli·ca·to·ry
ex·plic·it
ex·ploit·able
ex·ploit·er
ex·plor·a·to·ry
ex·plor·er
ex·plo·sion
ex·po·nent
ex·port·able
ex·port·er
ex·po·sé
    (disclosure)
ex·pos·i·tor
ex·pos·i·to·ry
ex·pos·tu·late
ex·pos·tu·la·tor
ex·pos·tu·la·to·ry
ex·pound·er
ex·press·er

ex·press·ible
ex·pro·pri·ate
ex·pro·pri·a·tor
ex·pul·sion
ex·punge
ex·pung·er
ex·pur·gate
ex·pur·ga·tor
ex·qui·site
ex·tant (existing)
ex·tem·po·ra·ne·ous
ex·tem·po·rary
ex·tem·po·re
ex·tem·po·rize
ex·tend·er
ex·tend·ible
ex·ten·si·ble
ex·ten·sion
ex·ten·sor
ex·tent (space,
    scope)
ex·ten·u·ate
ex·ten·u·a·tor
ex·te·ri·or
ex·ter·mi·na·tor
ex·tern
ex·tinct
ex·tinc·tion
ex·tin·guish·able
ex·tin·guish·er
ex·tir·pate
ex·tir·pa·tor
ex·tol
ex·tolled
ex·tol·ler
ex·tol·ling
ex·tol·ment

ex·tort·er
ex·tor·tion·ary
ex·tor·tion·er
ex·tra (Compound
   words beginning
   with *extra* are
   written solid:
   extramural, except
   as otherwise
   shown below.)
ex·tra-base hit
ex·tract·able
ex·trac·tor
ex·tra·cur·ric·u·
   lar
ex·tra·dit·able
ex·tra·dite
ex·tra·ne·ous

ex·traor·di·nary
ex·trap·o·late
ex·trap·o·la·tor
ex·tra·sen·so·ry
ex·trav·a·gance
ex·trav·a·gan·cy
ex·trav·a·gant
ex·trav·a·gan·za
ex·trem·i·ty
ex·tri·ca·ble
ex·tri·cate
ex·tro·ver·sion
ex·tro·vert
ex·trud·er
ex·tru·sion
ex·u·ber·ance
ex·u·ber·ant

ex·u·date
ex·ude
ex·ul·tance
ex·ul·tant
eye (Compound
   words beginning
   with *eye* are
   written solid:
   eyebrow, except
   as otherwise
   shown below.)
eye bank
eye-catch·er
eye·ing
eye-open·er
eye shad·ow
eye·wit·ness

F

fa·ble
fab·ric
fab·ri·ca·tor
fab·u·lous
fa·çade
face card
face lift·ing (*noun*)
face-off
face pow·der
face-sav·ing
fac·et
fac·et·ed
fac·et·ing
fa·ce·tious
face val·ue
fa·cial
fac·ile
fa·cil·i·tate
fa·cil·i·ty
fac·sim·i·le
fac·tious
fac·ti·tious
fac·tor
fac·tor·able
fac·to·ry
fac·tu·al

fac·ul·ty
fad·dish
fad·dist
fade-in (*noun*)
fade-out (*noun*)
fag end
fagged
fag·ging
fag·ot
fag·ot·ing
Fahr·en·heit
fail-safe (*adj*)
faint·heart·ed
fair ball
fair catch
fair copy
fair game
fair·ground
fair-haired
fair-mind·ed
fair play
fair-spok·en
fair-trade (*adj* and
    verb)
fair·way
fair-weath·er (*adj*)

fait ac·com·pli
faith·ful (*noun sing*
    and *plural*)
fak·er (bluffer)
fak·ery
fa·kir (Moslem or
    Hindu beggar)
fal·con·er
fal·con·ry
fal·de·ral
fal·la·cious
fal·la·cy
fal·li·ble
fall·ing-out (*noun*),
    plural fallings-out
fall·off
fall·out (*noun*)
fal·low
false·hood
false step
false teeth
fal·set·to, *plural*
    falsettos
fal·si·fy
fal·si·ty
fal·ter (stumble)

133

fa·mil·iar
fa·mil·iar·ize
fam·ish
fa·nat·ic
fan·cied
fan·ci·er (*noun* and
   adj)
fan·ci·est
fan·ci·ful
fan·cy dress
fan·cy-free
fan·cy·ing
fan·cy·work
fan·fare
fan·jet
fanned
fan·ning
fan·tan
fan·ta·size
fan·ta·sy
far·away
far·ceur
far·ci·cal
fare-thee-well
   (*noun*)
far·fetched
far-flung
farm·hand
farm·house
far-off
far-out
far-reach·ing
far·row
far·see·ing
far·sight·ed
far·thest
fas·ces
fas·cia

fas·ci·cle
fas·ci·nate
fas·ci·na·tor
fash·ion·able
fast day
fas·ten·er
fas·tid·i·ous
fa·tal
fat·back
fa·ther-in-law,
   plural fathers-in-
   law
fath·om
fath·om·able
fa·tigue
fa·tigued
fa·tigu·ing
fat-sol·u·ble
fat·ted
fat·ten
fat·tened
fat·ten·er
fat·ten·ing
fat·ter
fat·ti·er
fat·ting
fat·tish
fat·ty
fa·tu·ity
fat·u·ous
fat-wit·ted
fau·cet
fault·find·ing
fault·i·ly
faux pas (*sing* and
   plural)
fa·vor
fa·vor·able

fa·vor·ite
fa·vor·it·ism
faze (disturb; *see*
   phase)
fe·al·ty
fea·si·ble
feat
   (accomplishment)
feath·er bed (*noun*)
feath·er·bed (*verb*
   and *adj*)
feath·er·bed·ding
   (*noun* and *verb*)
feath·er·brain
feath·er·head
feath·er·stitch
feath·er·weight
Feb·ru·ary
fe·cal
fe·ces
fe·cund
fed·er·al·ism
fed·er·al·ize
fed·er·ate
fee·ble·mind·ed
feed (*past of* fee)
feed·back
fee·ing
fee-split·ting
feign
feign·er
feint (*noun* and *verb*
   pretend)
feisty
fe·lic·i·tate
fe·lic·i·ta·tor
fe·lic·i·tous
fe·lic·i·ty

fel·low·man
fel·on
fe·lo·ni·ous
fel·o·ny
fem·i·na·cy
fem·i·nine
fem·i·nin·i·ty
fen·es·tra·tion
fen·nel
fe·ral (wild)
fer·ment·able
fe·ro·cious
fe·roc·i·ty
fer·ret (*noun* and
  verb)
fer·ret·ed
fer·ret·ing
fer·rule (metal cap)
fer·tile
fer·til·ize
fer·ule (flat stick)
fer·ven·cy
fer·vent
fer·vor
fes·ter
fes·tive
fes·toon
fes·toon·ery
fete (entertainment)
fet·ed
fet·id
fet·ing
fe·tish
fe·tish·ism
fet·ter
fet·tle
fe·tus, *plural*
  fetuses

feud
feu·dal
fez, *plural* fezzes
fi·an·cé (*masc*)
fi·an·cée (*fem*)
fi·as·co, *plural*
  fiascoes
fi·at
fib·ber
fib·bing
fi·ber
fi·bered
fi·ber glass
fick·le
fic·tion·eer
fic·ti·tious
fid·dle
fid·dle-fad·dle
fid·gety
fi·du·cia·ry
field corn
field day
field event
field goal
field house
field·piece
field test (*noun*)
field-test (*verb*)
field·work
fiend
fierce
fi·er·i·er
fi·ery
fif·ti·eth
fif·ty-fif·ty
fif·ty-first, etc.
fif·ty-one, etc.
fig·ment

fig·ure·head
fil·a·ment
fi·let mi·gnon,
  plural filets
  mignons
fil·ial
fil·i·bus·ter
fil·i·gree
fil·i·greed
fil·i·gree·ing
fil·let (thin strip of
  meat, fish, ribbon,
  etc.)
fil·lip
film pack
film·strip
fil·ter (device for
  separating
  materials; *see*
  philter)
fil·ter·able
fil·ter tip (*noun*)
fil·ter-tipped (*adj*)
fin·a·ble (subject to
  fines)
fi·na·gle
fi·na·gler
fi·na·le
fi·nal·i·ty
fi·nal·ize
fi·nan·cial
fi·nan·cier
fine-grained
fin·ery
fine·spun
fi·nesse
fine-toothed comb
fin·ger·board

fin·ger bowl
fin·ger·breadth
fin·ger mark
fin·ger·nail
fin·ger·print
fin·ger·tip
fin·ger wave
fin·i·cal
fin·icky
fin·ish·er
fi·nite
finned
fin·ny
fire alarm
fire·ball
fire·boat
fire·bomb
fire·brand
fire·break
fire·bug
fire chief
fire con·trol
fire·crack·er
fire-cured
fire door
fire drill
fire-eat·er
fire·fly
fire·house
fire hy·drant
fire irons
fire·light
fire·place
fire·pow·er
fire·proof
fire-re·sis·tant
fire sale

fire screen
fire·side
fire tow·er
fire·trap
fire wall
fire·wa·ter
fire·wood
fire·works
fir·ma·ment
first aid
first base
first base·man
first-born (*adj*)
first-class (*adj*)
first-de·gree burn
first fruits
first-gen·er·a·tion
   (*adj*)
first·hand
first la·dy
first mate
first mort·gage
first-night·er
first of fend·er
first-rate
first-string (*adj*)
first wa·ter
fis·cal
fish and chips
fish·bowl
fish cake
fish·ery
fish fry
fish·hook
fish meal
fish·mong·er
fish·pond

fish sto·ry
fish·tail
fish·wife
fis·sion
fis·sion·able
fis·sure
fist·ic
fit·ful
fit·ness
fit·ted
fit·ter
fit·test
fit·ting
five-and-ten-cent
   store
fix·a·tion
fix·a·tive
fixed
fix·i·ty
fix·ture
fiz·zle
fjord
flab·ber·gast
flab·bi·er
flab·bi·ly
flab·by
flac·cid
fla·gel·lant
fla·gel·late
flagged
flag·ging
flag·man
flag of·fi·cer
flag·on
flag·pole
fla·gran·cy
fla·grant

flag·ship
flag·staff
flag·stone
flag stop
flag-wav·ing
flail
flair (talent; *see*
    flare)
flaky
flam·beau, *plural*
    flambeaus
flam·boy·ance
flam·boy·ant
fla·men·co
fla·min·go, *plural*
    flamingos
flam·ma·ble
flan·nel
flan·neled
flan·nel·ette
flan·nel·ing
flan·nel-mouthed
flapped
flap·per
flap·pi·er
flap·py
flare (to blaze up,
    bright light,
    curve out; *see*
    flair)
flare-up
flash·back
flash·bulb
flash card
flash flood
flash gun
flash·i·er

flash·i·ly
flash lamp
flash·light
flash point
flash tube
flat (Compound
    words beginning
    with *flat* are
    written solid:
    flatboat, except as
    otherwise shown
    below.)
flat-bed
flat·foot
flat-foot·ed
flat·ten
flat·tened
flat·ten·ing
flat·ter
flat·ter·er
flat·ter·ing
flat·tery
flat·test
flat·tish
flat·top
flat·u·lence
flat·u·len·cy
flat·u·lent
flaunt
fla·vor
flawed
flax·en
flayed
flay·ing
flea·bite
flea·bit·ten
fledg·ling

fleecy
flesh-col·ored
flesh·pot
flex·i·ble
flex·or
flib·ber·ti·gib·bet
flick·er
flick·ery
fli·er
flight-test (*verb* and
    adj)
flim·flam
flim·flammed
flim·flam·ming
flim·si·ly
flim·sy
flip-flop
flip·pan·cy
flip·pant
flipped
flip·per
flip·pest
flip·ping
flip side
flir·ta·tious
flit·ted
flit·ter
flit·ting
floc·cu·lence
floc·cu·lent
flogged
flog·ger
flog·ging
flood·gate
flood·light
flood tide
floo·ey

137

floor·board
floor lead·er
floor-length
floor·mop
floor plan
floor plug
floor show
floor·walk·er
floor wax
flop·house
flopped
flop·per
flop·pi·er
flop·pi·ly
flop·ping
flo·res·cence
flo·res·cent
flor·id
flo·tage
flo·ta·tion
flo·til·la
flot·sam
flounce
flour·ish
floury (of flour)
flout
flowed
flow·er·bed
flow·ered
flow·er girl
flow·er·pot
flow·ery (covered
    with flowers,
    ornate)
flubbed
flub·bing

fluc·tu·ant
fluc·tu·ate
flue (pipe or shaft)
flu·en·cy
flu·ent
flu·id
fluke
fluky
flun·ky
flum·mery
flu·o·res·cence
flu·o·res·cent
flur·ried
flur·ry
flur·ry·ing
flus·tra·tion
flut·ter
flut·tery
flux
fly·able
fly·away
fly·blown
fly·by
fly-by-night
fly cast·ing
fly·catch·er
fly·leaf, *plural*
    flyleaves
fly·pa·per
fly·speck
fly swat·ter
fly·way
fly·weight
fly·wheel
fobbed
fob·bing

fo·cal
fo·cus, *plural*
    focuses
fo·cused
fo·cus·ing
fod·der
foe, *plural* foes
fog·bound
fogged
fog·gi·er
fog·gi·ly
fog·gi·ness
fog·ging
fog·gy
fog·horn
fo·gy (one who is
    old)
foi·ble
fo·liage
fo·lio, *plural*· folios
folk dance
folk·lore
folk song
folk·sy
folk tale
folk·way
fol·li·cle
fol·lowed
fol·low·er
fol·low through
    (*verb*)
fol·low-through
    (*noun*)
fol·low up (*verb*)
fol·low-up (*noun*
    and *adj*)

138

fo·ment·er
fon·dle
fon·due
fool·ery
fool·har·dy
fool·proof
foot (Compound
   words beginning
   with *foot* are
   written solid:
   foothill, except as
   otherwise shown
   below.)
foot-and-mouth
   dis·ease
foot-can·dle
foot fault
foot-pound
foot·sie
foot sol·dier
foot-ton
fop·pery
fop·pish
for·age
for·ag·er
for·ay, *plural*
   forays
for·ayed
for·ay·ing
for·bade
for·bear (*verb* to
   refrain)
for·bear·ance
for·bid·dance
for·bid·den
for·bid·ding

force-feed (*verb*)
for·ceps
forc·ible
fore (Compound
   words beginning
   with *fore* are
   written solid:
   forearm.)
fore·bear (ancestor)
fore·bode
fore·cast·er
fore·clo·sure
fore·deck
fore·doom
fore·fa·ther
fore·front
fore·go (*verb* to
   precede; *see*
   forgo)
fore·go·ing
fore·gone
fore·hand
fore·hand·ed
fore·head
for·eign
for·eign-born
for·eign·er
fore·judge
fore·knowl·edge
fore·man
fore·most
fo·ren·sic
fore·or·dain
fore·part
fore·run·ner
fore·see·able

fore·shad·ow
fore·short·en
fore·sight
fore·stall
fore·stall·er
fore·stall·ment
for·est·er
for·es·try
fore·tell
fore·thought
fore·word (preface;
   see forward)
for·feit
for·feit·able
for·fei·ture
for·fend
for·gath·er
forg·ery
for·get·ful
for·get-me-not
for·get·ta·ble
for·get·ting
for·giv·able
for·give·ness
for·go (*verb* do
   without; *see*
   forego)
for·go·ing
for·gone
for·got·ten
fork·fuls
for·lorn
for·mal·i·ty
for·mal·ize
for·mal·ly (in a
   formal manner)

for·ma·tive
for·mer·ly (before)
for·mi·da·ble
for·mu·la, *plural*
  formulas
for·mu·lary
for·mu·la·tor
for·sake
for·swear
for·sworn
for·syth·ia
forte (special
  competence)
forth (forward; *see*
  fourth)
forth·right
for·ti·eth
for·ti·fi·a·ble
for·ti·fied
for·ti·fy
for·ti·fy·ing
for·ti·tude
fort·night
for·tu·itous
for·tu·ity
for·tune hunt·er
for·tune tell·er
for·ty-first, etc.
for·ty-one, etc.
fo·rum, *plural*
  forums
for·ward (ahead;
  see foreword)
for·ward·er
for·ward-look·ing
fos·sil
fos·sil·ize

fos·ter
foul ball
foul line
foul·mouthed
foul play
foul tip
foul-up (*noun*)
found·er (*verb*)
found·er (*noun* one
  who founds)
found·ling
found·ry
foun·tain
four-col·or
four-di·men·sion·al
four-flush (*verb*)
four-flush·er
four·fold
four·foot·ed
four-hand·ed
Four-H Club
four-in-hand
four-leaf clo·ver
four-let·ter word
four-o'clock
  (flower)
four-post·er
four·score
four·some
four·square
fourth (number; *see*
  forth)
four-way (*adj*)
four-wheel (*adj*)
fowl (bird)
fox·i·er
foxy

foy·er
fra·cas, *plural*
  fracases
frac·tious
frac·ture
frag·ile
frag·men·tary
fra·grance
fra·grant
frail
frail·ty
frame house
frame-up (*noun*)
frame·work
fran·chise
fran·chis·er
fran·chis·ing
fran·gi·ble
frank·furt·er
frank·in·cense
fran·tic
frap·pé
frat·er·nize
frat·ri·cide
fraud·u·lence
frad·u·lent
fraught (laden)
frayed
fray·ing
fraz·zle
freck·le
free·board
free·boot·er
free·born
freed
freed·man
free en·ter·prise

free-for-all
free·hand (*adj*)
free·hand·ed
free·heart·ed
free·hold
free·ing
free lance (*noun*)
free-lance (*adj* and
  verb)
free-liv·ing
free·load (*verb*)
free·load·er
free love
free·man
free on board
fre·er
free sil·ver
free soil (territory)
free-soil (*adj*)
free·spo·ken
fre·est
free·stand·ing
free·stone
free·think·er
free throw
free trade
free verse
free·way
free·wheel (*noun*
  and *verb*)
free will (*noun*)
free·will (*adj*)
freeze-dry
freeze·out (*noun*)
freeze·up (*noun*)
freight
freight car

fright·er
freight train
fre·net·ic
fren·zied
fren·zy
fre·quence
fre·quen·cy
fre·quent
fres·co, *plural*
  frescoes
fresh·wa·ter (*adj*)
fret·ful
fret·ted
fret·ting
fri·a·ble
fri·ar (monk)
fric·as·see
fric·ca·seed
fric·as·see·ing
friend
frieze (building)
frig·id
frip·pery
frit·ted
frit·ter
frit·ter·er
frit·ter·ing
frit·ting
friv·ol
friv·oled
friv·ol·er
friv·ol·ing
fri·vol·i·ty
friv·o·lous
frizz (hairdo)
frog·man
frol·ic

frol·icked
frol·ick·er
frol·ick·ing
frol·ic·some
fron·tier
fron·tiers·man
fron·tis·piece
front man
front mat·ter
front of·fice
front-page (*adj*)
front-run·ner
fro·ward (unruly)
frow·zi·er
frow·zi·est
frow·zy
fru·gal
fru·gal·i·ty
fruit·cake
fruit cup
fruit fly
fru·ition
fruit jar
fruit tree
fruit·wood
frus·tra·tion
fry·er (chicken or
  utensil)
fud·dy-dud·dy
fu·el
fu·eled
fu·el·er
fu·el·ing
fu·ga·cious
fu·gal (fugue)
fu·gi·tive
fu·gle (to lead)

fu·gle·man (leader)
fugue (music)
ful·crum, *plural*
  fulcrums
ful·fill
ful·filled
ful·fill·ing
ful·fill·ment
full·back
full blood
full-blood·ed
full-blown
full-bod·ied
full dress (*noun*)
full-dress (*adj*)
full-fash·ioned
full-fledged
full-grown
full house (poker)
full-length
full moon
full-mouthed
full·ness
full-scale (*adj*)
full speed
full tilt
full time (*noun*)

full-time (*adj*)
ful·mi·nate
ful·some
fu·mi·gate
fu·mi·ga·tor
func·tion
func·tion·ary
fun·er·ary
fu·ne·re·al
fun·gi·cide
fun·go, *plural*
  fungoes
fun·gus, *plural*
  fungi
fu·nic·u·lar
fun·nel
fun·neled
fun·nel·ing
fun·ni·er
fun·ni·ly
fun·ni·ness
fun·ning
fun·ny
fur·be·low
fur·bish
fur·lough
fur·nace

fu·ror
furred
fur·ri·er
fur·ri·ery
fur·ring
fur·row
fur·ther·ance
fur·tive
fuse (*verb* to join;
  noun protective
  device or cord
  for igniting
  explosives)
fu·se·lage
fus·ible
fu·sil
fu·sil·ier
fu·sil·lade
fu·tile
fu·til·i·ty
fu·tu·ri·ty
fuze (electric device
  for detonating an
  explosive)
fuzz·i·ness
fuzzy

G

gab·ar·dine (fabric)
gabbed
gab·ber
gab·bi·er
gab·bing
gab·ble
gab·bler
gab·bling
gab·by
ga·ble
gad·about
gad·ded
gad·der
gad·ding
gad·ge·teer
gad·get·ry
gagged
gag·ger
gag·ging
gai·ety
gail·ly
gain·said
gain·say
gain·say·ing
gait (way of
   walking)
gal·axy

gal·lant
gal·lant·ry
gal·le·on
gal·lery
gal·ley, *plural*
   galleys
gall·ing (annoying)
gal·li·vant
gal·lop
gal·lop·er
gal·lows, *plural*
   gallowses
ga·lore
ga·losh
gal·va·nize
gam·bit
gam·bol (frolic)
gam·boled
gam·bol·ing
gam·brel
game laws
games·man·ship
game·ster
gam·ut
gamy
gan·gling
gan·grene

gan·gre·nous
gant·let (railroad)
gantry
gaped
   (open-mouthed)
gap·ing
gapped
gap·ping
gar·ble
gar·gle
gar·goyle
gar·ish
gar·licky
gar·nish·ee
gar·nish·eed
gar·nish·ee·ing
gar·nish·er
gar·ni·ture
   (trimming)
gar·ri·son
gar·rote
gar·rot·ed
gar·rot·er
gar·rot·ing
gar·ru·li·ty
gar·ru·lous
gas·bag

gas burn·er
gas cham·ber
gas·eous
gas·es, *plural*
　of gas
gas·house
gas·ify
gas·light
gas log
gas main
gas mask
gas me·ter
gas·o·line
gassed
gas·ser
gas·ses (*verb*)
gas sta·tion
gas·sy
gas·tro·nom·ic
gas·tron·o·my
gas·works
gate-crash·er
gate·house
gate·keep·er
gate·leg ta·ble
gate·post
gauche
gau·che·rie
gau·cho, *plural*
　gauchos
gaudy
gauge
gauge·able
gaunt (hollow-eyed)
gaunt·let (glove,
　ordeal)

gauze
gauzy
gav·el
gav·eled
gav·el·ing
ga·votte
ga·ze·bo (turret)
ga·zelle
ga·zette
gaz·et·teer
gear·box
gear·wheel
gei·sha
gel·a·tin
ge·la·ti·nize
gemmed
gem·ming
gem·mol·o·gy
gem·stone
gen·darme
gen·dar·mer·ie
ge·ne·al·o·gy
gen·er·al·cy
gen·er·al·ize
gen·er·al-pur·pose
　(*adj*)
gen·er·a·tor
gen·e·sis
ge·nial
gen·i·tal
ge·nius, *plural*
　geniuses
gen·o·cide
genre (kind)
gen·teel
gen·til·i·ty

gen·tle·man-
　farm·er
gen·tle·man's
　agree·ment
gen·try
gen·u·flect
gen·u·flec·tion
gen·nus, *plural*
　genera
ge·ol·o·gist
ge·ol·o·gy
ger·i·at·rics
ger·i·a·tri·cian
ger·mane (relevant)
ger·mi·ci·dal
ger·mi·cide
ger·mi·nal
ger·ry·man·der
ger·und
ges·tic·u·late
ges·tic·u·la·tor
ges·ture
get·at·able
get·ting
get-to·geth·er
get-up (*noun*)
gew·gaw
gey·ser
ghast·ly
gher·kin (small
　cucumber)
ghet·to, *plural*
　ghettos
ghost
ghost·writ·er
ghoul (grave robber)

GI, *plural* GI's
gib·ber
gib·bered
gib·ber·ing
gib·ber·ish
gib·bet (gallows)
gib·bous
gibe (taunt)
gib·let
gift-wrap
gift-wrapped
gift-wrap·ping
  (*verb*)
gift·wrap·ping
  (*noun*)
gi·gan·te·an
gig·gan·tic
gig·gle
gig·gler
gig·gly
gig·o·lo, *plural*
  gigolos
gilt-edged
gim·let
gim·let-eyed
gim·mick
gim·mick·ry
gin·ger·bread
gin·ger·ly
ging·ham
ginned
gin·ner
gin·ning
gi·raffe
gird·er
gir·dle

girth (circumfer-
  ence)
gist (main point)
give-and-take
give·away (*noun*)
giz·zard
gla·cé
gla·céed
gla·cé·ing
gla·cial
gla·ci·ate
gla·cier
glad·den
glad·dened
glad·den·ing
glad·der
glad·dest
glad·i·a·tor
gla·di·o·lus, *plural*
  gladioli
glair (egg white)
glam·or·ize
glam·or·ous
glam·our
glan·du·lar
glare (dazzling
  light, to stare)
glary
glass·blow·er
glass eye
glass·ware
glass·work
glau·co·ma
gla·zier
gleam
glean (collect)

glib·ber (more glib)
glib·best
glimpse
gloam·ing
gloat
glob·al
globe-trot·ter
glob·u·lar
glob·ule
glo·ri·fy
glo·ri·ous
glos·sa·ry
glow·er (scowl)
glu·cose
glue·pot
glu·ey
glu·i·er
glu·ing
glum·ly
glum·mer
glum·mest
glum·ness
glu·ti·nous (like
  glue)
glut·ted
glut·ting
glut·ton
glut·ton·ous
  (overindulgent)
gnarl
gnash
gnat
gnaw
gnome
go (*noun*), *plural*
  goes

goad
go-ahead (*noun* and *adj*)
goal·keep·er
goal line
goal-line stand
goal post
goat·herd
gob·ble
gob·ble·dy·gook
gob·bler
gob·let
go-by
go-cart
god (Compound words beginning with *god* are written solid: *godson*.)
god·damn
God-fear·ing
god·for·sak·en
God·giv·en
God·speed
go-get·ter
gog·gle
gog·gle-eyed
gog·gling
go-go
go·ing-over (*noun*), *plural* goings-over
go·ings-on
goi·ter
gold·brick
gold dust
gold·en age

gold·en mean
gold·en·rod
gold·en rule
gold·field
gold-filled
gold·finch
gold·fish
gold leaf
gold mine
gold plate
gold-plat·ed
gold rush
gold·smith
gold stand·ard
gol·li·wogg
gon·do·la
gon·do·lier
gon·or·rhea
Good Book
good-bye
good fel·low
good-fel·low·ship
good-for-noth·ing
good-heart·ed
good-hu·mored
good-na·tured
good-sized
good-tem·pered
good will
goody-goody
goo·ey
goo·i·er
goose, *plural* geese except tailor's gooses
goose·ber·ry

goose egg
goose·flesh
goose·neck
goose step (*noun*)
goose-step (*verb*)
goos·y
go·pher
gor·geous
go·ril·la
gor·man·dize
gos·pel
gos·pel·er
gos·sa·mer
gos·sip
gouache (painting)
gou·lash
gourd
gour·mand
gour·met
gov·ern·able
gov·er·nance
gov·ern·ment
gov·er·nor
gov·er·nor gen·er·al, *plural* governors general
grabbed
grab·ber
grab·bi·er
grab·bing
grab·by
grace note
gra·cious
gra·da·tion
gra·di·ent

146

graf·fi·to, *plural*
  graffiti
gram
gram·mar
gram·mar·i·an
gram·mat·i·cal
gra·na·ry
grand (Compound
  words beginning
  with *grand*
  which refer
  to family
  relationships are
  written solid:
  grandson. All
  others beginning
  with *grand* are
  written as
  separate words,
  except as
  otherwise shown
  below.)
gran·dam
grand·dad
gran·deur
gran·dil·o·quence
gran·dil·o·quent
gran·di·ose
grand ju·ry
grand lar·ce·ny
grand·stand
gran·ite
gran·ite·ware
gran·ny
grant·er
grant-in-aid

gran·tor (law)
gran·u·lar
gran·u·la·tor
grape·fruit
grape·shot
grape·vine
graph·ic
grap·nel
grap·ple
grap·pler
grass green
grass·land
grass·plot
grass roots (*noun*
  common people)
grass-roots (*adj*)
grass wid·ow
grat·i·fied
grat·i·fy
grat·i·fy·ing
gra·tis
grat·i·tude
gra·tu·itous
gra·tu·ity
gra·va·men
grave·dig·ger
grav·el
grav·eled
grav·el·ing
grave·stone
grave·yard
grav·i·tate
grav·i·ty
gray
graze
grease·paint

great (Compound
  words beginning
  with *great* which
  refer to family
  relationships are
  written with a
  hyphen: *great-*
  aunt. All others
  beginning with
  great are written
  as separate words,
  except as
  otherwise shown
  below.)
great·coat
great·heart·ed
green·back
green bean
green·belt
green·bri·er
green corn
green·ery
green-eyed
green·gage
green·gro·cer
green·horn
green·house
green light
green·room
green·sward
gre·gar·i·ous
grem·lin
gren·a·dier
grid·dle
grid·iron
grief

grief-strick·en
griev·ance
griev·ous
grif·fin
grill (for cooking)
grille (screen)
grill·room
grill·work
gri·mace
grime
grim·i·er
grim·i·ness
grim·mer
grim·mest
grim·ness
grimy
grinned
grin·ner
grin·ning
gripe (pain, to
    complain)
griped
grip·er
grip·ing
grippe (illness)
gripped (grip)
grip·per (grip)
grip·ping
grip·py (ill)
gris·ly
gris·tle
grit·ted
grit·ti·er
grit·ti·ness
grit·ting
grit·ty
griz·zled

griz·zly
gro·cery
grog·gery
grog·gi·er
grog·gi·ly
grog·gi·ness
grog·gy
grom·met
gros·beak
gross (all meanings)
gro·tesque
gro·tes·que·ry
grot·to, *plural*
    grottoes
ground ball
ground con·trol
ground cov·er
ground crew
ground floor
ground·hog
ground·nut
ground plan
ground rule
grounds·keep·er
ground·speed
ground swell
ground-to-air
ground wa·ter
ground·work
grout
grov·el
grov·eled
grov·el·er
grov·el·ing
grown·up (*noun*)
grown-up (*adj*)
grubbed

grub·ber
grub·bi·er
grub·bi·ly
grub·bi·ness
grub·by
gru·el
gru·el·ing
grue·some
Gru·yère (cheese)
guar·an·tee (*verb* to
    promise; *noun* an
    assurance)
guar·an·tor
guar·an·ty (*noun*
    pledge, security)
guard·house
guard·ian
guard·rail
gu·ber·na·to·ri·al
guer·ril·la (fighter)
guess·work
guf·faw
guid·ance
guide·book
guide·line
guide·post
guide word
guild (group)
guile
guile·less
guil·lo·tine
guin·ea
guise
gui·tar
gul·let
gull·ible
gul·ly

gummed

gum·mi·er

gum·mi·ness

gum·ming

gum·my

gump·tion

gun (Compound
   words beginning
   with *gun* are
   written solid
   except as
   otherwise shown
   below.)

gun bar·rel

gunned

gun·ner

gun·nery

gun·ning

gun·ny·sack

gun room

gun-shy

gun·wale

gur·gle

gus·set

gus·ta·to·ry

gut·ted

gut·ter

gut·ting

gut·tur·al

guy

guyed

guy·ing

guz·zle

guz·zler

gym·na·si·um,
   plural
   gymnasiums

gyp·sum

gyp·sy

gy·rate

gy·ro·scope

H

ha·be·as cor·pus
hab·er·dash·er
hab·er·dash·ery
ha·bil·i·ment
hab·it·able
hab·i·tat
hab·it-form·ing
ha·bit·u·al
ha·bit·u·ate
hab·i·tude
ha·bi·tué, *plural*
  habitués
hack·le
hack·ney, *plural*
  hackneys
hack·neyed
had·dock
hag·gard
hag·gish
hag·gle
hag·gler
hag·rid·den
ha-ha
hail-fel·low
hail·stone
hail·storm

hair (Compound
  words beginning
  with *hair* are
  written solid:
  hairpin, except as
  otherwise shown
  below.)
hair·breadth
hair-rais·er
hair-rais·ing
hairs·breadth
hair shirt
hair trig·ger (*noun*)
hair-trig·ger (*adj*)
hal·cy·on
half-afraid
half-alive
half-and-half
half-awake
half·back
half-baked
half-blood (*noun*
  person)
half-blood·ed
half-breed
half broth·er

half-caste
half-cocked
half day
half dol·lar
half-doz·en
half gain·er
half·heart·ed
half hitch
half-hour
half-hour·ly
half-life
half-light
half-mast
half-mile
half-moon
half note
half past
half pint
half sis·ter
half size (*noun*)
half sole (*noun*)
half-sole (*verb*)
half speed
half-staff
half step
half time

half ti·tle
half·tone
  (engraving)
half tone (music)
half-track (*noun*)
half-truth
half·way
half-wit
half-wit·ted
hal·le·lu·jah
hall·mark
hal·low
hal·lowed
Hal·low·een
hal·lu·ci·nate
hal·lu·ci·na·to·ry
ha·lo, *plural* halos
hal·yard
ham·mer
ham·mock
ham·string
ham·strung
hand (Compound
  words beginning
  with *hand* are
  written solid:
  handshake, except
  as otherwise
  shown below.)
hand and foot
  (completely)
hand ax
hand·breadth
hand-feed
hand·fuls
hand glass

hand gre·nade
hand·i·cap
hand·i·capped
hand·i·cap·per
hand·i·cap·ping
hand·i·craft
hand·i·er
hand in glove
hand·i·work
hand·ker·chiefs
hand-me-down
hand over fist
hand run·ning
hands-down
hand·sel
hand·seled
hand·sel·ing
hands-off (*adj*)
hand-to-hand
hand-to-mouth
hand-wo·ven
handy·man
han·gar (for
  aircraft)
hang·dog
hang·er-on, *plural*
  hangers-on
han·ky-pan·ky
hap·haz·ard
hap·less
hap·pened
hap·pen·ing
hap·pen·stance
hap·pi·er
hap·pi·ly
hap·pi·ness

hap·py-go-lucky
hara-kiri
ha·rangue
ha·rangued
ha·rangu·er
ha·rangu·ing
ha·rass
har·bin·ger
har·bor
har·bor·er
hard-and-fast
hard-bit·ten
hard-boiled
hard cash
hard ci·der
hard coal
hard-core (*adj*)
hard·ened
hard·en·er
hard·fist·ed
hard·hand·ed
hard hat (helmet)
hard-hat (*noun* and
  adj construction
  worker)
hard·head·ed
hard·heart·ed
har·di·hood
har·di·ness
hard la·bor
hard li·quor
hard ma·ple
hard·nosed
hard-of-hear·ing
hard·pan
hard-pressed (*adj*)

hard sauce
hard sell
hard-shell (*noun* and
   adj)
hard·ship
hard·ware
hard·wood
hare·brained
hare·lip
har·em
har·lot
har·lot·ry
har·mo·ni·ous
har·mo·nize
harp·si·chord
har·ried
har·ri·er
har·row
har·ry (*verb* to
   harass)
har·ry·ing
har·um-scar·um
has-been
hash·ish
has·sle
has·sock
hast·i·er
hast·i·ly
hasty
hatch·able
hatch·ery
hatch·et-faced
hatch·et man
hate·a·ble
hat·ted
hat·ter

haugh·ti·ly
haugh·ty
haunch
haute cou·ture
hau·teur
have-not (*noun*)
hav·oc
hav·ocked
hav·ock·ing
hawk-eyed
haw·ser
hay (Compound
   words beginning
   with *hay* are
   written solid:
   haystack, except
   as otherwise
   shown below.)
hay fe·ver
haz·ard
haze
ha·zel
haz·i·ly
hazy
head (Compound
   words beginning
   with *head* are
   written solid:
   headset, except as
   otherwise shown
   below.)
head cold
head-on
head start
head tone
head wind

hear·ing aid
hear·ken
hear·say
hearse
heart (Compound
   words beginning
   with *heart* are
   written solid:
   heartache, except
   as otherwise
   shown below.)
heart at·tack
heart block
heart dis·ease
heart fail·ure
hearth (fireplace)
heart·i·ly
hearts·ease
heart-strick·en
heart-to-heart
hearty
heat ex·haus·tion
hea·then, *plural*
   heathens
heath·er
heat light·ning
heat rash
heat·stroke
heat wave
heav·i·er
heav·i·ly
heav·i·ness
heavy-du·ty (*adj*)
heavy-eyed
heavy-foot·ed
heavy-hand·ed

heavy heart·ed
heavy-lad·en
heavy·set
heavy·weight
heck·le
heck·ler
hec·tic
hec·tor
hedge·hop
hedged·hopped
hedge·hop·per
hedge·hop·ping
hee·bie-jee·bies
hee·haw
heel-and-toe (*adj*)
he·ge·mo·ny
heif·er
height·en
hei·nous
heir ap·par·ent,
    plural heirs
    apparent
hel·i·cop·ter
hel·met
hel·met·ed (*adj*)
hel·ter-skel·ter
he-man
hemi·sphere
hemmed
hem·mer
hem·ming
he·mo·glo·bin
hem·or·rhage
hem·or·rhag·ic
hem·or·rhoid
hen·na

hen·naed
hen·na·ing
hen·nery
her·ald·ry
her·ba·ceous
Her·cu·le·an
here·about
he·red·i·tary
he·red·i·ty
her·e·sy
her·e·tic
here·to·fore
here·with
her·i·ta·ble
her·i·tage
her·met·ic
her·mit
her·nia
he·ro (person or
    sandwich), *plural*
    heroes
her·o·in (drug)
her·o·ine (*fem for*
    hero)
he·ro wor·ship
    (*noun*)
he·ro-wor·ship
    (*verb*)
he·ro-wor·shiped
he·ro-wor·ship·er
he·ro-wor·ship·ing
hes·i·tance
hes·i·tan·cy
hes·i·tant
het·er·o·ge·neous
het·er·o·sex·u·al

heu·ris·tic
hewed
hew·ing
hey·day
hi·a·tus, *plural*
    hiatuses
hi·bis·cus
hic·cup
hic·cuped
hic·cup·ing
hick·ey, *plural*
    hickeys
hick·o·ry
hide-and-seek
hide·away
hid·eous
hie
hied
hi·er·ar·chy
hi·er·o·glyph·ic
hi-fi
high·ball
high beam
high·bind·er
high·born
high·boy
high·brow
high·chair
high-class
high·er-up (*noun*)
high·fa·lu·tin
high fi·del·i·ty
high·fli·er
high-flown
high·fly·ing
high fre·quen·cy

153

high-grade (*adj*)
high·hand·ed
high jump
high-keyed
high·land
high-lev·el
high·light
High Mass
high-mind·ed
high noon
high-oc·tane
high-pow·ered
high-pres·sure (*adj*
and *verb*)
high-priced
high-proof
high-rise (*noun* and
adj)
high·road
high sign
high-sound·ing
high-speed (*adj*)
high-spir·it·ed
high-strung
high·tail (*verb*)
high-ten·sion
high-test (*adj*)
high wa·ter
high·way
hi·jack
hi·jack·er
hi·lar·i·ous
hi·lar·i·ty
hill·ock
hin·drance
hind·sight

hipped
hip·pie (*noun*)
hip·po·drome
hip·po·pot·a·mus,
   plural
   hippopotamuses
hip·py (*adj*)
hir·a·ble
hire·ling
hir·sute
his·ta·mine
his·tri·on·ic
hit-and-run
hith·er·to
hit-or-miss (*adj*)
hit·ter
hit·ting
hoard·er
hoar·frost
hoarse (husky)
hoary (old)
hoax·er
hob·ble
hob·bler
hob·by·horse
hob·gob·lin
hob·nob
hob·nobbed
hob·nob·bing
ho·bo, *plural*
   hoboes
ho·cus
ho·cused
ho·cus·ing
ho·cus-po·cus
ho·cus-po·cused

ho·cus-po·cus·ing
hodge·podge
hoed
ho·er
hoe·ing
hogged
hog·ging
hog·gish
hogs·head
hog·tie
hog·tied
hog·ty·ing
ho-hum
hoi pol·loi
hoi·ty-toi·ty
ho·key·po·key
hold·all
hold·back (*noun*)
hold·out (*noun*)
hold·over (*noun*)
hold up (*verb*)
hold·up (*noun*)
hol·ey (full of holes)
ho·li·er-than-thou
ho·li·ness
hol·lan·daise
hol·low-eyed
hol·low·ware
hol·ly·hock
ho·lo·caust
ho·lo·graph
hol·ster
home (Compound
   words beginning
   with *home* are
   written solid:

154

homebody, except
as otherwise
shown below.)
home·com·ing
home eco·nom·ics
home front
home-grown
home·li·ness
home·ly
home·made
home plate
home·room
home rule
home run
home·stretch
home·ward
hom·ey
hom·i·ci·dal
hom·i·cide
hom·i·er
hom·i·ly
ho·mo·ge·ne·ity
ho·mo·ge·ne·ous
hom·o·logue
hon·ey, *plural* honeys
hon·ey·bee
hon·ey·comb
hon·ey·dew
hon·eyed (*verb* and
   adj)
hon·ey·ing
hon·ey·moon
hon·ey·suck·le
hon·or·able
hon·o·rar·i·um,
   plural honoraria

hon·or·ary
hon·or·if·ic
hoo·doo, *plural*
   hoodoos
hood·wink
hoof, *plural* hoofs
hook shot
hook·up (*noun*)
hook·worm
hooky
hoot·chy-koot·chy
hop·ing (hope)
hopped
hop·per
hop·ping
hore·hound
ho·ri·zon
hor·mone
hor·o·scope
hor·ren·dous
hor·ri·ble
hor·rid
hor·ri·fy
hor·ror
hors d'oeu·vre,
   plural hors
   d'oeuvres
horse (Compound
   words beginning
   with *horse* are
   written solid:
   horseman,
   except
   as otherwise
   shown below.)
horse chest·nut

horse mack·er·el
horse sense
horse trade (*noun*)
horse-trade (*verb*)
horse trad·er
horsy
hor·ta·to·ry
hor·ti·cul·ture
ho·sier
ho·siery
hos·pice
hos·pi·ta·ble
hos·pi·tal·ize
hos·tage
hos·tel
hos·tel·er
   (innkeeper)
hos·tel·ry
hos·tile
hos·til·i·ty
host·ler (groom)
hot·bed
hot-blood·ed
hot·box
hot cake
hot dog
hot flash
hot·foot, *plural*
   hotfoots
hot·head
hot·head·ed
hot·house
hot line
hot·pep·per
hot plate
hot-tem·pered

hot·ter
hot·test
hot war
hound's-tooth check
hour·glass
hour hand
house (Compound
  words beginning
  with *house* are
  written solid:
  housecoat, except
  as otherwise
  shown below.)
house ar·rest
house·bro·ken
house call
house·clean·ing
house·keep·er
House of
  Com·mons
House of
  Rep·re·sen·ta·
  tives
house or·gan
house par·ty
house-rais·ing
hov·el
hov·eled
hov·el·ing
hov·er
hov·er·craft
hov·er·er
how-do-you-do
  (*noun* awkward
  situation)
how·it·zer
how-to (*adj*)

hoy·den
hub·bub
hu·bris
huck·le·ber·ry
huck·ster
hud·dle
hue, *plural* hues
hued (colored)
hugged
hug·ger-mug·ger
hug·ging
hul·la·ba·loo
hu·mane
  (sympathetic,
  civilizing)
hu·man·i·tar·i·an
hu·man·ize
hum·ble
hum·ble pie
hum·bug
hum·bugged
hum·bug·gery
hum·bug·ging
hum·drum
hu·mid·i·fied
hu·mid·i·fi·er
hu·mid·i·fy
hu·mid·i·fy·ing
hu·mid·i·ty
hu·mi·dor
hu·mil·i·ate
hu·mil·i·ty
hummed
hum·mer
hum·ming
hum·mock
hu·mor

hump·back
hump·backed
hu·mus
hunch·back
hunch·backed
hun·dred-
  per·cent·er
hun·dredth
hun·dred·weight
hun·ger strike
hun·gri·er
hun·gri·ly
hur·dle
hur·dy-gur·dy
hurl·er
hur·ly-bur·ly
hur·rah
hur·ri·cane
hur·ried
hur·ri·er
hur·ry·ing
hur·ry-scur·ry
hurt·ful
hur·tle
hus·band·ry
hush-hush
hus·sy
hus·tle
hus·tler
hy·a·cinth
hy·brid
hy·brid·ize
hy·drant
hy·drau·lic
hy·drom·e·ter
hy·dro·pho·bia
hy·dro·plane

hy·e·na

hy·giene

hy·gi·en·ic

hy·ing (hie)

hym·nal

hy·per·bo·le

hy·per·crit·i·cal

  (overly critical)

hy·per·ten·sion

hy·phen

hyp·no·sis

hyp·not·ic

hyp·no·tize

hy·po·chon·dria

hy·poc·ri·sy

hyp·o·crite

hyp·o·crit·i·cal

hy·po·der·mic

hy·pot·e·nuse

hy·poth·e·cate

hy·poth·e·sis,

  plural hypotheses

hy·po·thet·i·cal

hys·te·ria

hys·ter·i·cal

I

ibi·dem
ice age
ice bag
ice·berg
ice·boat
ice·break·er
ice-cold (*adj*)
ice cream (*noun*)
ice-cream (*adj*)
ice field
ice·house
ice sheet
ice skate (*noun*)
ice-skate (*verb*)
ice skat·er
ici·cle
ic·i·er
ic·i·ly
ic·i·ness
ic·ing
icon·o·clast
ide·al·ist
ide·al·ize
iden·ti·cal
iden·ti·fi·able
iden·ti·fied
iden·ti·fi·er
iden·ti·fy
iden·ti·fy·ing

ide·ol·o·gy
id·i·o·cy
id·i·om
id·i·o·syn·cra·sy
idler
idol (image)
idol·a·ter
idol·a·trous
idol·a·try
idol·ize
idyll (poem)
idyl·lic
ig·loo
ig·ne·ous
ig·nit·able
ig·nit·er
ig·no·ble
ig·no·min·i·ous
ig·no·mi·ny
ig·no·ra·mus
ig·no·rance
ig·no·rant
ill (Compound
   words beginning
   with *ill* are
   hyphenated:
   ill-bred, except as
   otherwise shown
   below.)

il·le·gal
il·leg·i·ble
il·le·git·i·ma·cy
il·le·git·i·mate
ill fame
ill hu·mor
il·lib·er·al
il·lic·it
il·lim·it·able
il·lit·er·a·cy
il·lit·er·ate
ill na·ture
ill·ness
il·log·i·cal
il·lu·mi·nate
il·lu·mi·na·tor
ill-us·age
il·lu·sion (false
   notion)
il·lu·sive (unreal;
   see elusive)
il·lu·so·ry
il·lus·tra·tor
il·lus·tri·ous
ill will
im·age·ry
imag·in·able
im·ag·i·nary
im·bal·ance

im·be·cile
im·bro·glio
im·brue
im·brued
im·bru·ing
im·bue
im·bued
im·bu·ing
im·i·ta·ble
im·i·ta·tor
im·mac·u·late
im·ma·nence
im·ma·nent
(existing within,
inherent; *see*
eminent,
imminent)
im·ma·te·ri·al
im·ma·ture
im·mea·sur·able
im·me·di·a·cy
im·me·mo·ri·al
im·mense
im·men·si·ty
im·merge
im·merse
im·mers·ible
im·mi·grant
im·mi·grate (to
enter; *see*
emigrate)
im·mi·nence
im·mi·nent (near at
hand; *see*
immanent,
eminent)
im·mit·i·ga·ble
im·mo·bile

im·mo·bi·lize
im·mod·er·a·cy
im·mod·er·ate
im·mod·est
im·mo·late
im·mo·la·tor
im·mo·ral·i·ty
im·mor·tal
im·mor·tal·ize
im·mov·able
im·mu·ni·ty
im·mu·nize
im·mure
im·mu·ta·ble
im·pair (to damage)
im·pale
im·pale·ment
im·pal·pa·ble
im·pan·el
im·pan·eled
im·pan·el·ing
im·part·able
(revealable)
im·part·er
im·par·tial
im·par·ti·ble
(indivisible)
im·pass·able (bad
roads, mountains)
im·passe (deadlock)
im·pas·si·ble
(incapable of
feeling)
im·pas·sioned
im·pas·sive
im·pa·tience
im·pa·tient
im·peach·able

im·pec·ca·ble
im·pe·cu·nious
im·ped·ance
im·ped·i·ment
im·pel
im·pelled
im·pel·lent
im·pel·ler
im·pel·ling
im·pen·e·tra·ble
im·pen·i·tent
im·per·cep·ti·ble
im·pe·ri·al
im·per·il
im·per·iled
im·per·il·ing
im·pe·ri·ous
im·per·ish·able
im·per·ma·nence
im·per·ma·nent
im·per·me·able
im·per·mis·si·ble
im·per·son·a·tor
im·per·ti·nence
im·per·ti·nent
im·per·turb·able
im·per·vi·ous
im·pet·u·ous
im·pe·tus
im·pi·ety
im·pinge
im·pi·ous
im·pla·ca·ble
im·plau·si·ble
im·ple·ment
im·ple·men·tal
im·pli·ca·tion
im·plic·it

im·plied
im·ply·ing
im·pol·i·tic
im·pon·der·a·ble
im·port·able
im·por·tance
im·por·tant
im·port·er
im·por·tu·nate
im·por·tune
im·por·tu·ni·ty
im·po·si·tion
im·pos·si·ble
im·pos·tor
im·po·tence
im·po·tent
im·prac·ti·ca·ble
im·prac·ti·cal
im·pre·cate
im·pre·ca·tor
im·preg·na·ble
im·preg·na·tor
im·pre·sa·rio,
    plural
    impresarios
im·press·ible
im·pres·sion·able
im·pri·ma·tur
im·pris·on
im·prob·a·ble
im·promp·tu
im·pro·pri·ety
im·prov·able
im·prove·ment
im·prov·i·dence
im·prov·i·dent
im·pro·vi·sa·tion
im·pro·vise

im·pro·vis·er
im·pru·dence
im·pru·dent
im·pu·dence
im·pu·dent
im·pugn
im·pugn·able
im·pugn·er
im·pul·sive
im·pu·ni·ty
im·pu·ri·ty
im·put·able
in·ac·ces·si·ble
in·ac·cu·ra·cy
in·ad·e·qua·cy
in·ad·mis·si·ble
in·ad·ver·tence
in·ad·ver·ten·cy
in·ad·ver·tent
in·ad·vis·able
in·alien·able
in·ane
in·an·i·mate
in·an·i·ty
in·ap·par·ent
in·ap·pli·ca·ble
in·ap·pro·pri·ate
in·ar·tic·u·late
in·as·much as
in·au·di·ble
in·au·gu·ral
in·au·gu·rate
in·au·gu·ra·tor
in·aus·pi·cious
in·cal·cu·la·ble
in·can·des·cence
in·can·des·cent
in·ca·pa·ble

in·ca·pac·i·tate
in·car·cer·ate
in·car·cer·a·tor
in·car·nate
in·cau·tious
in·cen·di·a·rism
in·cen·di·ary
in·cense (all
    meanings)
in·cen·tive
in·cep·tion
in·cer·ti·tude
in·ces·sant
in·ces·tu·ous
inch·meal
in·cho·ate
in·ci·dence
in·ci·dent
in·ci·den·tal
in·cin·er·a·tor
in·cip·i·ence
in·cip·i·ent
in·cise
in·ci·sion
in·ci·sive
in·ci·sor
in·clem·en·cy
in·clem·ent
in·clud·able
in·clu·sion
in·clu·sive
in·co·erc·ible
in·cog·ni·to
in·co·her·ence
in·co·her·ent
in·com·bus·ti·ble
in·com·men·
    su·ra·ble

160

in·com·men·
  su·rate
in·com·mu·
  ni·ca·ble
in·com·mu·
  ni·ca·do
in·com·pa·ra·ble
in·com·pat·i·ble
in·com·pe·tence
in·com·pe·tent
in·com·pre·
  hen·si·ble
in·com·press·ible
in·con·ceiv·able
in·con·dens·able
in·con·gru·ence
in·con·gru·ent
in·con·gru·ity
in·con·gru·ous
in·con·se·quence
in·con·se·quent
in·con·sid·er·able
in·con·sis·ten·cy
in·con·sis·tent
in·con·sol·able
in·con·spic·u·ous
in·con·stan·cy
in·con·test·able
in·con·ti·nence
in·con·ti·nent
in·con·tro·vert·
  ible
in·con·ve·nience
in·con·ve·nient
in·con·vert·ible
in·con·vinc·ible
in·cor·po·rate
in·cor·po·ra·tor

in·cor·po·re·al
in·cor·ri·gi·ble
in·cor·rupt·ible
in·cred·i·ble
in·cre·du·li·ty
in·cred·u·lous
in·cre·ment
in·crim·i·nate
in·crim·i·na·to·ry
in·crust
in·crus·ta·tion
in·cu·ba·tor
in·cu·bus
in·cul·cate
in·cul·pa·ble
in·cul·pate
in·cum·ben·cy
in·cum·bent
in·cur
in·cur·able
in·curred
in·cur·rence
in·cur·ring
in·cur·sion
in·debt·ed
in·de·cen·cy
in·de·cent
in·de·ci·pher·able
in·dec·o·rous
in·de·fat·i·ga·ble
in·de·fea·si·ble
in·de·fen·si·ble
in·de·fin·able
in·del·i·ble
in·del·i·ca·cy
in·del·i·cate
in·dem·ni·fied
in·dem·ni·fy

in·dem·ni·fy·ing
in·dem·ni·ty
in·den·ture
in·de·pen·dence
in·de·pen·dent
in-depth (*adj*)
in·de·scrib·able
in·de·struc·ti·ble
in·de·ter·min·able
in·de·ter·mi·na·cy
in·dex (pointer, list),
  plural indexes;
  (math), *plural*
  indices
in·dic·a·tive
in·di·ca·tor
in·di·cia
in·dict (accuse; *see*
  indite)
in·dict·able
in·dict·er
in·dict·ment
in·dif·fer·ence
in·dif·fer·ent
in·di·gence
in·dig·e·nous
in·di·gent
in·di·gest·ible
in·dig·nant
in·dig·ni·ty
in·di·go, *plural*
  indigos
in·dis·cern·ible
in·dis·creet
  (imprudent)
in·dis·crete (not
  separated)
in·dis·cre·tion

in·dis·crim·i·nate
in·dis·pens·able
in·dis·put·able
in·dis·sol·u·ble
in·dis·tin·guish·
   able
in·dite (compose,
   put in writing;
   see indict)
in·di·vert·ible
in·di·vid·u·al·i·ty
in·di·vid·u·al·ize
in·di·vis·i·ble
in·doc·tri·na·tor
in·do·lence
in·do·lent
in·dom·i·ta·ble
in·du·bi·ta·ble
in·duce
in·duc·er
in·duce·ment
in·duc·ible
in·duc·tance
in·duct·ee
in·duc·tor
in·dul·gence
in·dul·gent
in·du·rate
in·dus·tri·al·ize
in·dus·tri·ous
in·e·bri·at·ed
in·e·bri·ety
in·ed·i·ble
in·ed·u·ca·ble
in·ef·fa·ble
in·ef·face·able
in·ef·fec·tu·al
in·ef·fi·ca·cy

in·ef·fi·cien·cy
in·ef·fi·cient
in·elas·tic
in·el·e·gance
in·el·e·gant
in·el·i·gi·ble
in·eluc·ta·ble
in·elud·ible
in·ept·i·tude
in·equal·i·ty
in·eq·ui·ta·ble
in·eq·ui·ty
in·e·rad·i·ca·ble
in·ert
in·er·tia
in·es·cap·able
in·es·ti·ma·ble
in·ev·i·ta·ble
in·ex·cus·able
in·ex·haust·ible
in·ex·o·ra·ble
in·ex·pe·di·en·cy
in·ex·pe·di·ent
in·ex·pe·ri·ence
in·ex·pi·a·ble
in·ex·plain·able
in·ex·pli·ca·ble
in·ex·press·ible
in·ex·tin·guish·
   able
in·ex·tri·ca·ble
in·fal·li·ble
in·fa·mous
in·fa·my
in·fan·cy
in·fan·ti·cide
in·fan·tile
in·fat·u·ate

in·fec·tious
in·fec·tor
in·fe·lic·i·ty
in·fer
in·fer·able
in·fer·ence
in·fer·en·tial
in·fe·ri·or
in·fe·ri·or·i·ty
in·fer·nal
in·ferred
in·fer·ring
in·fi·del
in·fight·ing
in·fil·tra·tor
in·fin·i·tes·i·mal
in·fin·i·tude
in·fin·i·ty
in·fir·ma·ry
in·fir·mi·ty
in·flame
in·flam·ma·ble
in·flam·ma·tion
in·flat·er
in·fla·tion·ary
in·flec·tion
in·flex·i·ble
in·flict·er
in-flight (*adj*)
in·flu·ence
in·flu·en·tial
in·flu·en·za
in·for·mal·i·ty
in·for·mant
in·frac·tor
in·fra·red
in·fra·struc·ture
in·fre·quence

in·fre·quent
in·fringe·ment
in·fu·ri·ate
in·fus·ible
in·gen·ious
  (skillful)
in·gé·nue
in·ge·nu·ity
in·gen·u·ous
  (frank)
in·glo·ri·ous
in·gra·ti·ate
in·grat·i·tude
in·gre·di·ent
in·gress
in-group
in·grown
in·hab·it·an·cy
in·hab·it·ant
in·hal·ant
in·ha·la·tor
in·hal·er
in·har·mo·ni·ous
in·here
in·her·ent
in·her·it·able
in·her·i·tance
in·her·i·tor
in·hi·bi·tion
in·hib·i·tor
in·hib·i·to·ry
in·hos·pi·ta·ble
in-house (*adj*)
in·im·i·cal
in·im·i·ta·ble
in·iq·ui·tous
in·iq·ui·ty
in·i·tialed

in·i·tial·ing
in·i·ti·a·tor
in·ject·able
in·jec·tor
in·ju·di·cious
in·junc·tion
in·ju·ri·ous
in·jus·tice
ink·ling
in·laid
in-law
in·lay, *plural* inlays
in·nate
in·ner·most
in·ner·sole
in·ner·vate (to
  stimulate)
in·no·cence
in·no·cent
in·noc·u·ous
in·no·va·tion
in·no·va·tor
in·nu·en·do, *plural*
  innuendoes
in·nu·mer·a·ble
in·ob·ser·vance
in·ob·ser·vant
in·oc·u·late
in·oc·u·la·tor
in·op·er·a·ble
in·op·por·tune
in·or·di·nate
in·qui·etude
in·quire
in·quir·er
in·qui·ry
in·quis·i·tive
in·quis·i·tor

ins and outs
in·san·i·tary
in·san·i·ty
in·sa·tia·ble
in·scrib·er
in·scrip·tion
in·scru·ta·ble
in·sec·ti·cide
in·se·cu·ri·ty
in·sem·i·na·tor
in·sen·sate
in·sen·si·ble
in·sep·a·ra·ble
in-ser·vice
in·sid·i·ous
in·sig·nia (*sing* and
  plural)
in·sig·nif·i·cance
in·sig·nif·i·cant
in·sin·cer·i·ty
in·sin·u·ate
in·sin·u·a·tor
in·sip·id
in·sis·tence
in·sis·tent
in·so·bri·ety
in·so·far as
in·so·lence
in·so·lent
in·sol·u·ble
in·solv·able
in·sol·ven·cy
in·sol·vent
in·som·nia
in·sou·ci·ance
in·sou·ci·ant
in·spec·tor
in·spi·ra·tion

163

in·stall
in·stal·la·tion
in·stalled
in·stall·ing
in·stall·ment
in·stance
in·stan·ta·neous
in·sti·gate
in·sti·ga·tor
in·still
in·stilled
in·still·ing
in·still·ment
in·stinct
in·sti·tute
in·sti·tu·tor
in·struc·tor
in·stru·men·tal
in·sub·or·di·nate
in·sub·stan·tial
in·suf·fer·able
in·suf·fi·cien·cy
in·suf·fi·cient
in·su·lar
in·su·la·tor
in·su·lin
in·su·per·a·ble
in·sup·port·able
in·sup·press·ible
in·sur·able
in·sur·ance
in·sure (to buy or
    sell an insurance
    policy; *see*
    ensure)
in·sur·er
in·sur·gen·cy
in·sur·gent

in·sur·mount·able
in·sur·rec·tion
in·sur·rec·tion·ary
in·sus·cep·ti·ble
in·ta·glio, *plural*
    intaglios
in·ta·glioed
in·ta·glio·ing
in·tan·gi·ble
in·te·ger
in·te·gral
in·te·gra·tor
in·teg·ri·ty
in·tel·lect
in·tel·li·gence
in·tel·li·gent
in·tel·li·gen·tsia
in·tel·li·gi·ble
in·tem·per·ance
in·tem·per·ate
in·ten·dance
in·ten·dan·cy
in·ten·dant
in·tense
in·ten·si·fied
in·ten·si·fi·er
in·ten·si·fy
in·ten·si·fy·ing
in·ten·si·ty
in·ten·tion
in·ter (to bury)
in·ter·cede
in·ter·cep·tor
in·ter·ces·sion
in·ter·ces·sor
in·ter·change·able
in·ter·de·pen·
    dence

in·ter·de·pen·dent
in·ter·dict
in·ter·dic·tor
in·ter·dis·ci·
    plin·ary
in·ter·fer·ence
in·te·ri·or
in·ter·jec·tor
in·ter·jec·to·ry
in·ter·lin·ear
in·ter·loc·u·tor
in·ter·loc·u·to·ry
in·ter·lop·er
in·ter·lude
in·ter·lu·nar
in·ter·me·di·ary
in·ter·ment (burial)
in·ter·mi·na·ble
in·ter·min·gle
in·ter·mit·tence
in·ter·mit·tent
in·tern
in·ter·nal·ize
in·ter·ne·cine
in·tern·ee
in·tern·ment
    (detention)
in·ter·plan·e·tary
in·ter·po·late (to
    insert)
in·ter·po·la·tor
in·ter·pret
in·ter·pret·able
in·ter·pret·er
in·ter·pre·tive
in·ter·ra·cial
in·terred (inter)
in·ter·re·late

in·ter·ring
in·ter·ro·gate
in·ter·ro·ga·tor
in·ter·rog·a·to·ry
in·ter·rupt
in·ter·rupt·er
in·ter·rupt·ible
in·ter·sperse
in·ter·stice
in·ter·sti·tial
in·ter·twine
in·ter·val
in·ter·ven·er
in·ter·ve·nor (law)
in·ter·view·er
in·tes·ta·cy
in·tes·tate
in·ti·ma·cy
in·ti·mate
in·tim·i·date
in·tim·i·da·tor
in·tol·er·a·ble
in·tol·er·ance
in·tol·er·ant
in·tox·i·cant
in·trac·ta·ble
in·tra·mu·ral
in·tran·si·gence
in·tran·si·gent
in·tra·ve·nous
in·trep·id
in·tri·ca·cy
in·tri·gant
in·tri·gante (*fem* only)
in·trigue
in·trigu·er
in·trigu·ing

in·trin·sic
in·tro·duc·to·ry
in·tro·spec·tion
in·tro·ver·sion
in·tro·vert
in·trud·er
in·tru·sion
in·tu·ition
in·tu·itive
in·un·da·tor
in·un·da·to·ry
in·ure
in·ure·ment
in·val·i·date
in·valu·able
in·vari·able
in·var·i·ance
in·var·i·ant
in·veigh
in·veigh·er
in·vei·gle
in·vei·gler
in·ven·tor
in·ven·to·ry
in·verse
in·ver·sion
in·ver·te·brate
in·vert·ible
in·vest·able
in·ves·ti·ga·tor
in·ves·tor
in·vet·er·a·cy
in·vet·er·ate
in·vid·i·ous
in·vig·o·ra·tor
in·vin·ci·ble
in·vi·o·la·ble
in·vi·o·late

in·vis·i·ble
in·vo·ca·tion
in·voice
in·voke
in·vol·un·tary
in·vul·ner·a·ble
in·ward
io·dine
ion·ize
iras·ci·ble
irate
ire
ir·i·des·cence
ir·i·des·cent
iris, *plural* irises
irk
iron·bound
iron·clad
iron cur·tain
iron hand
iron·ic
iron·i·cal
iron lung
iron·ware
iron·wood
iron·work
iro·ny
ir·ra·di·ate
ir·ra·di·a·tor
ir·ra·tion·al
ir·re·claim·able
ir·rec·on·cil·able
ir·re·cov·er·able
ir·re·deem·able
ir·re·duc·ible
ir·re·fut·able
ir·reg·u·lar
ir·rel·e·vance

165

ir·rel·e·vant
ir·re·li·gious
ir·re·me·di·a·ble
ir·re·mov·able
ir·rep·a·ra·ble
ir·re·place·able
ir·re·press·ible
ir·re·proach·able
ir·re·sist·ible
ir·res·o·lute
ir·re·solv·able
ir·re·spec·tive
ir·re·spon·si·ble
ir·re·triev·able

ir·rev·er·ence
ir·rev·er·ent
ir·re·vers·ible
ir·re·vo·ca·ble
ir·ri·gate
ir·ri·ga·tor
ir·ri·ta·ble
ir·ri·tant
isin·glass
is·land
is·land·er
iso·late
iso·tope
is·su·able

is·su·ance
is·sued
is·su·er
is·su·ing
isth·mus, *plural*
   isthmuses
ital·ic, *plural*
   italics
ital·i·cize
item·ize
it·er·ate
itin·er·ant
itin·er·ary
ivo·ry

J

jabbed
jab·ber
jab·bered
jab·ber·er
jab·ber·ing
jab·bing
jack (Compound
   words beginning
   with *jack* are
   written solid:
   jackpot, except as
   otherwise shown
   below.)
jack·al
jack·a·napes
Jack Frost
jack-in-the-box,
   plural jack-in-
   the-boxes
jack-in-the-pul·pit,
   plural jack-in-
   the-pulpits
jack-o'-lan·tern,
   plural jack-o'-
   lanterns
jack pine
jack rab·bit
jack·tar

jac·ta·tion
jad·ed
jade·ite
jag·ged
jag·ging
jag·gy
jag·uar
jail·break
jail·er
ja·lopy
jal·ou·sie
   (a window blind)
jam·bo·ree
jammed
jam·ming
jan·gle
jan·is·sary
jan·i·tor
Jan·u·ary
jape (to joke)
jap·ery
jar·gon
jarred
jar·ring
jas·mine
jas·per
jaun·dice
jaunt

jaun·ti·ly
jaun·ti·ness
jav·e·lin
jay·walk
jeal·ou·sy
jeer (to mock)
je·june
jel·ly·bean
jel·ly·fish
jel·ly roll
jeop·ar·dize
jeop·ar·dy
jer·ry-build
jer·ry-build·er
jer·ry-built
jer·sey
jet-black
jet en·gine
jet·lin·er
jet·port
jet-pro·pelled
jet pro·pul·sion
jet·sam
jet set
jet stream
jet·ted
jet·ting
jet·ti·son

167

jet·ty
jew·el
jew·eled
jew·el·er
jew·el·ry
jew's-harp
jibbed (refused)
jib·bing
jibed (sailing)
jigged
jig·ger
jig·ging
jig·gled
jig·gling
jig·gly
jin·gle
jin·go, *plural*
  jingoes
jin·go·ist
jit·tery
jobbed
job·ber
job·bery
job·bing
job·hold·er
job lot
jock·ey, *plural*
  jockeys
jock·eyed
jock·ey·ing
jo·cose
jo·cos·i·ty
joc·u·lar
joc·u·lar·i·ty
jo·cund
jogged
jog·ger

jog·ging
jog·gle
jog·gled
jog·gling
John·ny-come-
  late·ly
John·ny-on-the-
  spot
join·ery
join·ture
joist (beam)
jol·li·fy
jol·li·ty
jon·quil
jos·tle
jot·ted
jot·ting
jour·nal
jour·nal·ese
jour·nal·ize
jour·ney, *plural*
  journeys
jour·neyed
jour·ney·er
jour·ney·ing
jour·ney·man
ju·bi·lance
ju·bi·lant
ju·bi·lee
judg·mat·ic
judg·ment
ju·di·ca·to·ry
ju·di·cial
ju·di·cia·ry
ju·di·cious
ju·do
jug·fuls

jugged
jug·ging
jug·gle
jug·gled
jug·gler
jug·glery
jug·gling
jug·u·lar (vein)
juic·i·est
juic·i·ness
juicy
ju·jit·su
ju·lep
ju·li·enne
jum·ble
jum·bo, *plural*
  jumbos
jump bid
jump·ing-off place
jump-off
jun·co, *plural*
  juncos
junc·tion
junc·ture
jun·gle
ju·nior
jun·ket
jun·ke·teer (*noun*)
jun·to, *plural*
  juntos
ju·rid·i·cal
ju·ris·dic·tion
ju·ris·pru·dence
ju·ror
ju·ry-rigged
jus·tice
jus·ti·cia·ble

jus·ti·cia·ry

jus·ti·fi·able

jus·ti·fied

jus·ti·fy

jus·ti·fy·ing

jute

jut·ted

jut·ting

ju·ve·nile

jux·ta·pose

K

kaf·ir
kai·ser
ka·lei·do·scope
kan·ga·roo
ka·pok
kar·at (gold
   refinement)
ka·ra·te
kay·ak (canoe)
ke·bab
ken·nel
ken·neled
ken·nel·ing
ken·ning
ker·chief, *plural*
   kerchiefs
ker·nel (inner part)
ker·neled
ker·nel·ing
ker·o·sene
ketch·up
ket·tle
ket·tle·drum
key·board
keyed
key·hole
key·ing
key·note

key·not·er
key punch
key ring
key sig·na·ture
key·stone
kha·ki
ki·bitz
ki·bitz·er
kick·back
kick·off (*noun*)
kick off (*verb*)
kid·ded
kid·der
kid·ding
kid·dish
kid·dy
kid·like
kid·naped
kid·nap·er
kid·nap·ing
kid·ney, *plural*
   kidneys
kill·joy
kil·o·gram
ki·lo·me·ter
ki·mo·no, *plural*
   kimonos
kin·der·gart·ner

kind·heart·ed
kin·dle
kind·li·ness
kin·dling
kin·dred
kin·e·scope
ki·net·ic
kin·folk
king crab
king·fish
king mack·er·el
king·mak·er
king·pin
king·size (*adj*)
king snake
kin·ship
kins·man
kins·wom·an
ki·osk
kiss·able
kitch·en cab·i·net
kitch·en·ette
kitch·en gar·den
kitch·en·ware
klep·to·ma·nia
klieg light
knack
knap·sack

knav·ery
knav·ish
knead (to mix and
    work)
knee ac·tion
knee bend
knee·cap
knee-deep
knee-high
knee·hole
knee jerk
knee·pad
knell
knick·knack
knife-edge
knight·hood
knit·ted
knit·ter

knit·ting
knit·wear
knobbed
knob·bi·er
knob·bi·ness
knob·by
knock·down (*noun*
    and *adj*)
knock·kneed
knock·out (*noun*)
knoll (mound)
knot·hole
knot·ted
knot·ter
knot·ti·er
knot·ting
knot·ty
know·able

know-how
know-it-all
knowl·edge·able
know-noth·ing
knuck·le
knuck·le ball
knuck·le·bone
knuck·le-dust·er
knuck·le joint
knuck·ler
ko·ala
kohl·ra·bi
ko·sher
kow·tow
kraft (wrapping
    paper)
ku·dos (praise)
kum·quat

L

la·bel
la·beled
la·bel·er
la·bel·ing
la·bi·al (of the lips)
lab·o·ra·to·ry
la·bor·er
la·bo·ri·ous
la·bor·sav·ing
lab·y·rinth
lac·er·ate
lace·work
lach·ry·mal
lach·ry·mose
lack·a·dai·si·cal
lack·ey, *plural*
　lackeys
lack·lus·ter
la·con·ic
lac·quer
lac·te·al
lac·tic
la·cu·na, *plural*
　lacunae
lacy
la-di-da
la·dies' man

lad·ing
la·dle
lad·le·fuls
la·dy·bird
la·dy·bug
la·dy·fin·ger
la·dy-in-wait·ing
la·dy·like
la·ger (beer)
lag·gard
lagged
lag·ger
lag·ging
la·gniappe
la·goon
la·ic
la·i·cize
lais·sez faire (*noun*)
la·i·ty
la·ma (monk; *see*
　llama)
lam·baste
lam·ben·cy
lam·bent
la·men·ta·ble
lam·i·nate
lam·i·na·tor

lamp·black
lamp·light
lamp·light·er
lam·poon
lam·poon·ery
lamp·post
lan·cet
land (Compound
　words beginning
　with *land* are
　written solid:
　landfall, except as
　otherwise shown
　below.)
lan·dau
land bank
land breeze
land·fall
land·fill
land-grant (*adj*)
land of·fice
land-of·fice
　busi·ness
land-poor
land·ward
lang·syne
lan·guid

lan·guish
lan·guor
lan·guor·ous
lan·yard
lap dog
la·pel
lap·fuls
lap·i·dary
lapped
lap·per
lap·ping
lapse
lar·ce·nist
lar·ce·nous
lar·ce·ny
large·heart·ed
large-mind·ed
large-scale (*adj*)
lar·gess
larg·ish
lar·go, *plural* largos
lar·i·at
lar·va, *plural* larvae
lar·yn·gi·tis
lar·ynx
la·sa·gna
las·civ·i·ous
la·ser
las·si·tude
las·so, *plural* lassos
las·soed
las·so·er
las·so·ing
last-dich (*adj*)
la·ten·cy

la·tent
lat·er·al
lath (thin strip), *plural* laths
lathe (machine)
lath·er
lath·ery
lath·ing (lath and lathe)
lat·i·tude
lat·ter-day (*adj*)
lat·tice
laud·able
laud·a·to·ry
laugh·able
laugh·ing·stock
Laun·dro·mat (trademark)
laun·dry
lau·re·ate
lau·rel (*noun* and *verb*)
lau·reled
lau·rel·ing
la·va·liere
lav·a·to·ry
lav·en·der
law-abid·ing
law·book
law·break·er
law court
law·mak·er
lax·a·tive
lax·i·ty
lay·ette
lay·man
lay·off (*noun*)
lay·out (*noun*)

lay·over (*noun*)
lay read·er
lay-up (*noun*)
lay·wom·an
la·zi·ly
lea (meadow; *see* lee)
leach (to pass water through)
leach·able
lead-in (*noun*)
lead·off (*noun* and *adj*)
lead-pipe cinch
lead time
league
leagued
leagu·er
leagu·ing
leaned (*past of* lean)
lean-to, *plural* lean-tos
leaped
leap·frog
leap·frogged
leap·frog·ger
leap·frog·ging
leap year
learn·able
learn·ed (*adj*)
lease-back
lease·hold
lease·hold·er
leath·ery
leav·en (fermenter)
leav·en·ing
leave-tak·ing
lech·er

lech·er·ous
lech·ery
lec·tern
lec·tor
lec·tur·er
led·ger
lee (shelter; *see* lea)
leech (worm, parasite)
leer·i·er
leery
lee·ward
lee·way
left field
left field·er
left-hand (*adj*)
left-hand·ed
left-hand·er
left·over
left·ward
left-wing (*adj*)
left-wing·er
leg·a·cy
le·gal·ese
le·gal·ize
leg·a·tee
leg·end·ary
leg·er·de·main
legged
leg·gi·er
leg·gi·ness
leg·ging
leg·gy
leg·i·ble
le·gion·ary
le·gion·naire
leg·is·la·tor

le·git·i·ma·cy
le·git·i·mate
le·git·i·mize
leg·ume
lei (flowers)
lei·sure
leit·mo·tif
lend-lease
length·wise
le·ni·ence
le·ni·ent
len·i·ty
lens, *plural* lenses
len·til
le·o·nine
leop·ard
le·o·tard
lep·er
lep·ro·sy
lep·rous
le·sion
les·see (tenant)
les·sor (landlord)
let·down (*noun*)
le·thal
leth·ar·gy
let·ter car·ri·er
let·tered
let·ter·head
let·ter·ing
let·ter-per·fect
let·ter·press
let·ting
let·tuce
let·up (*noun*)
leu·ke·mia
lev·ee (*noun* embankment)

lev·eed
lev·ee·ing
lev·el
lev·eled
lev·el·er
lev·el·head·ed
lev·el·ing
le·ver
le·ver·age
le·vi·a·than
lev·ied
lev·ies
lev·i·tate
lev·i·ta·tor
lev·i·ty
levy·ing
lewd
lex·i·cal
lex·i·cog·ra·phy
lex·i·con
li·a·bil·i·ty
li·a·ble
li·ai·son
li·ba·tion
li·bel (defamation)
li·beled
li·bel·er
li·bel·ing
li·bel·ous
lib·er·al·ize
lib·er·a·tor
lib·er·tar·i·an
lib·er·tine
li·bid·i·nous
li·bi·do
li·bret·tist
li·bret·to, *plural* librettos

li·cens·able
li·cense
li·cens·ee
li·cens·er
li·cen·sor (law)
li·cen·ti·ate
li·cen·tious
li·chen
lic·it
lick·e·ty-split
lic·o·rice (flavor)
lid·ded
lief (willing)
liege·man
lien (legal claim)
lieu (instead)
lieu·ten·an·cy
lieu·ten·ant
lieu·ten·ant
  gov·er·nor
life belt
life·blood
life·boat
life buoy
life cy·cle
life ex·pec·tan·cy
life-giv·ing
life·guard
life·like
life·line
life·long
life raft
life·sav·er
life·sav·ing
life-size (*adj*)
life span
life·time
life·work

lift-off (*noun*)
lig·a·ment
lig·a·ture
light bulb
light·en·ing
  (making lighter;
  see lightning)
light·er-than-air
light·faced
light-fin·gered
light-foot·ed
light-hand·ed
light·head·ed
light·heart·ed
light·house
light house·keep·
  ing
light me·ter
light-mind·ed
light·ning (in the
  sky; *see*
  lightening)
light op·era
light·proof
light·ship
light-struck
light verse
light·weight
light-year
lik·able
like·li·hood
like-mind·ed
li·lac
lily-liv·ered
lily of the val·ley,
  plural lilies of the
  valley
lily-white

lim·ber
lim·bo, *plural*
  limbos
lime·ade
lime·light
lime·stone
lime·wa·ter
lim·it·able
lim·i·tary
limn (to draw)
limned
limn·er
limn·ing
lim·ou·sine
lim·pet
lim·pid
lin·age (number of
  printed lines)
lin·eage (descent
  from common
  ancestor)
lin·eal
lin·ea·ment
lin·ear
line·back·er
line cut
line draw·ing
line drive
line·man
lin·en
lines·man
line squall
line storm
line·up (*noun*)
lin·ge·rie
lin·go, *plural*
  lingoes
lin·gual

lin·guist
lin·i·ment
lin·ing
li·no·le·um
lin·tel
li·on·heart·ed
li·on·ize
lipped
lip·ping
lip·read (*verb*)
lip·read·er
lip read·ing (*noun*)
lip ser·vice
lip·stick
liq·ue·fi·able
liq·ue·fied
liq·ue·fi·er
liq·ue·fy
liq·ue·fy·ing
li·queur
liq·ui·date
liq·ui·da·tor
li·quor
lisle (thread)
lis·some
lis·ten·er
lit·a·ny
li·ter (measure)
lit·er·a·cy
lit·er·al
lit·er·ary
lit·er·ate
lithe
lithe·some
lith·o·graph
lit·i·ga·ble
lit·i·gant

lit·i·gate
lit·i·ga·tor
li·ti·gious
lit·mus
lit·tle (Compound
    words beginning
    with *little* are
    written as
    separate words:
    little finger, except
    as otherwise
    shown below.)
lit·tle·neck clam
lit·to·ral (shore)
li·tur·gi·cal
lit·ur·gy
liv·able
live·li·hood
live·li·ness
live load
live·long (*adj*)
live·ly
live oak
liv·ery
live steam
live·stock
live wire
liv·id
liv·ing room
liz·ard
lla·ma (animal; *see*
    lama)
loath (unwilling)
loathe (dislike)
loath·ing (dislike)
loath·some
lo·bar

lobbed
lob·ber
lob·bied
lob·bies
lob·bing
lob·by
lob·by·ing
lob·by·ist
lo·cale (place of an
    event)
lo·cal·ize
lo·ca·ter
lock·er
lock·er room
lock·et
lock·jaw
lock·nut
lock·out (*noun*)
lock·smith
lock step
lock·stitch
lock·up (*noun*)
lo·co, *plural* locos
lo·coed
lo·co·ing
lo·co·mo·tive
lo·cus, *plural* loci
lode·star
lode·stone
lodg·ment
lo·gan·ber·ry
log·a·rithm
log·book
logged
log·ger
log·ger·heads
log·ging

lo·gi·cian
lo·gi·ness (logy)
lo·gis·tics
log·jam
log·o·type
log·roll·er
log·roll·ing
lo·gy
loi·ter
loi·ter·er
loll (lounge about)
lol·li·pop
lone hand
lone·li·ness
long-dis·tance (*adj*)
long dis·tance
   (*noun*)
long-drawn
long-drawn-out
lon·gev·i·ty
long·hair
long·hand
long·head·ed
long·horn (cattle)
lon·gi·tude
lon·gi·tu·di·nal
long-lived
long-play·ing
long-range (*adj*)
long run (*noun*)
long-run (*adj*)
long·shore·man
long shot
long·stand·ing (*adj*)
long-suf·fer·ing
   (*adj*)
long suit

long-term (*adj*)
long·time (*adj*)
long-wind·ed
look·er-on, *plural*
   lookers-on
look-in (*noun*)
look·ing glass
look·out (*noun*)
loop·hole
loose ends
loose-joint·ed
loose-leaf
loose-limbed
loose-tongued
lop-eared
lopped
lop·ping
lop·sid·ed
lo·qua·cious
lo·quac·i·ty
lor·ry
los·able
loss lead·er
lo·tion
lot·ted
lot·tery
lot·ting
lo·tus
lo·tus-eat·er
loud·mouth
loud·mouthed
loud·speak·er
lousy
lou·ver
lov·able
love af·fair
love·bird

love feast
love·li·ness
love·mak·ing
love seat
love·sick
lov·ing cup
lov·ing-kind·ness
low blow
low·born
low·boy
low·bred
low·brow
low-cost (*adj*)
low·down (*noun*)
low-down (*adj*)
low·er-case (*adj*)
low·er case (*noun*)
low·er·class·man
   (school)
low·er·ing
   (scowling,
   overcast)
low fre·quen·cy
low-grade (*adj*)
low-key (*adj*)
low·land
low-lev·el (*adj*)
low·ly
low-mind·ed
low-necked
low-pitched
low-pres·sure (*adj*)
low-priced (*adj*)
low re·lief
low-spir·it·ed
low-ten·sion (*adj*)
low-test (*adj*)

low tide
low-wa·ter mark
loz·enge
lu·bri·cant
lu·bri·ca·tor
lu·bri·cious
lu·bric·i·ty
lu·cid
lu·cra·tive
lu·cre
lu·cu·brate
lu·cu·bra·tor
lu·di·crous
lug·gage
lugged
lug·ger
lug·ging
lu·gu·bri·ous
luke·warm

lul·la·by
lum·ba·go
lu·mi·nance
lu·mi·nary
lu·mi·nes·cence
lu·mi·nes·cent
lu·mi·nous
lump·sum
lu·na·cy
lu·nar
lu·na·tic
lurch
lu·rid
lus·cious
lus·ter
lus·ter·ware
lus·trous
lux·u·ri·ance
lux·u·ri·ant

lux·u·ri·ate
lux·u·ri·ous
lux·u·ry
lye (alkaline
    substance)
ly·ing (speaking
    falsely, reclining)
ly·ing-in, *plural*
    lyings-in
lymph
lynch
lynch law
lynx-eyed
ly·on·naise
lyre (musical
    instrument)
lyr·ic
lyr·i·cist

M

ma·ca·bre
mac·ad·am
mac·a·ro·ni, *plural*
  macaronis
mac·a·roon
mace (club and
  spice)
ma·cé·doine
mac·er·ate
mac·er·a·tor
ma·che·te
ma·chin·able
mach·i·nate
mach·i·na·tor
ma·chine gun
  (*noun*)
ma·chine-gun (*verb*)
ma·chin·ery
ma·chine shop
ma·chine tool
ma·chin·ist
mack·er·el
mack·i·naw
mack·in·tosh
mac·ro·cosm
mac·ro·scop·ic
mad·cap
mad·den
mad·den·ing

mad·der
mad·dest
mad·dish
ma·de·moi·selle
made-to-or·der
made-up (*adj*)
ma·don·na
ma·dras
mad·ri·gal
ma·dri·lène (soup)
mael·strom
mae·stro, *plural*
  maestros
Ma·fia
mag·got
ma·gi·cian
mag·is·te·ri·al
mag·is·tra·cy
mag·is·tral
mag·is·trate
mag·na·nim·i·ty
mag·nan·i·mous
mag·nate
  (important
  person)
mag·ne·tism
mag·ne·tize
mag·ne·to, *plural*
  magnetos

mag·nif·i·cence
mag·nif·i·cent
mag·nif·i·co, *plural*
  magnificoes
mag·ni·fied
mag·ni·fi·er
mag·ni·fy
mag·ni·fy·ing
mag·nil·o·quence
mag·nil·o·quent
mag·ni·tude
mag·no·lia
ma·hog·a·ny
maid of hon·or
maid·ser·vant
mail·able
mail drop
mail·er
mail·man
mail or·der (*noun*)
mail-or·der (*adj*)
main·land
main line (railroad)
main·mast
main·sail
main·spring
main·stay
main·stream
main·tain·able

main·te·nance
maî·tre d', *plural*
   maître d's
maî·tre d'hô·tel
maize (corn; *see*
   maze)
maj·es·ty
ma·jor-do·mo,
   plural major-
   domos
ma·jor league
   (*noun*)
ma·jor-league (*adj*)
mak·able
make-be·lieve
   (*noun* and *adj*)
make-do
make·ready
make·shift (*noun*
   and *adj*)
make·up (*noun* and
   adj)
make·weight
mal·adapt·ed
mal·ad·just·ed
mal·adroit
mal·a·dy
mal·aise
ma·lar·ia
mal·con·tent
mal·e·dic·tion
mal·e·dic·to·ry
mal·e·fac·tor
ma·lev·o·lence
ma·lev·o·lent
mal·fea·sance
mal·for·ma·tion

mal·func·tion
mal·ice
ma·li·cious
ma·lign
ma·lig·nan·cy
ma·lig·nant
ma·lign·er
ma·lig·ni·ty
ma·lin·ger
ma·lin·ger·er
mall (public walk;
   see maul)
mal·le·a·ble
mal·let
mal·nour·ished
mal·nu·tri·tion
mal·odor
mal·odor·ous
mal·prac·tice
mam·mal
mam·ma·ry
mam·mon
mam·moth
man about town
man·a·cle
man·age·able
man·a·ge·ri·al
man-child
man·da·rin
man·da·tary (*noun*)
man·da·to·ry (*adj*)
man-day
man·di·ble
man-eat·er
ma·neu·ver
ma·neu·ver·able
mange

man·ger (feedbox)
man·gi·ness
man·gle
man·go, *plural*
   mangoes
mangy
man·han·dle
man·hole
man-hour
man·hunt
ma·nia
ma·ni·a·cal
man·ic
man·i·cure
man·i·fest
man·i·fes·to, *plural*
   manifestoes
man·i·fold
man·i·kin (pygmy)
ma·nila
Ma·nila pa·per
man in the street
ma·nip·u·late
ma·nip·u·la·tor
man·like
man-made
manned
man·ne·quin
   (model, tailor's
   dummy)
man·ning
man·nish
man-of-war
man·or
man·or house
ma·no·ri·al
man·pow·er

manse
man·ser·vant
man-size (*adj*)
man·slaugh·ter
man·tel (fireplace)
man·tel·piece
man·tle (cloak)
man-to-man
man·u·fac·to·ry
man·u·fac·tur·er
many-sid·ed
ma·ple
mapped
map·per
map·ping
mar·a·schi·no
mar·a·thon
ma·raud
ma·raud·er
mar·ble·ize
mar·bling
mar·cel
Mar·di gras
mare's-nest
mar·ga·rine
mar·gin·al
mar·i·gold
mar·i·jua·na
mar·i·nate
mar·i·o·nette
mar·i·tal (marriage;
  see martial)
mar·i·time
mar·jo·ram
mark·down (*noun*)
mar·ket·able
mar·ket·er

mar·ket·place
mar·ket price
mar·ket val·ue
mark·up (*noun*)
mar·line
mar·ma·lade
mar·quee (tent,
  awning)
mar·quis
  (nobleman)
marred
mar·riage
mar·ried
mar·ring
mar·ron (sweet
  chestnut)
mar·ry·ing
mar·shal
mar·shaled
mar·shal·ing
marsh·mal·low
  (candy)
mar·tial (warlike;
  see marital)
mar·tin·gale
mar·tyr
mar·tyr·dom
mar·tyr·ize
mar·vel
mar·veled
mar·vel·ing
mar·vel·ous
mar·zi·pan
mas·cara
mas·cu·line
mash·ie
mas·och·ism

ma·son·ry
mas·quer·ade
mas·sa·cre
mas·sage
mas·seur (*masc*)
mas·seuse (*fem*)
mas·sif (mountain)
mas·sive (large)
mass-pro·duce
mass-pro·duced
mass-pro·duc·ing
mass pro·duc·tion
mas·ter hand
mas·ter key
mas·ter·mind (*noun*
  and *verb*)
mas·ter·piece
mas·ter·stroke
mas·ter·work
mas·ti·cate
mas·ti·ca·tor
mas·tiff
mas·toid
mat·a·dor
match·able
match·book
match·box
match·mak·er
match play
match point
match·wood
ma·te·ri·al·i·ty
ma·te·ri·al·ize
ma·te·ri·el
  (equipment and
  supplies)
mat·i·née

ma·tri·arch
ma·tri·cide
ma·tric·u·lant
ma·tric·u·late
ma·trix, *plural*
　matrices
ma·tron
mat·ted
mat·ter of course
　(*noun*)
mat·ter-of-course
　(*adj*)
mat·ter of fact
　(*noun*)
mat·ter-of-fact (*adj*)
mat·ting
mat·tock (tool)
mat·tress
mat·u·rate
ma·tu·ri·ty
mat·zo, *plural*
　matzoth
maud·lin
maul (*noun* hammer;
　verb injure; *see*
　mall)
maun·der
mau·so·le·um,
　plural
　mausoleums
mauve (color)
mav·er·ick
mawk·ish
max·il·lary
max·im
max·i·mal
max·i·mize

max·i·mum, *plural*
　maximums
may·hem
may·on·naise
may·or
may·or·al·ty
maze (confusing
　network; *see*
　maize)
ma·zur·ka
mead·ow
mea·ger
meal tick·et
meal·time
mealy-mouthed
me·an·der
mean·ness
means test
mea·sles
mea·sly
mea·sur·able
meat·ball
meat loaf
meat·pack·er
me·chan·ic
mech·a·nism
mech·a·nize
med·aled
med·al·ist
me·dal·lion
med·dle (interfere)
med·dler
med·dle·some
med·dling
me·di·an
me·di·a·tor
me·di·a·to·ry

med·i·ca·ble
Med·ic·aid (the
　state and federal
　program)
med·i·ca·ment
Med·i·care (federal
　only)
me·dic·i·nal
med·i·cine
me·di·eval
me·di·o·cre
me·di·oc·ri·ty
med·i·ta·tor
me·di·um, *plural*
　media (channels of
　communication,
　cell cultures) or
　mediums (all
　other meanings)
med·ley
meer·schaum
meg·a·lo·ma·nia
meg·a·lop·o·lis
meg·a·phone
mel·an·cho·lia
mel·an·choly
mé·lange
me·lee
me·lio·rate
me·lio·ra·tor
mel·lif·lu·ence
mel·lif·lu·ent
mel·lif·lu·ous
mel·low
me·lo·di·ous
me·lo·dize
mel·o·dra·ma

mel·on
mem·brane
mem·bra·nous
me·men·to, *plural*
   mementos
mem·oir
mem·o·ra·bil·ia
mem·o·ra·ble
mem·o·ran·dum,
   plural
   memorandums
me·mo·ri·al·ize
mem·o·rize
men·ace
me·nag·er·ie
men·da·cious
   (untruthful)
men·dac·i·ty
   (untruthfulness)
men·di·can·cy
   (practice of
   begging)
men·di·cant
   (beggar)
men·dic·i·ty
   (begging)
men·o·pause
men·su·ra·ble
men·tion·able
men·tor
menu, *plural* menus
me·ow
mer·can·tile
mer·ce·nary
mer·chan·dise
mer·chan·dis·er
mer·ci·ful

mer·ci·less
mer·cu·ri·al
mer·e·tri·cious
merg·er
me·rid·i·an
me·ringue
mer·i·toc·ra·cy
mer·i·to·ri·ous
mer·ri·ment
mer·ry-go-round
mer·ry·mak·ing
mes·mer·ize
mes·quite
Mes·si·ah
me·tab·o·lism
me·tab·o·lize
met·al
met·aled
met·al·ing
met·al·ize
met·al·lic
met·al·lur·gy
met·al·ware
met·al·work
met·a·mor·phose
met·a·mor·pho·sis
met·a·phor
me·tas·ta·sis
mete (to allot,
   a boundary)
me·te·or
me·te·or·ic
me·te·o·rol·o·gy
me·thod·i·cal
me·tic·u·lous
mé·tier (trade,
   profession)

met·o·nym
me·ton·y·my
met·ro·nome
me·trop·o·lis
met·tle (spirit)
met·tle·some
mez·za·nine
mi·as·ma, *plural*
   miasmas
mi·ca
mi·cro (Words
   beginning with the
   combining form
   micro are written
   solid:
   microorganism.)
mi·cro·cosm
mi·cro·fiche
mi·crom·e·ter
mi·cro·or·gan·ism
mid (Words
   beginning with the
   combining form
   mid are written
   solid: *midpoint,*
   unless the second
   element begins
   with a capital
   letter:
   mid-Victorian.)
mid·dle age (*noun*)
mid·dle-aged (*adj*)
mid·dle class (*noun*)
mid·dle-class (*adj*)
mid·dle·man
mid·dle-of-the-road
mid·dle·weight

mid·dling
midg·et
mid·riff
mien (bearing)
might·i·er
might·i·ly
might·i·ness
mi·graine
mi·grant
mi·gra·tor
mi·gra·to·ry
mil·dew
mile·age
mile·post
mile·stone
mi·lieu
mil·i·tan·cy
mil·i·tant
mil·i·ta·rism
mil·i·ta·rist
mil·i·tary
mil·i·tate
mi·li·tia
milk·liv·ered
milk run
milk shake
milk toast
milk train
milk·weed
mill·age (taxes)
mil·le·na·ry
(thousand)
mil·len·ni·al
mil·len·ni·um,
plural
millenniums
mil·let
mil·li·gram

mil·li·me·ter
mil·li·ner
mil·li·nery (ladies'
hats)
mil·lion·aire
mill·pond
mill·race
mill·run (*noun*)
mill-run (*adj*)
mill·stone
mill·stream
mill wheel
mill·work
mill·wright
mim·eo·graph
mim·ic
mim·icked
mim·ick·ing
mim·ic·ry
min·able (mine)
min·a·ret
mi·na·to·ry
mince·meat
mince pie
mind read·er
mind's eye
min·er·al·ize
min·er·al·o·gy
min·e·stro·ne
min·i·a·ture
min·i·mal
min·i·mize
min·i·mum, *plural*
minimums
min·ion
min·i·skirt
min·is·te·ri·al
min·is·trant

min·is·try
min·ne·sing·er
min·now
mi·nor (lesser)
min·strel
min·strel·sy
min·u·et
mi·nus (*noun*),
plural minuses
mi·nus·cule
min·ute hand
min·ute·man
min·ute steak
mi·nu·tia, *plural*
minutiae
mir·a·cle
mi·rac·u·lous
mi·rage
mir·ror
mir·rored
mir·ror·ing
mis·ad·vise
mis·al·li·ance
mis·an·thrope
mis·an·thro·py
mis·ap·ply
mis·ap·pre·hend
mis·ap·pro·pri·ate
mis·be·come
mis·be·got·ten
mis·be·lief
mis·cal·cu·late
mis·call
mis·car·riage
mis·ce·ge·na·tion
mis·cel·la·neous
mis·cel·la·ny
mis·chief

mis·chief-mak·er
mis·chie·vous
mis·ci·ble
mis·con·ceive
mis·con·strue
mis·con·strued
mis·con·stru·ing
mis·cre·ant
mis·cue
mis·cued
mis·cu·ing
mis·de·mean·or
mi·ser
mis·er·a·ble
mis·er·ly
mis·ery
mis·fea·sance
mis·guid·ance
mis·judg·ment
mis·la·beled
mis·la·bel·ing
mis·man·age
mi·sog·a·my
    (hatred of
    marriage)
mi·sog·y·ny
    (hatred of women)
mis·pri·sion
mis·sal
mis·send
mis·shaped
mis·sile
mis·sile·man
mis·sile·ry
mis·sion·ary
mis·sive
mis·speak
mis·spell

mis·spend
mis·state
mis·step
mis·tak·able
mis·tle·toe
mis·tri·al
mite (small sum,
    insect)
mi·ter
mi·tered
mi·ter·ing
mit·i·ga·tor
mitt
mitz·vah
mix·able
mixed
mix-up
miz·zen
mne·mon·ic
moat (ditch; *see*
    mote)
mobbed
mob·bing
mob·bish
mo·bile
mo·bi·lize
mob·oc·ra·cy
moc·ca·sin
mo·cha
mock·ery
mock-he·ro·ic
mock-up (*noun*)
mod·al (pertaining
    to modes)
mod·el (example,
    ideal, etc.)
mod·eled
mod·el·er

mod·el·ing
mod·er·ate
mod·er·a·tor
mod·ern·ize
mod·es·ty
mod·i·cum
mod·i·fi·able
mod·i·fied
mod·i·fi·er
mod·i·fy·ing
mod·ish
mod·u·lar
mod·u·la·tor
mod·ule
mo·gul
mo·hair
Mo·ham·med·an
moi·ety
mo·lar
mo·las·ses
mold (all meanings)
mold·er
mold·i·ness
mold·ing
mo·lec·u·lar
mol·e·cule
mol·li·fied
mol·li·fi·er
mol·li·fy
mol·li·fy·ing
mol·lusk
mol·ly·cod·dle
molt (to shed)
mol·ten
mo·men·tary
mo·men·tum,
    plural
    momentums

mon·arch
mo·nar·chi·cal
mon·ar·chist
mon·as·tery
mo·nas·tic
mon·au·ral
mon·e·tary
mon·e·tize
mon·ey, *plural*
  moneys
mon·ey·bag
mon·ey·box
mon·ey·chang·er
mon·eyed
mon·ey·lend·er
mon·ey·mak·er
mon·ey or·der
mon·ger
mon·grel
mon·grel·ize
mon·i·tor
mon·i·to·ry
mon·key, *plural*
  monkeys
mon·key busi·ness
mon·keyed
mon·key·ing
mon·key·shine
mon·key wrench
mono (Words
  beginning with the
  combining form
  mono are written
  solid:
  monogram.)
mon·o·chord
mon·o·chrome
mon·o·cle

mon·oc·u·lar
mo·nog·a·my
mon·o·gram
mon·o·gram·
  mat·ic
mon·o·grammed
mon·o·gram·ming
mon·o·graph
mon·o·lith
mo·no·lo·gist
mon·o·logue
mo·nop·o·lize
mo·nop·o·ly
mon·o·syl·la·ble
mo·not·o·nous
mo·not·o·ny
Mon·si·gnor, *plural*
  Monsignors
mon·soon
mon·strance
mon·stros·i·ty
mon·strous
mon·tage
mon·u·ment
mood·i·ly
mood·i·ness
moon (Compound
  words beginning
  with *moon* are
  written solid:
  moonbeam,
  except as
  otherwise shown
  below.)
moon-blind
moon blind·ness
moon-eyed
moon-faced

moot (debatable)
moped
mop·er (mope)
mop·ery
mop·ing
mop·ish
mopped (mop)
mop·per
mop·pet
mop·ping
mop-up (*noun*)
mo·rale (attitude)
mo·ral·i·ty
mor·al·ize
mo·rass
mor·a·to·ri·um,
  plural
  moratoriums
mor·bid
mor·bid·i·ty
mor·dan·cy
mor·dant (biting,
  caustic)
mor·dent (music)
morgue
mor·i·bund
mo·ron
mo·rose
mor·phine
mor·sel
mor·tal
mor·tal·i·ty
mor·tar
mort·gage
mort·gag·ee
  (lender)
mort·ga·gor
  (borrower)

mor·ti·cian
mor·ti·fied
mor·ti·fy
mor·ti·fy·ing
mor·tise
mor·tu·ary
mo·sa·ic
mo·sa·icked
mo·sa·ick·ing
mosque
mos·qui·to, *plural*
  mosquitoes
mos·qui·to·ey
moss·back
moss-grown
mote (speck; *see*
  moat)
mo·tet
moth·ball (*noun* and
  verb)
moth-eat·en
moth·er-in-law,
  plural mothers-in-
  law
moth·er·land
moth·er-of-pearl
moth·er of
  vin·e·gar
moth·er tongue
moth·er wit
mo·tif
mo·tile
mo·ti·va·tor
mot·ley
mo·tor·bus
mo·tor·car
mo·tor court
mot·or·drome

mo·tor·ize
mo·tor pool
mo·tor truck
mo·tor ve·hi·cle
mot·tle
mot·to, *plural*
  mottoes
mount·able
moun·tain·eer
moun·tain·ous
moun·tain·side
Moun·tain
  Stand·ard Time
moun·tain·top
moun·te·bank
mousse (dessert)
mousy
mouth·fuls
mouth or·gan
mouth·part
mouth·piece
mouth-to-mouth
mouth·wash
mouth·wa·ter·ing
mov·able
mu·ci·lage
mu·ci·lag·i·nous
muck·rak·er
muck·rak·ing
mu·cous (*adj*)
mu·cus (*noun*)
mud·der
mud·died
mud·di·er
mud·ding
mud·dle
mud·dled
mud·dle·head·ed

mud·dler
mud·dling
mud·dy
mud·dy·ing
mud flat
mud·guard
mud hen
mud·sling·er
muf·fin
muf·fle
muf·fler
muf·ti
mugged
mug·ger
mug·gi·er
mug·gi·ness
mug·ging
mug·gy
mu·lat·to, *plural*
  mulattoes
mul·ber·ry
mulct
mu·le·teer
mul·let
mul·lion
mul·ti (Words
  beginning with the
  combining form
  multi are written
  solid:
  multicolored.)
mul·ti·dis·ci·pli·
  nary
mul·ti·far·i·ous
mul·ti·lat·er·al
mul·ti·mil·lion·aire
mul·ti·ple-choice
mul·ti·pli·able

mul·ti·plic·i·ty
mul·ti·plied
mul·ti·pli·er
mul·ti·ply·ing
mul·ti·tu·di·nous
mul·ti·ver·si·ty
mum·ble
mum·bler
mum·bo jum·bo
mum·mery
mum·mi·fied
mum·mi·fy
mum·mi·fy·ing
mun·dane
mu·nic·i·pal
mu·nif·i·cence
mu·nif·i·cent
mur·der·er
mur·der·ous
murk (gloom)
murk·i·er
murk·i·ness
murky
mur·mur

mur·mur·er
mur·mur·ous
mus·cle
mus·cle-bound
mus·cu·lar
mu·se·um
mu·si·cal (pertain-
　　ing to music)
mu·si·cale (social
　　event)
mu·si·cian
mus·ke·teer
mus·ket·ry
musk·mel·on
musk·rat
mus·sel (shellfish)
mus·tache
mus·ta·chio, *plural*
　　mustachios
mus·ta·chioed
mus·tard
mus·ter
mu·ta·ble

mu·tant
mu·ti·late
mu·ti·la·tor
mu·ti·neer
mu·ti·nous
mu·ti·ny
mu·tu·al
mu·tu·al·ize
muz·zle
my·o·pia
myr·i·ad
myr·mi·don
myrrh
myr·tle
mys·te·ri·ous
mys·tery
mys·tic
mys·ti·fied
mys·ti·fy
mys·ti·fy·ing
mys·tique
myth·i·cal
my·thol·o·gy

N

nabbed
nab·bing
na·bob
na·dir
nagged
nag·ger
nag·ging
nag·gy
nai·ad (nymph)
na·ive
na·ive·ty
nam·able
nam·by-pam·by
name-call·ing
name day
name-drop·per
name·plate
name·sake
na·pery
naph·tha
napped
nap·per
nap·ping
nar·cis·sus
nar·co·sis
nar·cot·ic
nar·rate
nar·ra·tion

nar·ra·tor
nar·row gauge
　(*noun*)
nar·row-gauge (*adj*)
nar·row-mind·ed
na·sal
na·sal·ize
na·scence
na·scent
nas·ti·er
nas·ti·ly
nas·ti·ness
nas·tur·tium
na·ta·to·ri·um,
　plural
　natatoriums
na·tion·al·ize
na·tion-state
na·tion·wide
na·tive-born
na·tiv·i·ty
nat·ti·ly
nat·ti·ness
nat·ty
nat·u·ral·ize
naught (nothing,
　zero)
naugh·ti·er

naugh·ti·ly
naugh·ti·ness
nau·sea
nau·se·ate
nau·seous
nau·ti·cal
na·val (ships)
nave (church)
na·vel (umbilicus)
nav·i·ga·ble
nav·i·ga·tor
nay, *plural* nays
Na·zism
Ne·an·der·thal
neap tide
near·sight·ed
neb·u·la, *plural*
　nebulas
neb·u·lous
nec·es·sar·i·ly
nec·es·sary
ne·ces·si·tate
ne·ces·si·tous
ne·ces·si·ty
neck·band
neck·er·chief,
　plural
　neckerchiefs

neck·line
neck-rein (*verb*)
ne·crol·o·gy
nec·ro·man·cy
ne·crop·o·lis
nec·tar
nec·tar·ine
nee (born)
need·i·er
need·i·est
need·i·ness
nee·dle·point
nee·dle·work
ne'er-do-well
ne·far·i·ous
neg·a·tive
ne·ga·tor
ne·glect·er
neg·li·gee
neg·li·gence
neg·li·gent
neg·li·gi·ble
ne·go·tia·ble
ne·go·ti·ate
ne·go·ti·a·tor
Ne·gro, *plural*
  Negroes
neigh·bor
nem·e·sis, *plural*
  nemeses
neo (The combining
  form *neo* is joined
  solid to the
  following element
  unless it begins
  with a capital
  letter, when a
  hyphen is

required:
Neo-Darwinism.
Exception:
Neoplatonism.)
neo·lith·ic
ne·ol·o·gism
ne·on
ne·phri·tis
nep·o·tism
nerve-rack·ing
nerv·i·est
nervy
nest egg
nes·tle
net·ted
net·ting
net·tle
net·tle·some
neu·ral
neu·ral·gia
neu·ri·tis
neu·rol·o·gist
neu·rol·o·gy
neu·ro·sis
neu·rot·ic
neu·ter
neu·tral
neu·tral·ize
nev·er-nev·er land
new·born (*noun* and
  adj)
new·com·er
new·el
new·fan·gled
new-fash·ioned
new·found
new·ly·wed
new moon

new-mown (*adj*)
news agen·cy
news·cast
news con·fer·ence
news·stand
news·wor·thy
newsy
next-door (*adj*)
next of kin
nex·us
nibbed
nib·bing
nib·ble
nib·bled
nib·bler
nib·bling
ni·ce·ty
niche
nick·el
nick·eled
nick·el·ing
nick·el·o·de·on
nic·o·tine
niece
nig·gard·ly
nig·gling
night-blind (*adj*)
night blind·ness
night clothes
night crawl·er
night·gown
night latch
night let·ter
night life
night light
night owl
night school
night ta·ble

night watch·man
ni·hil·ism
ni·mi·ety
nin·com·poop
nine·ti·eth
nine·ty-first, etc
nine·ty-one, etc.
ninth
nipped
nip·per
nip·pi·er
nip·ping
nip·ple
nip·py
nip-up
nir·va·na
ni·ter
nit-pick·ing
nit·ty-grit·ty
no (*noun*), *plural*
  noes
no·bil·i·ty
no·ble
no·ble·man
no·blesse oblige
noc·tur·nal
noc·turne (music)
nod·ded
nod·der
nod·ding
node
nod·u·lar
nod·ule
no-hit·ter
nois·i·er
nois·i·ly
nois·i·ness
noi·some

noisy
no-load (*adj*)
no·mad
no·men·cla·ture
nom·i·nal
nom·i·na·tor
non (The prefix
  non is joined solid
  to the following
  element unless it
  begins with a
  capital letter,
  when a hyphen is
  required:
  nonentity,
  non-American.)
non·ab·sor·bent
non·ac·cep·tance
non·ad·just·able
non·aes·thet·ic
non·af·fil·i·a·ted
non·ag·gres·sion
non·ag·gres·sor
non·aligned
non·ap·pear·ance
non·ap·pli·ca·ble
non·as·sess·able
non·as·sign·able
non·as·sim·i·la·ble
non·at·ten·dance
non·bel·lig·er·ence
non·bel·lig·er·ent
non·break·able
non·can·cel·able
non·can·cer·ous
non·cha·lance
non·cha·lant
non·charge·able

non·clas·si·fi·able
non·cler·i·cal
non·clin·i·cal
non·col·laps·ible
non·col·lect·ible
non·com·bat·ant
non·com·bus·ti·ble
non·com·mit·tal
non·com·mu·
  ni·ca·ble
non·com·pli·ance
non·com·pli·ant
non·com·press·ible
non·com·pul·so·ry
non·con·cur·rence
non·con·du·cive
non·con·duc·tor
non·con·fer·ra·ble
non·con·for·mance
non·con·trib·u·
  to·ry
non·con·trol·la·ble
non·con·vert·ible
non·co·op·er·a·
  tion
non·crit·i·cal
non·cul·pa·ble
non·cur·rent
non·de·duct·ible
non·de·fer·ra·ble
non·de·script
non·dis·ci·plin·ary
non·dis·par·ag·ing
non·di·vis·i·ble
non·dry·ing
non·du·ra·ble
non·du·ti·able
non·ed·i·ble

non·ed·u·ca·ble
non·en·force·able
non·en·ti·ty
non·equiv·a·lent
non·es·sen·tial
none·such
non·ex·change·
  able
non·ex·cus·able
non·ex·ist·ent
non·ex·pend·able
non·ex·port·able
non·ex·tra·dit·able
non·fat·ten·ing
non·fea·sance
non·flam·ma·ble
non·fraud·u·lent
non·ful·fill·ment
non·hab·it·able
non·he·red·i·tary
non·her·i·ta·ble
non·in·flam·ma·ble
non·in·tel·lec·tu·al
non·in·ter·fer·ence
non·in·ter·ven·tion
non·ir·ri·tant
non·ju·ror
non·lin·ear
non·mail·able
non·met·al·lic
non·ne·go·tia·ble
non·obe·di·ence
non·ob·ser·vance
non·oc·cur·rence
no-non·sense (*adj*)
non·pa·reil
non·par·lia·
  men·ta·ry

non·pa·ro·chi·al
non·par·tic·i·pant
non·par·ti·san
non·per·for·mance
non·per·ish·able
non·per·ma·nent
non·per·me·able
non·per·mis·si·ble
non·per·sis·tent
non·plus
non·plused
non·plus·es (*noun*
  and *verb*)
non·plus·ing
non·pro·fes·sion·al
non·pro·gres·sive
non·pro·pri·etary
non·re·cov·er·able
non·re·cur·rent
non·re·deem·able
non·re·new·able
non·res·i·dent
non·re·sis·tant
non·re·turn·able
non·re·vers·ible
non·re·vert·ible
non·rhym·ing
non·sal·able
non·sched·uled
non·scho·las·tic
non·sen·si·cal
non se·qui·tur
non·shrink·able
non·sked
non·sol·vent
non·stop
non·tax·able
non·trans·fer·able

non·vi·o·lent
non·vir·u·lent
noo·dle
no one
no-par (*adj*)
nor·mal·cy
nor·mal·ize
north (direction)
North (section of
  the country)
north·bound
north by east
north by west
north·east
North·ern·er
north-north·east
north-north·west
North Pole
North Star
north·ward
north·west
north·west by north
north·west by west
North·west·ern·er
nose·bag
nose·band
nose·bleed
nose cone
nose-dive (*verb*)
nose dive (*noun*)
nose-dived (*verb*)
nose·gay
no-show
nos·i·er
nos·tal·gia
nos·tril
nos·trum
nosy

nota be·ne
no·ta·ble
no·ta·rize
no·ta·ry pub·lic,
    plural notaries
    public
no·tice·able
no·ti·fied
no·ti·fy
no·ti·fy·ing
no·tion·al
no·to·ri·ety
no·to·ri·ous
no-trump (*noun* and
    adj)
nou·gat
nov·el
nov·el·ette
no·ve·na
nov·ice
no·vi·ti·ate

now·a·days
no·way
nox·ious
noz·zle
nu·ance
nub·bin
nu·bile
nu·cle·ar
nu·cle·us, *plural*
    nuclei
nu·di·ty
nu·ga·to·ry
nui·sance
null
nul·li·fied
nul·li·fy
nul·li·fy·ing
nul·li·ty
nu·mer·a·ble
nu·mer·a·tor
nu·mer·i·cal

nu·mer·ol·o·gy
nu·mis·mat·ic
num·skull
nun·nery
nup·tial
nurs·ery
nurs·ling
nur·tur·ance
nur·ture
nu·tri·ent
nu·tri·ment
nu·tri·tious
nu·tri·tive
nut·ted
nut·ti·er
nut·ti·est
nut·ti·ness
nut·ty
nymph
nym·pho·ma·nia

O

oa·kum
oars·man
oa·sis, *plural* oases
ob·bli·ga·to, *plural*
  obbligatos
ob·du·ra·cy
ob·du·rate
obe·di·ence
obe·di·ent
obei·sance
ob·e·lisk
obese
obe·si·ty
obeyed
obey·er
obey·ing
ob·fus·cate
obit·u·ary
ob·ject·ti·fied
ob·jec·ti·fy
ob·jec·ti·fy·ing
ob·jec·tion·able
ob·jec·tor
ob·jur·gate
ob·la·tion
ob·li·gate
oblig·a·to·ry
oblique
obliq·ui·ty

oblit·er·ate
oblit·er·a·tor
obliv·ion
obliv·i·ous
ob·lo·quy, *plural*
  obloquies
ob·nox·ious
oboe, *plural* oboes
obo·ist
ob·scene
ob·scen·i·ty
ob·scur·ant
ob·se·qui·ous
ob·se·quy, *plural*
  obsequies
ob·serv·able
ob·ser·vance
ob·ser·vant
ob·ser·va·to·ry
ob·sess
ob·ses·sion
ob·so·lesce
ob·so·les·cence
ob·so·les·cent
ob·so·lete
ob·sta·cle
ob·ste·tri·cian
ob·sti·na·cy
ob·strep·er·ous

ob·struc·tor
ob·tain·able
ob·trud·er
ob·tru·sive
ob·tuse
ob·verse
ob·vi·ate
ob·vi·ous
oc·ca·sion
oc·ci·den·tal
oc·clude
oc·clu·sion
oc·cult
oc·cu·pan·cy
oc·cu·pant
oc·cu·pied
oc·cu·pi·er
oc·cu·py·ing
oc·cur
oc·curred
oc·cur·rence
oc·cur·rent
oc·cur·ring
ocean·go·ing
ocean·og·ra·phy
ocher
oc·ta·gon
oc·tane
oc·tave

194

oc·tet
oc·to·ge·nar·i·an
oc·to·pus, *plural*
  octopuses
oc·to·roon
oc·u·lar
oc·u·list
oda·lisque
odds and ends
odds-on (*adj*)
odi·ous
odi·um
odor·ant
odor·if·er·ous
od·ys·sey
oeu·vre, *plural*
  oeuvres
of·fal
off-and-on (*adj*)
off and on (*adv*)
off·beat
Off Broad·way
off·cast
off-col·or (*adj*)
of·fend·er
of·fense
of·fen·sive
of·fer·er
of·fer·or (law)
of·fer·to·ry
off·hand
off-hours
of·fice boy
of·fice·hold·er
of·fice seek·er
of·fi·cial
of·fi·cial·ese
of·fi·ci·ate

of·fi·ci·a·tor
of·fi·cious
off-key
off-lim·its
off-line
off-load (*verb*)
off·peak
off-sea·son
off·set
off·shoot
off·shore
off·side
off·spring (*sing* and
  plural)
off·stage
off-the-cuff (*adj*)
off-the-rec·ord (*adj*)
off-the-shelf (*adj*)
off-white
off year (*noun*)
off-year (*adj*)
ogle
ogler
ogre
ogre·ish
ohs and ahs
oil·can
oil·cloth
oil field
oil paint·ing
oil·pa·per
oil·skin
oil slick
oil well
oint·ment
OK (*noun*), *plural*
  OK's
OK (*verb*)

OK'd
OK'ing
OK's (*verb*)
old (Compound
  words beginning
  with *old* are
  written as
  separate words:
  old hand, except
  as otherwise
  shown below.)
old-fash·ioned (*adj*)
old fash·ioned
  (drink)
old-line (*adj*)
old-maid·ish (*adj*)
old-time (*adj*)
old-tim·er
old-world (*adj*)
Old World
  (Europe)
ole·ag·i·nous
ole·an·der
oleo·mar·ga·rine
ol·fac·to·ry
ol·i·garch
olio (mixture),
  plural olios
ol·ive drab
ol·ive green
Olym·pic Games
om·bre (game)
om·buds·man
om·e·let
om·i·nous
omis·si·ble
omis·sion
omit

omit·ted
omit·ting
om·ni·bus, *plural*
  omnibuses
om·nip·o·tence
om·nip·o·tent
om·ni·science
om·ni·scient
om·niv·o·rous
once-over (*noun*)
on·com·ing
one-base hit
one-eyed
one-horse
one hun·dred first,
  etc.
one hun·dred one,
  etc.
one-night stand
on·er·ous
one·self
one-shot (*adj*)
one-sid·ed (*adj*)
one-time (former)
one-to-one (*adj*)
one-track (*adj*)
one-up
one-up·man·ship
one-way (*adj*)
on·go·ing
on-line (*adj*)
on·side
on·slaught
on stream (*adv* into
  operation)
onus
on·ward

on·yx
ooz·ier
ooz·i·ness
ooz·ing
oozy
opac·i·ty
opal
opal·es·cent
opaque
open-air (*adj*)
open-and-shut (*adj*)
open door (*noun*)
open-door (*adj*)
open end (*noun*)
open-end (*adj*)
open-eyed
open-faced
open·hand·ed
open·heart·ed
open-hearth (*adj*)
open-heart sur·gery
open house
open let·ter
open-mind·ed
open-mouthed
open sea·son
open se·cret
open shop
open stock
open work
op·er·a·ble
op·era glass·es
op·era·go·er
op·era house
op·er·ant
op·er·a·tor
op·er·et·ta

oph·thal·mic
opi·ate
opos·sum
op·po·nent
op·por·tune
op·pos·able
op·po·site
op·press
op·pres·sor
op·pro·bri·ous
op·pro·bri·um
op·pugn
op·ti·cian
op·ti·mal
op·ti·mism
op·ti·mize
op·ti·mum, *plural*
  optima
op·tom·e·try
op·u·lence
op·u·lent
opus, *plural* opuses
or·a·cle (person of
  great knowledge;
  see auricle)
orac·u·lar
or·ange·ade
orang·utan
or·a·tor
or·a·tor·io, *plural*
  oratorios
or·a·to·ry
or·bit
or·bit·ed
or·bit·ing
or·ches·tra
or·ches·tra·tion

or·ches·tra·tor
or·chid
or·dain
or·dain·er
or·di·nal
or·di·nance
  (statute)
or·di·nar·i·ly
or·di·nary
or·di·na·tion
ord·nance
  (weapons)
or·gan·dy
or·gan·iz·able
or·gan·ize
or·gan·iz·er
or·gasm
or·gi·as·tic
or·gy
ori·en·ta·tion
or·i·fice
or·i·gin
orig·i·nal
orig·i·na·tor
ori·ole
or·i·son
or·na·men·tal
or·nate
or·ner·i·est
or·ner·i·ness
or·nery
oro·tund
or·phan
or·tho·don·tia
or·tho·dox
or·thog·ra·phy
or·tho·pe·dics

os·cil·late (back
  and forth)
os·cil·la·tion
os·cil·la·tor
os·cu·late (to kiss)
os·mo·sis
os·mot·ic
os·si·fied
os·si·fy
os·si·fy·ing
os·su·ary
os·ten·si·ble
os·ten·ta·tion
os·te·o·path
os·te·op·a·thy
os·tra·cism
os·tra·cize
os·trich
oti·ose
ot·ter
ot·to·man
ought (*verb* should;
  see aught)
oust·er
out (Compound
  words beginning
  with *out* are
  written solid:
  outboard, except
  as otherwise
  shown below.)
out-and-out
out-and-out·er
out·bid·ding
out·cries
out·cropped
out·crop·ping

out·er space
out·field·er
out·fit·ted
out·fit·ter
out·fit·ting
out·gen·er·aled
out·gen·er·al·ing
out·go, *plural*
  outgoes
out-group
out-Her·od
out·laid (*verb*)
out·law·ry
out·lay·ing
out·ly·ing
out·ma·neu·ver
out·manned
out·man·ning
out-of-bounds
out-of-date (*adj*)
out-of-doors
out-of-pock·et (*adj*)
out-of-print (*adj*)
out-of-the-way (*adj*)
out-of-town·er
out·ra·geous
out·rig·ger
out·run·ner
out·run·ning
out·sell·ing
out·stripped
out·strip·ping
out·ward
out·wit·ted
out·wit·ting
ou·zel
ova·ry

ova·tion
over (Compound
   words beginning
   with *over* are
   written solid:
   oversight, except
   as otherwise
   shown below.)
over·achiev·er
over·bid·ding
over·buy·ing
over·con·fi·dent
over·cor·rec·tion
over·cropped
over·crop·ping
over·in·dul·gence
over·in·dul·gent
over·laid
over·lapped
over·lap·ping
over·lay·ing

over·ly·ing
over·manned
over·man·ning
over·paid
over·pay·ing
over·rate
over·reach
over·re·act
over·re·fine
over·rid·den
over·ride
over·ripe
over·rule
over·run
over·run·ning
over·seas
over·seer
over·stepped
over·step·ping
over·stuffed

over·sup·plied
over·sup·ply·ing
overt
over-the-count·er
   (*adj*)
over·topped
over·top·ping
over·ture
over-un·der (*adj*)
over·writ·ten
over·wrought
ovu·lar
ovu·late
ow·ing
ox-eyed
ox·ford
ox·i·dize
ox·y·gen
oys·ter
ozone

P

pab·u·lum
pace·set·ter
pach·y·derm
pac·i·fi·able
pac·i·fied
pac·i·fi·er
pac·i·fism
pac·i·fist
pac·i·fy
pac·i·fy·ing
pack·able
pack·ag·er
pack·et
pack·ing house
pad·ded
pad·ding
pad·dle
pad·dler
pad·dling
pad·dock
pae·an
pa·gan
pa·gan·ize
pag·eant
pag·eant·ry
pag·i·na·tion
pa·go·da

pail·ful, *plural*
  pailfuls
pais·ley
pa·ja·mas
pal·at·able
pal·ate (mouth)
pa·la·tial
pa·la·ver
pale (lacking color,
  boundary)
pal·ette (artist's
  board)
pal·frey, *pluraal*
  palfreys
pa·limp·sest
pal·in·drome
pal·ing
pal·i·sade
pall
pall·bear·er
palled (from *pal* and
  pall)
pal·let (small bed)
pal·li·ate
pal·li·a·tor
pal·lid
pal·lor

pal·met·to,
  plural palmettos
palm·ist·ry
pal·pa·ble
pal·pi·tant
pal·pi·tate
pal·sied
pal·sy
pal·ter
pal·try
pam·phlet
pam·phle·teer
pan·a·cea
Pan-Amer·i·can
Pan Amer·i·can
  Union
pan·a·tela
pan·cre·as
pan·der
pan·der·er
pane (flat sheet)
pan·e·gy·ric
pan·el
pan·eled
pan·el·ing
pan·el·ist
pan·el truck

pan-fried
pan-fry
pan-fry·ing
pan·han·dle
pan·ic
pan·icked
pan·ick·ing
pan·icky
pan·ic-strik·en
panned
pan·nier
pan·ning
pan·o·ply
pan·o·ra·ma
pan·sy
pan·ta·lets
pan·the·ism
pan·the·on
pan·tie
pan·to·mime
pant·suit
pan·ty gir·dle
pan·ty hose
pan·ty·waist
pa·pa·cy
pa·pal
pa·per·back
pa·per·board
pa·per·bound
pa·per car·ri·er
pa·per clip
pa·per·hang·er
pa·per knife
pa·per·mill
pa·per mon·ey
pa·per·weight
pa·per·work

pa·pier-mâ·ché
pa·poose
pa·pri·ka
pa·py·rus, *plural*
   papyri
par·a·ble
pa·rab·o·la
par·a·chute
par·a·digm
par·a·dise
par·a·di·si·a·cal
par·a·dox
par·a·dox·i·cal
par·af·fin
par·a·gon
par·al·lel
par·al·leled
par·al·lel·ing
par·al·lel·ism
pa·ral·y·sis
par·a·lyt·ic
par·a·lyze
pa·ram·e·ter
par·a·mount
par·a·mour
par·a·noia
par·a·noid
par·a·pet
par·a·pher·na·lia
par·a·phrase
par·a·ple·gia
par·a·ple·gic
par·a·site
par·a·sol
par·a·troops
par·cel
par·celed

par·cel·ing
Par·chee·si
   (trademark)
par·don·able
pa·ren·the·sis,
   plural
   parentheses
pa·re·sis
par·fait
pa·ri·ah
pa·ri·e·tal
pari·mu·tu·el
pa·rish·ion·er
par·i·ty
par·lance
par·lay (*noun* and
   verb bet)
par·ley (*verb*
   confer; *noun*
   conference)
par·lia·ment
par·lia·men·ta·ry
par·lor
pa·ro·chi·al
par·o·dist
par·o·dy
pa·rol (word of
   mouth)
pa·role (word of
   honor, release)
pa·roled
pa·rol·ee
pa·rol·ing
par·ox·ysm
par·quet
par·queted
par·quet·ing

par·quet·ry
par·ra·keet
parred (par)
par·ri·cide
par·ried
par·ring
par·rot
par·ry
par·ry·ing
par·si·mo·ni·ous
par·si·mo·ny
pars·ley
par·tial
par·tial·i·ty
par·ti·ble
par·tic·i·pant
par·ti·ci·pa·tor
par·ti·cle
par·ti-col·ored
par·tic·u·lar
par·tic·u·lar·ize
par·ti·san
part-time
pass·able (tolerable)
pas·sel
pas·ser-by, *plural*
  passers-by
pas·si·ble (capable
  of feeling)
pass·key
pass·word
pas·ta
pas·tel
pas·tel·ist
pas·teur·ize
pas·teur·iz·er
pas·tiche

pas·tille (lozenge)
pas·time
pas·tor
pasty
patch·work
pâ·té
pa·tel·la, *plural*
  patellas
pat·ent·able
pat·en·tee (receiver
  of a patent)
pat·en·tor (giver of
  a patent)
pa·ter·nal
pa·thet·ic
pa·thol·o·gy
pa·thos
pa·tience
pa·tient
pa·ti·na
pa·tio, *plural* patios
pa·tri·arch
pa·tri·cian
pat·ri·cide
pat·ri·mo·ny
pa·trol
pa·trolled
pa·trol·ling
pa·trol·man
pa·trol wag·on
pa·tron·ize
pat·sy
pat·ted
pat·ter
pat·tern
pat·ting
pat·ty

pau·ci·ty
paunch
pau·per
pau·per·ize
pa·vil·ion
pawn·er
pay·able
pay·check
pay·day
pay dirt
pay·ee
pay·er
pay·load
pay·mas·ter
pay·off (*noun*)
pay phone
pay·roll
pay sta·tion
peace·able
peace·mak·er
peace of·fer·ing
peace pipe
peace·time (*noun*
  and *adj*)
peal (loud sound;
  see peel)
pear-shaped
peas·ant
peas·ant·ry
pea·vey
peb·ble
peb·bly
pec·ca·dil·lo,
  plural peccadilloes
pec·u·la·tion
pec·u·la·tor
pe·cu·liar

pe·cu·li·ar·i·ty
pe·cu·ni·ary
ped·a·gogue
ped·a·gogu·ish
ped·a·go·gy
ped·aled
ped·al·ing
ped·ant
ped·ant·ry
ped·dle
ped·dler
ped·dlery
ped·es·tal
ped·es·taled
ped·es·tal·ing
pe·des·tri·an
pe·di·a·tri·cian
pe·di·at·rics
ped·i·cure
ped·i·gree
ped·i·ment
peel (to cut away
    rind, etc; *see*
    peal)
peer (same rank, a
    noble; *see* pier)
pee·vish
pegged
peg·ging
pe·jo·ra·tive
pel·i·can
pel·let
pel·let·ize
pell-mell
pel·vis, *plural*
    pelvises

pe·nal
pe·nal·ize
pen·ance
pen·chant
pen·cil
pen·ciled
pen·cil·er
pen·cil·ing
pen·dant (*noun*)
pen·den·cy
pen·dent (*adj*)
pen·du·lous
pen·du·lum
pen·e·tra·ble
pen·e·trance
pen·e·trant
pen·e·trate
pen·guin
pen·i·cil·lin
pen·in·su·la
pen·in·su·lar
pen·i·tence
pen·i·tent
pen·i·ten·tia·ry
pen·knife
pen·man
pen name
pen·nant
penned
pen·ning
pen·ny an·te
pen·ny-pinch (*verb*)
pen·ny pinch·er
pen·ny-pinch·ing
pen·ny·weight
pen·ny-wise

pe·nol·o·gy
pen·sion·able
pen·sion·ary
pen·sion·er
pen·sive
pen·ta·gon
pent-up (*adj*)
pe·nu·che
pe·nu·ri·ous
pen·u·ry
pe·on, *plural* peons
peo·ple
pepped (pep)
pep·per-and-salt
    (*adj*)
pep·per·box
pep·per·corn
pep·per mill
per·per pot
pep·pery
pep·pi·er
pep·ping
pep·py
pep·sin
per·am·bu·la·tor
per an·num
per cap·i·ta
per·ceiv·able
per·ceive
per·cent
per·cent·age
per·cen·tile
per cen·tum
per·cep·ti·ble
per·cep·tu·al
per·chance

per·cip·i·ence
per·cip·i·ent
per·co·late
per·co·la·tor
per·cuss
per·cus·sion
per di·em
per·di·tion
per·e·grin·ate
per·e·gri·na·tor
per·emp·to·ry,
　(decisive,
　imperious)
per·en·ni·al
per·fect·ible
per·fid·i·ous
per·fi·dy
per·fo·rate
per·fo·ra·tor
per·form·able
per·form·ance
per·fum·ery
per·func·to·ry
per·fuse
per·il
per·iled
per·il·ing
pe·rim·e·ter
per·i·pa·tet·ic
pe·riph·er·al
pe·riph·ery
per·i·scope
per·ish·able
per·i·stal·sis
per·i·to·ni·tis
per·jur·er

per·ju·ry
per·ma·nence
per·ma·nent
per·me·able
per·me·ate
per·mis·si·ble
per·mis·sion
per·mis·sive
per·mit·ted
per·mit·ting
per·ni·cious
per·nick·e·ty
per·pen·dic·u·
　lar
per·pe·tra·tor
per·pet·u·al
per·pet·u·a·tor
per·pe·tu·ity
per·plex·i·ty
per·qui·site
per se
per·se·cu·tor
per·se·ver·ance
per·se·ver·ant
per·se·vere
per·si·flage
per·sim·mon
per·sis·tence
per·sis·tent
per·snick·e·ty
per·son·able
per·son·al·ize
per·son·i·fied
per·son·i·fy
per·son·i·fy·ing
per·son·nel

per·spec·tive
　(view)
per·spi·ca·cious
　(shrewd)
per·spi·cac·i·ty
per·spi·cu·i·ty
per·spic·u·ous
　(clear)
per·spir·a·to·ry
per·spire
per·suad·able
per·suad·er
per·sua·si·ble
per·sua·sion
per·tain
per·ti·na·cious
per·ti·nac·i·ty
per·ti·nence
per·ti·nent
per·turb
per·turb·able
per·tur·ba·tion
per·turb·er
pe·ru·sal
pe·ruse
per·vade
per·va·sive
per·verse
per·ver·sion
per·ver·si·ty
per·vi·ous
pes·si·mism
pes·ti·cide
pes·tif·er·ous
pes·ti·lence
pes·ti·lent

pes·ti·len·tial
pes·tle
pet·al
pet·aled
pe·tit four, *plural*
   petits fours
pe·ti·tion·ary
pe·ti·tion·er
pet·it ju·ry
pet·it lar·ce·ny
pet·it point
pe·trel
pet·ri·fied
pet·ri·fy
pet·ri·fy·ing
pe·tro·le·um
pet·ted
pet·ti·coat
pet·ti·fog
pet·ti·fogged
pet·ti·fog·gery
pet·ti·fog·ging
pet·ti·ness
pet·ting
pet·u·lance
pet·u·lant
pew·ter
pha·lanx
phal·lic
phan·tasm
phan·tom
Phar·i·sa·ic
Phar·i·see
phar·ma·ceu·
   ti·cal
phar·ma·cy

phar·ynx, *plural*
   pharynxes
phase (stage,
   aspect; *see* faze)
phase-out (*noun*)
pha·sic
pheas·ant
phe·nom·e·nal
phe·nom·e·non,
   plural
   phenomenons
   (exceptional
   persons) or *plural*
   phenomena (all
   other meanings)
phi·lan·der
phi·lan·der·er
phi·lan·thro·py
phil·a·tel·ic
phi·lat·e·list
phi·lat·e·ly
phi·los·o·pher
phi·los·o·phize
phil·ter (potion,
   charm;
   see filter)
phlegm
phleg·mat·ic
pho·bia
phoe·be
phoe·nix
pho·net·ics
phon·ics
pho·ny, *plural*
   phonies
phos·phate

phos·pho·res·
   cence
phos·pho·res·cent
phos·pho·rous
   (*adj*)
phos·pho·rus
   (*noun*)
pho·to (Words
   beginning with
   the combining
   form *photo* are
   written solid:
   photograph,
   except as
   otherwise shown
   below.)
pho·to fin·ish
pho·to-off·set
pho·to·stat
pho·to·stat·ed
pho·to·stat·ing
phras·al
phy·si·cian
phys·i·cist
phys·icked
phys·ick·ing
phys·i·ol·o·gy
phy·sique
pi·an·ism
pi·an·ist
pi·ano, *plural*
   pianos
pi·az·za, *plural*
   piazzas
pi·ca
pic·a·resque

pic·a·yune
pic·ca·lil·li
pic·co·lo, *plural*
   piccolos
pic·co·lo·ist
pick·ax
pick·er·el
pick·le
pick·up (*noun* and
   adj)
pic·nic
pic·nicked
pic·nick·er
pic·nick·ing
pic·to·ri·al
pic·to·ri·al·ize
pic·tur·esque
pid·gin (language)
piece
piece·meal
piece·work
pied (*past of* pi)
pier (breakwater,
   promenade, etc;
   see peer)
pierce
pi·etism
pi·ety
pi·geon (bird)
pi·geon-heart·ed
pi·geon·hole
pi·geon-liv·ered
pi·geon-toed
pigged
pig·gi·er
pig·gi·est

pig·ging
pig·gish
pig·gy
pig·gy·back
pig·gy bank
pig·head·ed
pig iron
pig·men·tary
pi·ing (pi)
pi·laf
pil·fer
pil·grim
pil·ing (structure of
   piles)
pil·lage
pil·lar
pil·lo·ried
pil·lo·ry
pil·lo·ry·ing
pil·low·case
pil·low·slip
pi·mien·to, *plural*
   pimientos
pim·per·nel
pim·ple
pim·ply
pin (Compound
   words beginning
   with *pin* are
   written solid:
   pinball, except as
   otherwise shown
   below.)
pin·a·fore
pince-nez
pin·cers

pinch-hit
pinch hit·ter
pin curl
Ping-Pong
   (trademark)
pin·ing (*verb* pine)
pink·eye
pink·ie
pin mon·ey
pin·na·cle (highest
   point)
pinned
pin·ning (pin)
pi·noch·le (game)
pin stripe
pin·to, *plural* pintos
pint-size
piny (woods)
pi·o·neer
pi·ous
pip·age
pipe dream
pipe·line
pipe or·gan
pi·pette
pip·ing (pipe)
pip-squeak
pi·quan·cy
pi·quant
pique
piqued
piqu·ing
pi·ra·cy
pir·ou·ette
pis·ta·chio, *plural*
   pistachios

pis·til (plant part)
pis·tol
pis·toled
pis·to·leer
pis·tol·ing
pis·tol-whip
pis·tol-whipped
pis·tol-whip·ping
pis·ton
pitch-black
pitch-dark
pitch·fork
pitch·out (*noun*)
pitch pipe
pit·e·ous
pithy
pit·i·able
pit·ied
pit·i·less
pit·tance
pit·ted
pit·ter-pat·ter
pit·ting
pi·tu·itary
pity·ing
piv·ot
pix·ie·ish
pix·i·lat·ed
pixy
plac·ard
pla·cate
pla·cat·er
pla·ca·to·ry
place·able
pla·ce·bo, *plural*
  placebos
place card

place kick (*noun*)
place-kick (*verb*)
place-name
place set·ting
plac·id
pla·gia·rism
pla·gia·ry
plague
plagu·ing
plaguy
plain·clothes man
plain sail·ing
plain-spo·ken
plain·tiff
plain·tive
plait (hair)
plan·e·tar·i·um,
  plural
  planetariums
plan·e·tary
plaque
plas·ma
pla·teau, *plural*
  plateaus
plate·fuls
plat·en
plat·i·num
plat·i·tude
plat·i·tu·di·nous
pla·toon
plat·ted (mapped)
plat·ter
plat·ting
plau·si·ble
play (Compound
  words beginning
  with *play* are

written solid:
playbill, except
as otherwise
shown below.)
play·able
play·act
play·back (*noun*)
play-by-play
play-off
plead·able
pleas·ance (estate)
pleas·ant·ry
plea·sur·able
pleat (fold of cloth)
ple·be·ian
pleb·i·scite
pledg·er
pledg·or (law)
ple·na·ry
plen·i·po·ten·tia·
  ry
plen·i·tude
plen·te·ous
plen·ti·ful
pleth·o·ra
pleu·ri·sy
plex·us
pli·able
pli·ant
plied (*verb* ply)
pli·ers
plod·ded
plod·der
plod·ding
plopped
plop·ping
plot·ted

plot·ter
plot·ting
plow
plow·able
plugged
plug·ger
plug·ging
plug-ug·ly
plum·age
plum·met
plun·der·er
plu·ral·i·ty
plus, *plural* pluses
plu·toc·ra·cy
ply·ing (ply)
P.M. (after noon)
pneu·mat·ic
pneu·mo·nia
pock·et·book
   (small case)
pock·et book
   (small book)
pock·et·fuls
pock·et-size (*adj*)
pock·et ve·to
   (*noun*)
pock·et-ve·to
   (*verb*)
po·di·um
   (platform), *plural*
   podiums
po·esy
po·ets lau·re·ate
po·go stick
po·grom
poi·gnan·cy
poi·gnant

poin·set·tia
point-blank
poi·son
poi·son·er
poi·son-pen (*adj*)
poky
po·lar
po·lar·i·ty
po·lar·ize
pole·ax
po·lem·ic
pole vault (*noun*)
pole-vault (*verb*)
pole-vault·er
pol·i·cy
pol·ish
pol·i·tic (shrewd,
   practical)
pol·i·ti·cian
po·lit·i·cize
pol·i·tick (*verb*)
pol·i·tick·er
pol·i·tick·ing
po·lit·i·co, *plural*
   politicos
pol·i·ty
poll (head, vote, vot-
   ing place, survey)
pol·len
pol·li·nate
pol·li·na·tor
poll·ster
pol·lu·tant
pol·lute
pol·lut·er
pol·ter·geist
pol·troon

pol·troon·ery
po·lyg·a·mist
po·lyg·a·my
pol·y·glot
pol·y·gon
pol·y·mer
pol·yp (growth)
pol·y·phon·ic
pol·y·syl·la·ble
pom·ace (crushed
   fruit pulp)
po·made
pome·gran·ate
pom·mel
pom·meled
pom·mel·ing
pom·pa·dour
pom·pom (orna-
   mental tuft on
   costumes)
pom·pon (flower)
pom·pos·i·ty
pomp·ous
pon·cho, *plural*
   ponchos
pon·der·a·ble
pon·tiff
pon·tif·i·cal
pon·tif·i·ca·tor
pon·toon
pooh-pooh
pooh-poohed
pooh-pooh·ing
poor-mouth (*verb*)
pop·ery
pop·eyed
pop fly

pop·lar
pop·lin
popped
pop·ping
pop·u·lace
pop·u·lar
pop·u·lar·ize
pop·u·lar·iz·er
pop·u·lous
por·ce·lain
por·ce·la·ne·ous
por·cu·pine
pore (to gaze
  intently, skin
  opening)
po·ros·i·ty
po·rous
por·phy·ry
por·poise
por·ridge
por·ta·ble
por·tal
por·taled
por·tal-to-por·tal
  (adj)
port·fo·lio, plural
  portfolios
por·ti·co, plural
  porticoes
por·tiere
por·tray·al
por·trayed
por·tray·er
por·tray·ing
po·seur
pos·se
pos·ses·sor

pos·ses·so·ry
pos·si·ble
post-bel·lum
post-com·mu·nion
pos·te·ri·or
post ex·change
post-free
post·haste
post·hole
post·hu·mous
pos·til·ion
post·mas·ters
  gen·er·al
post·me·rid·i·an
  (in the afternoon)
post me·ri·di·em
  (after noon, P.M.)
post-mor·tem
post of·fice
post·pon·able
post road
pos·tu·lant
pos·tu·la·tor
pos·ture
po·sy
po·ta·ble
po·ta·to, plural
  potatoes
po·ten·cy
po·tent
po·ten·tial
pot li·quor
pot roast
pot·shot
pot·tage
pot·ted
pot·ter

pot·tery
pot·ting
pot-val·iant
pouf
poul·ter·er
poul·tice
poul·try
pound-fool·ish
pov·er·ty-strick·en
pow·der blue
pow·er·boat
power·er dive (noun)
pow·er-dive (verb)
pow·er·house
pow·er plant
pow·er play
prac·ti·ca·ble
prac·tice (noun
  and verb)
prac·ticed (adj)
prac·tic·er
prac·ti·tion·er
prai·rie
prate
prat·tle
prat·tler
prayed (begged,
  worshiped; see
  preyed)
prayer
pray·ing
pre (Words
  beginning with
  the prefix pre
  are written solid:
  predawn. If
  the second

208

element begins
with a capital
letter, a
hyphen is used:
pre-Christian.)
pre·ad·o·les·cence
pre·am·ble
pre·am·pli·fi·er
pre·ar·range
pre·can·celed
pre·can·cel·la·tion
pre·car·i·ous
pre·cau·tion·ary
pre·cede
pre·ce·dence
pre·ce·dent
pre·cen·sor (*verb*)
pre·cep·tor
pre·cinct
pre·ci·os·i·ty
pre·cious
prec·i·pice
pre·cip·i·tance
pre·cip·i·tant
pre·cip·i·tate
pré·cis
pre·cise
pre·co·cious
pre·con·ceive
pre·con·scious
pre·cur·sor
pre·cur·so·ry
pre·da·cious
pred·a·tor
pred·a·to·ry
pre·de·cease
pre·de·ces·sor

pre·des·tine
pre·de·ter·mine
pred·i·ca·ble
pre·dic·a·ment
pre·dict·able
pre·dic·tor
pre·di·lec·tion
pre·dom·i·nance
pre·dom·i·nant
pre·dom·i·nate
pre·elec·tion
pre·em·i·nence
pre·em·i·nent
pre·empt
pre·emp·tion
pre·emp·tive
pre·emp·tor
preen
pre·ex·ist
pre·ex·is·tence
pref·ace
pref·a·to·ry
pre·fect
pre·fer
pref·er·a·ble
pref·er·ence
pref·er·en·tial
pre·fer·ment
pre·ferred
pre·fer·ring
preg·na·ble
preg·nan·cy
preg·nant
pre·hen·sile
pre·judg·ment
prej·u·dice
prej·u·di·cial

prel·a·cy
prel·ate
pre·lim·i·nary
pre·mar·i·tal
pre·mier (chief,
   first)
pre·miere (first
   performance)
prem·ise
pre·mi·um
pre·mon·i·to·ry
pre·na·tal
pre·oc·cu·pan·cy
pre·oc·cu·pied
pre·oc·cu·py·ing
pre·paid
pre·par·a·to·ry
pre·pay·ing
pre·pense
pre·pon·der·ance
pre·pon·der·ant
   (*adj*)
pre·pon·der·ate
   (*verb*)
pre·pos·sess·ing
pre·pos·ses·sion
pre·pos·ter·ous
prepped
prep·ping
pre·req·ui·site
pre·rog·a·tive
pres·age
pres·by·ter
pres·by·tery
pre·science
   (foreknowledge)
pre·scient

pres·ence
pre·sent·able
pres·ent-day (*adj*)
pre·sen·ti·ment
  (foreboding)
pre·sent·ment
  (grand jury
  report,
  presentation)
pre·shrunk
pres·i·den·cy
pres·i·dent-elect
press agent
press box
press con·fer·ence
press gang
press·man
press re·lease
press room
press·run
pres·sure-cook
  (*verb*)
pres·sure cook·er
pres·sur·ize
pres·ti·dig·i·ta·tor
pres·tige
pres·ti·gious
pre·sum·able
pre·sump·tion
pre·sump·tu·ous
pre·tense
pre·ten·sion
pre·ten·tious
pret·tied
pret·ti·fy
pret·ty·ish
pret·zel
pre·vail

prev·a·lence
prev·a·lent
pre·var·i·cate
pre·var·i·ca·tor
pre·vent·able
pre·view
preyed (plundered;
  see prayed)
prey·ing
prick·le
prick·ly
pri·er (one that
  pries; *see* prior)
prig·gery
prig·gish
pri·ma·cy
pri·ma fa·cie
pri·ma·ry
prim·er (first
  reader, first
  coat, etc.)
pri·me·val
prim·ing (*verb*
  prime)
prim·i·tive
prim·mer (more
  prim)
prim·mest
prim·ness
pri·mo·gen·i·tor
pri·mo·gen·i·ture
pri·mor·di·al
prin·ci·pal (chief,
  employer, capital)
prin·ci·pal·i·ty
prin·ci·ple (rule,
  doctrine)
print·able

print·out
pri·or (earlier, head
  of religious house;
  see prier)
pri·or·i·ty
pri·o·ry
prism
pris·on
pris·tine
pri·va·cy
pri·va·teer
priv·et (shrub)
priv·i·lege
priv·i·ly
priv·i·ty
privy
prize·fight
prob·a·ble
pro·ba·tion·ary
pro·ba·tion·er
prob·er
pro·bi·ty
pro·bos·cis, *plural*
  proboscises
pro·ce·dur·al
pro·ce·dure
pro·ceed
pro·ces·sion
pro·ces·sor
pro·claim
pro·claim·er
proc·la·ma·tion
pro·cliv·i·ty
pro·cre·a·tor
proc·tor
pro·cur·able
pro·cur·ance
proc·u·ra·tor

pro·cur·er
prod·ded
prod·ding
prod·i·gal
pro·di·gious
prod·i·gy
pro·duc·er
pro·duc·ible
pro·duc·tiv·i·ty
pro·fa·na·tion
pro·fa·na·to·ry
pro·fan·i·ty
pro·fes·sor
prof·fer
prof·fered
prof·fer·ing
pro·fi·cien·cy
pro·fi·cient
prof·it·able
prof·i·teer
prof·li·ga·cy
prof·li·gate
pro·fun·di·ty
pro·fuse
pro·fu·sion
pro·gen·i·tor
prog·e·ny
prog·no·sis
prog·nos·tic
pro·gram
pro·gram·mat·ic
pro·grammed
pro·gram·mer
pro·gram·ming
pro·gres·sive
pro·hib·it
pro·hib·it·or
pro·hib·i·tive

pro·hib·i·to·ry
pro·ject·able
pro·jec·tile
pro·jec·tor
pro·le·tar·i·an
pro·lif·er·ate
pro·lif·ic
pro·lix
pro·lix·i·ty
pro·logue
pro·logu·ize
prom·e·nade
prom·i·nence
prom·i·nent
pro·mis·cu·ity
pro·mis·cu·ous
prom·is·so·ry
prom·on·to·ry
pro·mot·able
pro·mot·er
prompt·er
promp·ti·tude
pro·mul·ga·tor
pro·nounce·able
pro·nounce·ment
pro·nun·ci·a·tion
proof·read
pro·pae·deu·tic
pro·pa·gan·da
pro·pa·gan·dize
prop·a·gate
prop·a·ga·tor
pro·pel
pro·pel·lant (*noun*)
pro·pelled
pro·pel·lent (*adj*)
pro·pel·ler
pro·pel·ling

pro·pen·si·ty
proph·e·cy (*noun*)
proph·e·sied
proph·e·sy (*verb*)
proph·e·sy·ing
proph·et
pro·phy·lac·tic
pro·pin·qui·ty
pro·pi·ti·able
pro·pi·ti·ate
pro·pi·ti·a·tor
pro·pi·tious
pro·po·nent
pro·por·tion·al
pro·pos·al
pro·pos·er
pro·pound·er
propped
prop·ping
pro·pri·etary
pro·pri·etor
pro·pri·ety
pro·rogue
pro·sa·ic
pro·sce·ni·um,
    plural proscenia
pros·e·cut·able
pros·e·cu·tor
pros·e·lyte
pros·e·lyt·er
pros·e·ly·tize
pros·i·er
pros·i·ness
pros·o·dy
pros·pec·tor
pro·spec·tus, *plural*
    prospectuses
pros·per·i·ty

pros·tra·tion
prosy
pro·tag·o·nist
pro·te·an
  (changeable)
pro·tec·tor
pro·té·gé (*masc*)
pro·té·gée (*fem*)
pro·tein (complex
  chemical
  substance)
Prot·es·tant
  (church)
prot·es·tant
  (objector)
pro·to·col
pro·to·colled
pro·to·col·ling
pro·to·plasm
pro·to·type
pro·to·zo·an
pro·trac·tor
pro·tu·ber·ance
pro·tu·ber·ant
prov·able
prov·e·nance
prov·en·der
prov·i·dence
prov·i·dent
prov·i·den·tial
pro·vid·er
prov·ince
pro·vin·cial
pro·vi·sion
pro·vi·sion·ary
pro·vi·so, *plural*
  provisos
pro·vi·so·ry

prov·o·ca·tion
pro·voke
pro·vok·er
prow·ess
prox·im·i·ty
proxy, *plural*
  proxies
pru·dence
pru·dent
prud·ery
pru·ri·ence
pru·ri·ent
pry·ing (*verb* pry)
psalm
psal·tery
pseu·do (*adj*)
pseu·do·nym
psit·ta·co·sis
pso·ri·a·sis
psy·che·del·ic
psy·chi·a·try
psy·chic
psy·cho (Words
  beginning with
  the combining
  form *psycho* are
  written solid:
  psychosomatic.)
psy·cho·an·a·lyst
psy·chol·o·gist
psy·chol·o·gy
psy·cho·sis, *plural*
  psychoses
psy·chot·ic
pto·maine
pu·ber·ty
pub·lic-ad·dress
  sys·tem

pub·lic·i·ty
pub·li·cize
pub·lic-ser·vice
  cor·po·ra·tion
pub·lic-spir·it·ed
pud·ding
pud·dle
pud·dler
pud·dling
pueb·lo, *plural*
  pueblos
pu·er·ile
pu·gi·list
pug·na·cious
puis·sance
puis·sant
pul·chri·tude
pull·back (*noun*)
pul·ley, *plural*
  pulleys
pull·out (*noun*)
pull·over (*adj*)
pul·mo·nary
pul·mo·tor
pul·pit
pul·sa·tor
pul·ver·ize
pul·ver·iz·er
pum·ice (for
  scouring)
pum·iced
pum·ic·ing
pum·mel
pum·meled
pum·mel·ing
pum·per·nick·el
punch·board
punch card

punch-drunk
punch line
punc·til·io, *plural*
  punctilios
punc·til·i·ous
punc·tu·al
punc·tu·a·tor
pun·dit
pun·gen·cy
pun·gent
pun·ish·able
pu·ni·tive
punned
pun·ning
pun·ster
pu·ny (small size,
  unimportant)
pu·pil
pu·pil·age
pup·pet
pup·pe·teer
pup·py
pup·py·hood
pup·py·ish
pur·blind
pur·chas·able
pure·bred
pu·rée
pu·réed
pu·ré·ing
pur·ga·to·ry

pu·ri·fied
pu·ri·fy
pu·ri·fy·ing
pu·ri·ty
pur·lieu
pur·loin
pur·port
purr (cat)
purse-proud
purs·er
purse strings
pur·su·ance
pur·su·ant
pur·su·er
pur·sued
pur·su·ing
pur·suit
pu·ru·lence
pu·ru·lent
pur·vey·ance
pur·vey·or
pur·view
push·ball
push but·ton (*noun*)
push-but·ton (*adj*)
push·cart
push·i·er
push·i·ness
push·off (*noun*)
push·over

push-pull (*adj*)
push-up (*noun*)
pu·sil·la·nim·i·ty
pu·sil·lan·i·mous
pus·tu·lar
pus·tule
put-on (*adj*)
put·out (*noun*)
pu·tre·fac·tion
pu·tre·fied
pu·tre·fy
pu·tre·fy·ing
pu·tres·cence
pu·tres·cent
pu·trid
putt (golf)
put·ter
put·ting (put and
  putt)
put-up (*adj*)
put-up·on (*adj*)
puz·zle
pyg·my
py·lon
py·or·rhea
pyr·a·mid
pyre (funeral)
py·ro·ma·nia
py·ro·tech·nic
pyr·rhic

Q

quack·ery
quad·ran·gle
quad·ran·gu·lar
quad·rant
quad·ren·ni·al
quad·ren·ni·um,
  plural
  quadrenniums
qua·drille
quad·ru·ped
quad·ru·ple
quad·ru·plet
quag·mire
qua·hog
quail (all meanings)
qual·i·fi·ca·tion
qual·i·fied
qual·i·fi·er
qual·i·fy
qual·i·fy·ing
qual·i·ta·tive
qualm
quan·da·ry
quan·ti·fi·able
quan·ti·fied
quan·ti·fi·er
quan·ti·fy
quan·ti·fy·ing
quan·ti·ty

quan·tum, *plural*
  quanta
quar·an·tine
quar·rel
quar·reled
quar·rel·er
quar·rel·ing
quar·ried
quar·ri·er
quar·ry (object of
  hunt, place for
  excavating stone)
quar·ry·ing
quar·ter·back
quar·ter-deck
quar·ter·fi·nal
quar·ter horse
quar·ter-hour
quar·ter·mas·ter
quar·ter note
quar·tet
quar·tile
quar·to, *plural*
  quartos
quartz
qua·sar
qua·si (Compound
  words beginning
  with *quasi* are

written with a
  hyphen joining
  quasi to the
  second element:
  quasi-historical.)
qua·ter·na·ry
quat·rain
qua·ver
quay
quay·age
quea·si·er
quea·si·ly
quea·si·ness
quea·sy
queen-size
quell
quench·able
quer·u·lous
que·ry (question)
ques·tion·able
ques·tion·naire
queue
queued
queu·ing
quib·ble
quick as·sets
quick bread
quick-change (*verb*
  and *adj*)

quick-fire
quick-freeze
quick·lime
quick·sand
quick·sil·ver
quick·step
quick-tem·pered
quick time
quick-wit·ted
quid·di·ty
quid pro quo
qui·es·cence
qui·es·cent

qui·etude
quince
quin·sy
quin·tes·sence
quin·tet
quin·tu·plet
quipped
quip·ping
quire (paper)
quirk
quit·rent
quit·tance
quit·ted

quit·ter
quit·ting
quiv·er
quix·ot·ic
quiz, *plural* quizzes
quizzed
quiz·zer
quiz·zi·cal
quiz·zing
quo·rum
quot·able
quo·tient

R

rab·bet (groove)
rab·bi, *plural* rabbis
rab·bin·i·cal
rab·ble-rous·er
rab·ble-rous·ing
rab·id
ra·bies
rac·oon
race·horse
race·track
ra·cial
rac·ism
rac·ist
rack (frame or
    torture)
rack·et
rack·e·teer
rack·ety
ra·con·teur
racy
ra·dar
ra·di·al
ra·di·ance
ra·di·ant
ra·di·a·tor
rad·i·cal (politics,
    math, chemistry)
rad·i·cle (biology)
ra·dio, *plural* radios

ra·dio·ac·tive
ra·di·oed
ra·di·o·ing
ra·di·um
ra·di·us, *plural*
    radii
raff·ish
raf·fle
rag·a·muf·fin
raged
rag·ged
rag·gedy
rag·ging
rag·gle-tag·gle
rag·ing (rage)
rag·lan
ra·gout (*noun*
    stew)
rail·lery
rail-split·ter
rai·ment
rain check
rain for·est
rain gauge
rain·i·er
rain·i·est
rain·wa·ter
rai·sin
rake-off (*noun*)

rak·ish
ral·ly (all meanings)
ram·ble
ram·bler
ram·bunc·tious
ram·e·kin
ram·i·fi·ca·tion
ram·i·fied
ram·i·fy
ram·i·fy·ing
rammed
ram·mer
ram·ming
ram·pa·geous
ram·pan·cy
ram·pant
ram·shack·le
ranch house
ran·cho, *plural*
    ranchos
ran·cid
ran·cor
ran·cor·ous
ran·dom
ran·dom·ize
rang·i·ness
rang·ing
rangy
ran·kle

ran·sack
ran·som
ran·somed
ran·som·ing
rant
rant·er
ra·pa·cious
ra·pac·i·ty
rap·id-fire (*adj*)
ra·pi·er
rapped
rap·per (one who raps)
rap·ping
rap·port
rap·proche·ment
rapt (absorbed)
rap·ture
rar·e·fied
rar·e·fy
rar·e·fy·ing
rar·i·ty
ras·cal
rasp·ber·ry
rat·able (rate)
ratch·et
rat·i·fied
rat·i·fi·er
rat·i·fy
rat·i·fy·ing
ra·tio, *plural* ratios
ra·tion
ra·tion·al (able to reason, sensible)
ra·tio·nale (explanation)
ra·tion·al·ize

rat·tan
rat·ted
rat·ter
rat·ting
rat·tle
rat·tle·brained
rat·tle·snake
rat·tle·trap
rat·tling
rat·trap
rat·ty
rau·cous
rav·age
rav·ag·er
rav·el
rav·eled
rav·el·er
rav·en (*noun* bird; *verb* to feed greedily, to seek prey
rav·en·ous
ra·vi·o·li
raw·boned
raw deal
raw·hide
raw ma·te·ri·al
raze (demolish)
ra·zor
raz·zle-daz·zle
re-act (to do again)
re·ac·tant
re·ac·tion·ary
re·ac·tor
read·able
read·i·ly
read·i·ness
re·ad·mit·tance
read·out (*noun*)

ready-made
ready-mix
ready-to-wear
ready-wit·ted
re·af·firm
re·align
re·al·ize
real-life (*adj*)
re·ap·pear·ance
re·ap·ply
re·ap·point
re·ap·por·tion
re·ap·prais·al
re·ap·praise
rear guard
re·ar·ma·ment
re·ar·range
re·ar·range·ment
rear·ward
rea·son·able
re·as·sem·ble
re·as·sess
re·as·sign
re·as·sur·ance
reb·el (*noun* and *adj*)
re·belled
re·bel·ling
re·bel·lion
re·bel·lious
re·bid·da·ble
re·broad·cast
re·buff
re·buke
re·but
re·but·tal
re·but·ted
re·but·ting

re·cal·ci·trance
re·cal·ci·trant
re·cap
re·ca·pit·u·late
re·capped
re·cap·ping
re·cede
re·ceipt
re·ceipt·or
re·ceiv·able
re·ceiv·er
re·cen·cy
re·cep·ta·cle
re·cep·tor
re·ces·sion·al
re·ces·sion·ary
re·ces·sive
re·cid·i·vism
rec·i·pe
re·cip·i·ent
re·cip·ro·cal
re·cip·ro·ca·tor
rec·i·proc·i·ty
re·cit·al
rec·i·ta·tive
reck·on
re·claim·able
rec·la·ma·tion
re·cluse
rec·og·ni·tion
rec·og·niz·able
rec·og·ni·zance
rec·og·nize
re·coil (to fall back)
re-coil (to coil again)
rec·ol·lect
   (remember)

re-col·lect (collect
   again)
rec·om·mend
rec·om·mend·er
re·com·mit
re·com·mit·tal
rec·om·pense
rec·on·cil·able
rec·on·cile
re·con·dite
re·con·nais·sance
re·con·noi·ter
re·con·vey
re·con·vey·ance
re·count (tell)
re-count (*noun* and
   verb, count again)
re·coup
re·coup·able
re·course
re·cov·er (get back)
re-cov·er (cover
   again)
rec·re·ant
rec·re·ate (refresh,
   restore)
re-cre·ate (create
   again)
re·crim·i·nate
re·crim·i·na·to·ry
re·cru·des·cence
re·cru·des·cent
re·cruit
re·cruit·er
rec·tan·gu·lar
rec·ti·fi·able
rec·ti·fi·er

rec·ti·fy
rec·ti·fy·ing
rec·ti·lin·ear
rec·ti·tude
rec·tor
rec·to·ry
re·cum·bent
re·cu·per·ate
re·cur
re·curred
re·cur·rence
re·cur·rent
re·cur·ring
rec·u·sant
re·dac·tor
red-blood·ed
red·breast
red·cap (porter)
red-car·pet (*adj*)
red·den
red·dened
red·den·ing
red·der
red·dest
red·dish
re·deem·able
re·deem·er
red-hand·ed
red·head
red-head·ed
red·her·ring
red-hot
red-let·ter (*adj*)
red-neck
red·o·lence
red·o·lent
re·doubt·able

red-pen·cil (*verb*)
red poll
re·dress (set right)
re-dress (dress
  again)
re·dress·able
re·dress·er
red·skin
red tape
re·duc·ible
re·dun·dan·cy
re·dun·dant
re·echo, *plural*
  reechoes
re·echoed
re·echo·ing
re·ed·u·cate
re·ed·u·ca·tion
re·elect
re·elec·tion
re·emerge
re·emer·gence
re·em·pha·size
re·em·ploy
re·en·act
re·en·gage
re·en·list
re·en·list·ment
re·en·ter
re·en·trance
re·en·trant
re·en·try
re·es·tab·lish
re·eval·u·ate
re·ex·am·i·na·tion
re·ax·am·ine
re·ex·port

re·ex·port·er
re·fec·to·ry
re·fer
re·fer·able
ref·er·ee
ref·er·eed
ref·er·ee·ing
ref·er·ence
ref·er·en·dum,
  plural
  referendums
ref·er·ent
ref·er·en·tial
re·fer·ral
re·ferred
re·fer·rer
re·fer·ring
re·fill·able
re·fin·ery
re·flec·tion
re·flec·tor
re·flex·ive
re·form·able
re·for·ma·to·ry
re·form·er
re·frac·tor
re·frac·to·ry
re·frain
re·frig·er·ant
re·frig·er·a·tor
re·fu·eled
re·fu·el·ing
ref·u·gee
re·ful·gence
re·ful·gent
re·fur·bish
re·fus·al

re·fut·able
re·gale (entertain)
re·ga·lia
re·gat·ta
re·gen·cy
re·gen·er·ate
re·gen·er·a·tor
reg·i·cide
re·gime
reg·i·men
re·gion
reg·is·ter
reg·is·tra·ble
reg·is·trant
reg·is·trar
reg·is·try
reg·nant
re·gress
re·gres·sive
re·gres·sor
re·gret·ta·ble
re·gret·ted
re·gret·ting
reg·u·lar
reg·u·lar·ize
reg·u·la·tor
re·gur·gi·tate
re·ha·bil·i·tate
re·hears·al
re·hearse
reign (rule)
re·im·burs·able
re·im·burse
re·im·burse·ment
rein (check)
re·in·car·na·tion
re·in·cur

re·in·curred
re·in·cur·ring
rein·deer
re·in·force
re·in·force·ment
re·in·state
re·in·sur·ance
re·in·ter·pret
re·is·sue
re·it·er·ate
re·ject·er
re·joice
re·join·der
re·ju·ve·nate
re·ju·ve·na·tor
re-laid (laid again)
re·lapse
re·lat·able
re·la·tor (one who
    relates)
re·lax·ant
re·lax·er
re·lay (convey)
re-lay (lay again)
re·layed (conveyed)
re·lay·ing
    (conveying)
re-lay·ing (laying
    again)
re·leas·able
re-lease (lease
    again)
rel·e·gate
rel·e·vance
rel·e·vant
re·li·able
re·li·ance

re·li·ant
rel·ic
re·lied (rely)
re·lief
re·liev·able
re·lieve
re·liev·er
re·li·gious
re·lin·quish
rel·i·quary
re·luc·tance
re·luc·tant
re·ly·ing
re·main·der
re·mark·able
re·me·di·a·ble
re·mem·brance
rem·i·nisce
rem·i·nis·cence
rem·i·nis·cent
re·miss
re·mis·si·ble
re·mis·sion
re·mit
re·mit·ment
re·mit·ta·ble
re·mit·tance
re·mit·ted
re·mit·tent
re·mit·ter
re·mit·ting
rem·nant
re·mod·el
re·mod·eled
re·mod·el·er
re·mod·el·ing
re·mon·strance

re·mon·strant
re·mon·stra·tor
re·mov·able
re·mov·al
re·mu·ner·ate
re·mu·ner·a·tive
re·mu·ner·a·tor
re·nais·sance
    (rebirth)
Re·nais·sance
    (historic period)
ren·coun·ter
ren·der·able
ren·dez·vous
ren·e·gade
re·nege
re·neged
re·neg·er
re·neg·ing
re·ne·go·tia·ble
re·new·able
re·new·al
re·nounce
re·nounc·er
ren·o·va·tor
re·nown (fame)
rent·able
rent·al
re·nun·ci·a·tion
re·paid (repay)
re·pair·able
rep·a·ra·ble
rep·a·ra·tion
re·par·a·tive
rep·ar·tee
re·pa·tri·ate
re·pay·ing

re·peal·able
re·peal·er
re·peat·able
re·peat·er
re·pel
re·pelled
re·pel·lence
re·pel·lent
re·pel·ling
re·pen·tance
re·pen·tant
re·pent·er
re·per·cus·sion
rep·er·toire
rep·er·to·ry
rep·e·ti·tion
rep·e·ti·tious
re·pet·i·tive
re·place·able
re·place·ment
re·plete
rep·li·ca
rep·li·cate
re·pli·er
re·port·able
re·port·age
re·pos·i·to·ry
re·pos·sess
rep·re·hen·si·ble
rep·re·sent·able
re·press·ible
re·pres·sor
re·priev·al
re·prieve
rep·ri·mand
re·pri·sal
re·proach

rep·ro·bate
re·pro·duc·ible
re·prov·able
re·prove
rep·tile
re·pu·di·a·tor
re·pug·nance
re·pug·nant
re·pulse
re·pul·sive
rep·u·ta·ble
req·ui·site
re·quit·al
re·sal·able
re·scind
re·scind·a·ble
re·scis·sion
res·cu·a·ble
res·cue
res·cued
res·cu·er
res·cu·ing
re·search·able
re·search·er
re·sem·blance
re·sem·blant
re·sem·ble
re·serv·ist
res·er·voir
re·shuf·fle
res·i·dence
res·i·den·cy
res·i·dent
res·i·den·tial
re·sid·u·al
re·sid·u·ary
re·sid·u·um

res·i·due
re·sil·ience
re·sil·ient
res·in (material
    extruded from
    plants; *see* rosin)
re·sis·tance
re·sis·tant
re·sist·er
re·sist·ible
re·sis·tor
    (electricity)
res·o·lute
re·solv·able
re·solv·er
res·o·nance
res·o·nant
res·o·na·tor
re·sort·er
re·source·ful
re·spect·able
re·spect·er
res·pi·ra·tor
re·spi·ra·to·ry
re·splen·dence
re·splen·dent
re·spond·ence
re·spond·ent
re·spond·er
re·sponse
re·spon·si·ble
re·spon·sive
res·tau·rant
res·tau·ra·teur
re·stor·able
re·stor·a·tive
re·stor·er

re·strain·able
re·strain·er
re·sul·tant
re·sume (start
again)
ré·su·mé
(summary)
re·sump·tion
re·sur·gence
re·sur·gent
res·ur·rect
re·sus·ci·tate
re·sus·ci·ta·tor
re·tail·er
re·tain·er
re·tal·i·ate
re·tal·i·a·to·ry
re·tar·dant
retch (effort to
vomit; *see*
wretch)
ret·i·cence
ret·i·cent
ret·i·cle (network)
ret·i·cule (handbag)
ret·i·na, *plural*
retinas
ret·i·nue
re·trace·able
re·tract·able
re·trac·tile
re·trac·tor
re·tread (tires)
re-tread (tread
again)
re·treat
(withdrawal)

re-treat (treat again)
re·tri·al (second
trial)
ret·ri·bu·tion
re·trib·u·to·ry
re·tried (tried again)
re·triev·able
re·triev·al
re·triev·er
ret·ro·ac·tive
ret·ro·cede
ret·ro·ces·sion
ret·ro·grade
ret·ro·gres·sion
ret·ro·rock·et
ret·ro·spect
re·try (try again)
re·try·ing
re·turn·able
re·union
re·unite
re·us·able
re·val·u·ate
re·veal·able
rev·eil·le
rev·el
rev·e·la·tion
rev·eled
rev·el·er
rev·el·ing
rev·el·ry
rev·e·nue; *plural*
revenues
rev·e·nu·er
re·ver·ber·ant
re·ver·ber·a·tor
re·ver·ber·a·to·ry

re·vere
rev·er·ence
rev·er·end
rev·er·ent
re·ver·ie
re·ver·sal
re·vers·ible
re·ver·sion·ary
re·vert·er
re·vert·ible
re·vis·able
re·vis·al
re·vise
re·vis·er
re·vi·sion·ary
re·vi·so·ry
re·vi·tal·ize
re·viv·al
rev·o·ca·ble
rev·o·ca·tion
re·voke
rev·o·lu·tion·ary
rev·o·lu·tion·ize
re·volv·able
re·volv·er
re·vul·sion
revved
rev·ving
re·ward·able
re·writ·er
re·writ·ing
re·writ·ten
rhap·so·dize
rhap·so·dy
rhet·o·ric
rheum
rheu·ma·tic

rheu·ma·tism
rhi·noc·er·os,
  plural
  rhinoceroses
rho·do·den·dron
rhu·barb
rhyme (verse; *see*
  rime)
rhym·er
rhyme·ster
rhythm
rhyth·mic
rib·ald
rib·ald·ry
ribbed
rib·bing
rib·bon
rick·ets
rick·ett·sia
rick·ety
rick·shaw
ric·o·chet
ric·o·cheted
ric·o·chet·ing
rid·able (ride)
rid·dance
rid·ded
rid·dling
rid·dle
rid·i·cule
ri·dic·u·lous
rif·fle (leaf
  through, shuffle)
riff·raff
ri·fle
ri·fle·ry
ri·fling

rigged
rig·ger
rig·ging
right·about (all uses)
right·about-face
right an·gle (*noun*)
right-an·gled (*adj*)
righ·teous
right field
right field·er
right-hand (*adj*)
right-hand·ed
right-mind·ed
right of way
right-to-work (*adj*)
right-wing (*adj*)
right wing (*noun*)
right-wing·er
rig·id
rig·ma·role
rig·or
rill
rime (frost; *see*
  rhyme)
rimmed
rim·ming
ring·er
ring fin·ger
ring·lead·er
ring·mas·ter
ring-necked
ring·side (*noun* and
  adj)
ring-streaked
ring-tailed
ring·toss
ring·worm

rins·a·ble
rinse
rins·ing
ri·ot·er
ri·ot·ous
ri·poste
ripped
rip·per
rip·ping
rip·ple
rip·ply
rip-roar·ing
rip·snort·er
rip·snort·ing
ris·i·ble
risk·i·ness
ris·qué
rite (ceremony)
rite of pas·sage
rit·u·al
rit·u·al·ize
ri·val
ri·valed
ri·val·ing
ri·val·ry
riv·et
riv·et·ed
riv·et·ing
riv·u·let
road·a·bil·i·ty
road agent
road·bed
road·block
road gang
road hog
road·house
road·run·ner

road·show
toad test (*noun*)
road-test (*verb*)
road·work
roan
robbed
rob·ber
rob·bery
rob·bing
ro·bot
ro·bus·tious
rock and rye
rock bass
rock bot·tom (*noun*)
rock-bot·tom (*adj*)
rock-bound
rock can·dy
rock·e·teer
rock·et·ry
rock gar·den
rock·i·est
rock 'n' roll
rock-ribbed.
rock salt
rock wool
ro·co·co
ro·dent
ro·deo, *plural*
   rodeos
rod·o·mon·tade
rogue
rogu·ery
ro·guish
rois·ter
role (part, function)
roll·back (*noun*)
roll bar
roll call

roll·er skate (*noun*)
roll·er-skate (*verb*)
roll·er skat·er
roll·er-skat·ing
roll film
rol·lick
rol·lick·ing
roll-top (*adj*)
ro·ly-po·ly
ro·maine (lettuce)
ro·man·ti·cize
ron·del (verse)
ron·do, *plural*
   rondos
roof gar·den
roof·top
roof·tree
rook·ery
room·fuls
room·i·er
room·mate
roor·back
ropy (rope)
ro·sa·ry
ro·se·ate
rose·bush
rose-col·ored
ro·sette
ros·i·ly
ros·in (hard
   material resulting
   from distilling
   turpentine, used
   for violin bows;
   see resin)
ros·trum, *plural*
   ros·trums
rosy

ro·ta·ry
ro·ta·tor
ro·ta·to·ry
rote (routine, by
   memory)
ro·tis·ser·ie
ro·to·gra·vure
ro·tor
rot·ted
rot·ten
rot·ten·ness
rot·ter
rot·ting
ro·tund
ro·tun·da
roué
rough-and-ready
rough-and-tum·ble
rough·cast
rough-cut
rough-dry
rough-hew
rough·neck
rough·shod
rou·lade
rou·lette
round·about
roun·de·lay
round·house
round rob·in
round-shoul·dered
round steak
round-ta·ble (*adj*)
round-the-clock
   (*adj*)
round trip (*noun*)
round-trip (*adj*)
round·up (*noun*)

rout (*noun* mob,
  defeat; *verb* to
  defeat, to dig out)
route (*noun* course;
  verb to direct)
rou·tine
rou·tin·ize
roux (cooking; *see*
  rue)
row·di·ness
row·dy·ish
row·dy·ism
row·el
row·eled
row·el·ing
ru·ba·to (music)
rubbed
rub·ber band
rub·ber-base (*adj*)
rub·ber ce·ment
rub·ber·ize
rub·ber stamp
  (*noun*)
rub·ber-stamp
  (*verb*)
rub·bery (*adj*)
rub·bing
rub·bish
rub·ble (fragments
  of stone, brick,
  etc.)
ru·ble (money)
ru·bric
ruck·us

rud·di·er
rud·di·ness
rud·dy
ru·di·ment
ru·di·men·ta·ry
rue (regret; *see*
  roux)
rued (rue)
rue·ful
ruf·fle
rug·ged
ru·ing
ru·in·ous
rule of thumb
rum·ble
rum·bly
ru·mi·nant
ru·mi·na·tor
rum·mage
rum·mi·est
rum·my
ru·mor
ru·mored
ru·mor·mon·ger
rum·ple
rum·ply
rum·pus
rum·run·ner
rum·run·ning
run·about (*noun*)
run·around (*noun*)
run·away
run·back (*noun*)
run-down (*adj*)

run-down (*noun*)
run-in (*noun* and
  adj)
run·nel
run·ner-up, *plural*
  runners-up
run·ni·er
run·ning
run·ny
run·off (*noun*)
run-of-the-mill
run-of-the-mine
run-on (*adj*)
run·over (*noun* and
  adj)
run-through (*noun*)
rup·ture
ru·ral
ruse
rus·set
rust-col·ored
rus·tic
rus·ti·cate
rus·ti·ca·tor
rust·i·er
rus·tle
rus·tler
rust·proof
ru·ta·ba·ga
rut·ted
rut·ti·er
rut·ting
rut·tish
rut·ty

S

Sab·bath
sab·bat·i·cal
sa·ber
sa·ble
sab·o·tage
sab·o·taged
sab·o·tag·ing
sab·o·teur
sac·cha·rin
   (chemical)
sac·cha·rine (*adj*
   sweetish)
sac·er·do·tal
sa·chem
sa·chet
sack·cloth
sack·fuls
sac·ra·ment
sa·cred
sac·ri·fice
sac·ri·fi·cial
sac·ri·lege
sac·ri·le·gious
sac·ro·sanct
sad·den
sad·dened

sad·den·ing
sad·der
sad·dle·bag
sad·dle horse
sad·dlery
sad·dle shoe
sad·dle sore (*noun*)
sad·dle-sore (*adj*)
sa·dism
sa·fa·ri, *plural*
   safaris
safe-con·duct
safe·crack·er
safe-de·pos·it (*adj*)
safe·guard
safe·keep·ing
saf·fron
sa·ga·cious
sa·gac·i·ty
sagged
sag·gi·er
sag·ging
sag·gy
sail·er (boat)
sail·or (man, hat)
saint·li·ness

sal·able
sa·la·cious
sal·a·man·der
sa·la·mi
sal·a·ried
sal·a·ry
sales·clerk
sales pro·mo·tion
sales re·sis·tance
sales·room
sales talk
sales tax
sa·lience
sa·lient
sa·line
sa·li·va
sal·i·vary
sal·low
salm·on
salt-and-pep·per
   (*adj*)
sal·ta·to·ry
salt·box
salt·cel·lar
salt·i·er
salt·i·ness

salt lick
salt marsh
salt·pe·ter
salt pork
salt-ris·ing (*adj*)
salt·shak·er
salt·wa·ter (*adj*)
sa·lu·bri·ous
sal·u·tary
salv·able
sal·vage (rescue, save)
sal·vage·able
sal·vag·er
salve
sal·ver
sal·vo, *plural* salvos
sam·o·var
sam·ple
sanc·ti·fied
sanc·ti·fy
sanc·ti·fy·ing
sanc·ti·mo·nious
sanc·tion
sanc·tion·able
sanc·ti·ty
sanc·tu·ary
sanc·tum, *plural* sanctums
sand (Compound words beginning with *sand* are written solid: *sandbar*, except as otherwise shown below.)
san·dal

san·daled
sand·bagged
sand·bag·ger
sand·bag·ging
sand-blind
sand flea
sand·lot (*adj*)
sand ta·ble
sand trap
sang-froid
san·gui·nary
san·guine
san·guin·e·ous
san·i·tar·i·um, *plural* sanitariums
san·i·tary
san·i·tize
san·i·ty
sa·pi·ence
sa·pi·ent
sapped
sap·per
sap·phire
sap·pi·er
sap·ping
sap·py
sar·casm
sar·don·ic
sa·ri (garment)
sa·rong (garment)
sar·sa·pa·ril·la
sar·to·ri·al
satch·el
sat·el·lite
sa·tia·ble
sa·ti·ate
sa·ti·ety

sat·in·et
sat·ire
sa·tir·i·cal
sat·is·fac·to·ry
sat·is·fi·able
sat·u·rate
sat·ur·nine
sa·tyr
sau·er·bra·ten
sau·er·kraut
saun·ter
sau·té
sau·téed
sau·té·ing
sav·able
sav·age·ry
sa·van·na
sa·vant (learned person)
sav·ior
sa·vor
sa·vory
saw·buck
saw-edged
sawed-off
saw·mill
saw·tooth
saw-toothed
sax·o·phone
say·able
say-so
scab·bard
scabbed
scab·bi·er
scab·bi·ness
scab·bing
scab·by

sca·bies
sca·bi·ous
sca·brous
scaf·fold
scal·able
sca·lar (concerning
    scales)
scal·a·wag
scald
scal·i·er
scal·i·ness
scal·lion
scal·lop
scal·loped
scal·lo·pi·ne
scal·lop·ing
scal·pel
scaly
scan·dal
scan·dal·ize
scanned
scan·ner
scan·ning
scant·i·er
scant·i·ly
scant·i·ness
scape·goat
scar·ab
scarce
scarce·ly
scar·ci·ty
scare·mon·ger
scarf, *plural* scarfs
scar·i·est
scar·i·fied
scar·i·fy
scar·i·fy·ing
scarred

scar·ring
scar·ry (showing
    scars)
scary (frightening)
scath·ing
scat·ter
scav·enge
scav·en·ger
sce·nar·io, *plural*
    scenarios
sce·nery
scent (odor)
scep·ter
sched·u·lar (*adj*)
sched·ule
sche·mat·ic
sche·ma·tize
scheme
schem·er
scher·zo, *plural*
    scherzos
schism
schiz·o·phre·nia
schmaltz
schnapps
schnit·zel
schol·ar
scho·las·tic
school age
school board
school·book
school·boy
school bus
school day
school dis·trict
school·girl
school·room
school·teach·er

school·work
school year
schoon·er
sci·at·i·ca
scim·i·tar
scin·til·la
scin·til·late
scin·til·la·tor
sci·on (bud of a
    plant, offspring)
scis·sors
scle·ro·sis
scoff
scoff·law
sconce
scor·pi·on
scot-free
scoun·drel
scourge
scowl
scrab·ble
scrag·gi·er
scrag·gli·er
scrag·gly
scrag·gy
scram·ble
scrap·ing (scrape)
scrap iron
scrapped
scrap·per
scrap·pi·er
scrap·pi·ly
scrap·pi·ness
scrap·ping
scrap·ple
scrap·py
scrawl
scrawl·er

228

scrawl·i·est
scrawly
scraw·ni·er
scraw·ni·ness
scrawny
screech
screech·er
screen·land
screen pass
screen·play
screen test
scrib·ble
scrib·bler
scrim·mage
scrim·mag·er
scrim·shaw
scrip (paper
    currency, brief
    writing, etc.)
script (written text)
scrip·tur·al
script·writ·er
scrof·u·la
scrof·u·lous
scroll (roll of writing
    material)
scrolled
scroll saw
scroll·work
scrounge
scrubbed
scrub·ber
scrub·bi·est
scrub·bing
scrub·by
scruff
scruff·i·est
scruff·i·ness

scruffy
scrump·tious
scru·ple
scru·pu·lous
scru·ta·ble
scru·ti·nize
scru·ti·ny
scud·ded
scud·ding
scuff
scuf·fle
scull (racing boat)
scul·lery
scul·lion
sculp·tor
sculp·ture
scummed
scum·ming
scum·my
scup·per
scurf
scur·ril·i·ty
scur·ri·lous
scur·ried
scur·ry
scur·ry·ing
scur·vi·ly
scur·vy
scut·tle
scut·tle·butt
scythe
sea bag
sea bass
sea·beach
sea bird
sea·board
sea·borne
sea breeze

sea·coast
sea·far·er
sea·food
sea·go·ing
sea gull
sea lane
seal·ant
sea legs
sea lev·el
sea·man
seam·i·er
seam·stress
seamy
sé·ance
sea·plane
sea·port
sea pow·er
sear (scorch, burn;
    see sere)
search light
search war·rant
sea·scape
sea·shell
sea·shore
sea·sick·ness
sea·side
sea·son·able
sea·son·al
seat belt
seat·mate
seat·work
sea wall
sea·wa·ter
sea·way
sea·weed
se·cede
se·ces·sion
se·clu·sion

229

sec·ond·ary

sec·ond base

sec·ond base·man

sec·ond-best (*adj*)

sec·ond-class (*adj*)

sec·ond-de·gree

   (*adj*)

sec·ond·er

sec·ond fid·dle

sec·ond-guess

sec·ond hand

   (*noun*)

sec·ond·hand (*adj*)

sec·ond-rate

sec·ond-sto·ry (*adj*)

sec·ond-string

sec·ond thought

sec·ond wind

se·cre·cy

sec·re·tar·i·al

sec·re·tar·i·at

sec·re·tary

se·crete

se·cre·tion

se·cre·tive

se·cre·to·ry

   (glands, etc.)

sec·tar·i·an

sec·tor

sec·u·lar

sec·u·lar·ize

se·cur·able

se·cur·ance

se·cur·er

se·cu·ri·ty

se·date

sed·a·tive

sed·en·tary

sed·i·ment

sed·i·men·ta·ry

se·di·tion

se·di·tion·ary

se·di·tious

se·duce

se·duc·er

se·duc·i·ble

se·du·li·ty

sed·u·lous

see·able

seed·bed

seed·ling

seed mon·ey

seed pearl

seed plant

seed·pod

seed stock

seed·time

seem·li·er

seem·li·ness

seem·ly

seep·age

seer (one who sees)

seer·ess

seer·suck·er

seethe

seg·men·tary

seg·re·gate

sei·del

sei·gnior

seine

seis·mic

seis·mo·graph

seis·mol·o·gy

seize

sei·zure

se·lect·ee

se·lec·tor

self (Compound

   words beginning

   with *self* are

   written with a

   hyphen joining

   self to the second

   element:

   self-centered.)

self-ac·cu·sa·to·ry

self-ad·dressed

self-ag·gran·

   dize·ment

self-an·ni·hi·la·

   tion

self-ap·point·ed

self-as·sert·ing

self-as·sur·ance

self-com·pla·cent

self-con·ceit

self-con·demned

self-con·fessed

self-con·fi·dence

self-con·scious

self-con·sis·tent

self-con·tra·dic·

   to·ry

self-crit·i·cal

self-crit·i·cism

self-de·ceit

self-de·fense

self-de·ni·al

self-de·pen·dence

self-dis·ci·pline

self-ef·fac·ing

self-es·teem

self-ev·i·dent

self-ful·fill·ing

self-hyp·no·sis
self-im·por·tance
self-im·por·tant
self-im·prove·ment
self-in·duced
self-in·dul·gence
self-in·sur·ance
self-per·pet·u·at·ing
self-pos·sessed
self-pro·claimed
self-pro·pelled
self-re·li·ance
self-re·li·ant
self-righ·teous
self-ris·ing
self-sac·ri·fice
self-sub·sis·tence
self-suf·fi·cien·cy
self-suf·fi·cient
self-suf·fic·ing
sell-off (*noun*)
sell·out (*noun*)
sel·vage (edging)
sem·a·phore
sem·blance
se·mes·ter
semi (The prefix *semi* is joined to the following element without a hyphen: *semicircle*.)
semi·an·nu·al
semi·aquat·ic
semi·ar·id
semi·cen·ten·ni·al
semi·con·scious

semi·fi·nal
semi·lit·er·ate
sem·i·nal
sem·i·nar
sem·i·nary
semi·of·fi·cial
semi·trans·par·ent
semi·trop·i·cal
semi·week·ly
sen·a·tor
send-off (*noun*)
se·nes·cence
se·nes·cent
sen·ior
sen·ior·i·ty
sen·si·ble
sen·si·tive
sen·si·tize
sen·sor (device for sensing)
sen·so·ry
sen·su·al
sen·su·ous
sen·ten·tious
sen·tience
sen·tient
sen·ti·men·tal
sen·ti·nel
sen·ti·neled
sen·ti·nel·ing
se·paled
sep·a·ra·ble
sep·a·rate
sep·a·ra·tor
se·pia
sep·sis
sep·tet
sep·tic

sep·ul·cher
sep·ul·chered
se·pul·chral
se·quel
se·que·la, *plural* sequelae
se·quence
se·quen·tial
se·ques·ter
se·ques·trate
se·quin
se·quined
se·quoia
se·ra·glio, *plural* seraglios
sere (dried up; *see* sear)
ser·e·nade
ser·en·dip·i·ty
se·rene
se·ren·i·ty
serge (cloth; *see* surge)
ser·gean·cy
ser·geant
ser·geant-at-arms
ser·geants ma·jor
se·ri·al (in series, appearing in succession)
se·ri·al·ize
se·ri·a·tim
se·ries (*sing* and *plural*)
ser·if (printing)
se·ri·ous
se·ri·ous-mind·ed
ser·mon·ize

ser·pent
ser·pen·tine
ser·rat·ed
  (saw-tooth edge)
ser·ried (crowded)
se·rum, *plural*
  serums
ser·vant
ser·vice
ser·vice·able
ser·vice charge
ser·vice club
ser·vice en·trance
ser·vice·man
ser·vice sta·tion
ser·vile
ser·vil·i·ty
ser·vi·tor
ser·vi·tude
ser·vo·mech·a·
  nism
ses·a·me
ses·qui·pe·da·lian
ses·sion
set·back (*noun*)
set-in (*adj*)
set·off (*noun*)
set·screw
set·tee
set·ter
set·ting
set·tler
set-to, *plural* set-tos
set·up (*noun*)
sev·enth-day (*adj*)
sev·en·ti·eth
sev·en·ty-first, etc.
sev·en·ty-one, etc.

sev·er·able
sev·er·ance
se·ver·i·ty
sew·age (refuse)
sewed (with needle
  and thread; *see*
  sowed)
sew·er·age (sewer
  system)
sew·ing
sewn
sex·tant
sex·tet
sex·tu·plet
sex·u·al·i·ty
sexy
shab·bi·er
shab·bi·ly
shab·by
shack·le
shad·i·er
shad·i·ly
shad·i·ness
shad·ow·box (*verb*)
shad·ow box (*noun*)
shady
shag·gi·er
shag·gi·ness
shag·gy
shak·able
shake·down (*noun*
  and *adj*)
shak·i·er
shak·i·ly
shak·i·ness
sha·ko, *plural*
  shakos
shaky

shal·lot
sha·man
sham·ble
shame·faced
shammed
sham·mer
sham·ming
sham·poo
sham·pooed
sham·poo·er
sham·poo·ing
shang·hai
shang·haied
shang·hai·er
shang·hai·ing
shap·able
shape·li·er
shape·li·ness
shape·ly
shape-up (*noun*)
shard
share·cropped
share·crop·per
share·crop·ping
share·hold·er
shark·skin
sharp-eyed
sharp·ie
sharp-nosed
sharp-set
sharp·shoot·er
sharp-sight·ed
sharp-tongued
sharp-wit·ted
shat·ter·proof
sheaf, *plural*
  sheaves
shears (scissors)

sheath (*noun*)
sheathe (*verb*)
shed·ding
sheep-dip
sheep dog
sheep·fold
sheep·herd·er
sheep·skin
sheer (*verb* to swerve;
   noun thin texture)
sheik
sheik·dom
shel·lac
shel·lacked
shel·lack·ing
shell·fire
shell·fish
shell game
shell·proof
shell shock
shell-shocked (*adj*)
shel·ter·belt
shep·herd
sher·bet
sher·iff
shib·bo·leth
shied (to shy)
shield
shi·er (more shy)
shi·est
shil·le·lagh
shil·ling
shilly-shally
shim (thin wedge)
shimmed
shim·mer
shim·mered
shim·mer·ing

shim·mery
shim·ming
shin·dy, *plural*
   shindies
shin·er
shin·gle
shin·i·er (shiny)
shin·i·ness
shin·ing (shine)
shinned
shin·ning
shin·ny (game)
shiny (shine)
ship·board
ship·build·er
ship·load
ship·mate
ship·pa·ble
shipped
ship·per
ship·ping
ship·shape
ship·wreck
ship·yard
shirk
shirk·er
shirr (to cook eggs)
shirt·mak·er
shirt-sleeve (*adj*)
shirt sleeves (*noun*)
shirt·tail
shish ke·bab
shiv·a·ree
   (serenade)
shiv·ery
shock ab·sorb·er
shock·head·ed
shock·proof

shock troops
shock wave
shod (*past of* shoe)
shod·di·er
shod·di·ly
shod·di·ness
shod·dy
shoe·horn
shoe·lace
shoe·mak·er
shoe·pac
sho·er
shoe·shine
shoe·string
shoe tree
shooed (shoo)
shoo-in
shoo·ing
shoot-the-chutes
shop·keep·er
shop·lift·er
shopped
shop·per
shop·ping
shop stew·ard
shop·talk
shop·worn
short·cake
short·change (*verb*
   and *adj*)
short·chang·er
short cir·cuit (*noun*)
short-cir·cuit (*verb*)
short·com·ing
short·cut
short·en·ing
short·hand
short-hand·ed

short·horn (cattle)
short-lived
short-or·der (*adj*)
short-range
short shrift
short·sight·ed
short-spo·ken
short·stop
short-tem·pered
short-term (*adj*)
short·wave (*noun* and *adj*)
short-wind·ed
shot put
shot-put·ter
shot-put·ting
shoul·der
shov·el
shov·eled
shov·el·er
shov·el·fuls
shov·el·ing
show·case
show·down (*noun*)
show·i·er
show·i·ly
show·i·ness
show·man
show-me (*adj*)
show·off (*noun*)
show·piece
show·room
show win·dow
shrap·nel
shred·ded
shred·der
shred·ding

shrew
shrewd
shrew·ish
shriek
shrink·able
shriv·el
shriv·eled
shriv·el·ing
shroud
shrub·bery
shrub·bi·er
shrub·bi·ness
shrub·by
shrugged
shrug·ging
shud·der
shud·dery
shuf·fle
shunned
shun·ning
shut·down (*noun*)
shut-in (*noun* and *adj*)
shut·off (*noun*)
shut·out (*noun*)
shut·ter
shut·ting
shut·tle
shy·ly
shy·ness
sib·i·lance
sib·i·lant
sib·ling
sib·yl
sib·yl·line
sic (*verb*)
sick bay

sick·bed
sick call
sicked (sic)
sick·ing (sic)
sick·le
sick leave
sick·le cell ane·mia
sick·room
side (Compound words beginning with *side* are written solid: *sideline*, except as otherwise shown below.)
side arm (weapon)
side·arm (*adj* and *adv*)
side dish
side ef·fect
side-glance
side is·sue
side·ling (sideways, *adj* and *adv*)
side·show
side step (*noun*)
side·step (*verb*)
side street
side·stroke
side·wall (*noun*)
side·ward
side·ways
side-wheel (*adj*)
side whis·kers
si·dle (*verb*)
si·dled
si·dling (*verb*)

siege
si·en·na
si·er·ra
si·es·ta
sieve
sight-read
sight-read·er
sight-read·ing
sight·se·er
sight·see·ing
sig·nal
sig·naled
sig·nal·er
sig·nal·ing
sig·nal·ize
sig·na·to·ry
sig·na·ture
sig·ni·fi·able
sig·nif·i·cance
sig·nif·i·cant
sig·ni·fied
sig·ni·fy
sig·ni·fy·ing
si·lenc·er
sil·hou·ette
sil·i·con (element)
sil·i·cone (chemical
    compound)
sil·i·co·sis
silk·i·ness
silk-stock·ing (*adj*)
silk·worm
si·lo, *plural* silos
sil·ver (Compound
    words beginning
    with *silver* are
    written as

separate words:
silver fox, except
as otherwise
shown below.)
sil·ver·fish
sil·ver-plate (*verb*)
sil·ver·smith
sil·ver-tongued
sil·ver·ware
sim·i·lar
sim·i·lar·i·ty
sim·i·le
si·mil·i·tude
si·mo·nize
si·mon-pure
sim·per
sim·ple-mind·ed
sim·plic·i·ty
sim·pli·fied
sim·pli·fy
sim·pli·fy·ing
sim·plis·tic
sim·u·late
sim·u·la·tor
si·mul·ta·ne·ity
si·mul·ta·neous
sin·cere·ly
sin·cer·i·ty
si·ne·cure
sin·ew
singe
singe·ing
sin·gle-ac·tion
    (*adj*)
sin·gle-breast·ed
sin·gle-en·try (*adj*)
sin·gle file

sin·gle-foot (*noun
    and adj*), *plural*
    single-foots
sin·gle-hand·ed
sin·gle-heart·ed
sin·gle·mind·ed
sin·gle-space (*verb
    and adj*)
sin·gle-track (*adj*)
sin·gle·tree
sin·gu·lar
sin·gu·lar·i·ty
sin·is·ter
sinned
sin·ner
sin·ning
sin·u·ous
si·nus, *plural*
    sinuses
sin·us·i·tis
si·phon
sipped
sip·per
sip·ping
si·ren
si·roc·co, *plural*
    siroccos
sir·ree
sis·si·fied
sis·ter-in-law,
    plural
    sisters-in-law
sit-down (*noun
    and adj*)
site (location)
sit-in (*noun*)
sit·ter

sit·ting
sit-up (*noun*)
si·tus
six-foot·er
six-gun
six-pack
six-shoot·er
six·ti·eth
six·ty-first, etc.
six·ty-one, etc.
siz·able
siz·zle
siz·zler
skein (yarn)
skel·e·ton
skel·e·ton·ize
skep·tic
skep·ti·cal
skep·ti·cism
sketch·book
sketch·i·er
sketch·i·ly
sketch·i·ness
skew (swerve, twist)
skew·er
skew·ered
skid·ded
skid·der
skid·ding
skid·proof
skied
ski·er
ski·ing
ski jump
ski lift
skil·let
skill·ful
skill·ful·ness

skill-less
skimmed
skim·mer
skim·ming
skimp·i·er
skimp·i·ly
skimp·i·ness
skin-deep
skin-dive (*verb*)
skin-dived
skin div·er
skin-div·ing (*verb*)
skin div·ing (*noun*)
skin game
skin graft
skinned
skin·ner
skin·ni·er
skin·ning
skin·ny
skin test
skin·tight
ski·plane
skipped
skip·per
skip·ping
skirl (bagpipes)
skis
skit·ter
skit·tish
skul·dug·gery
sky blue (*noun*)
sky-blue (*adj*)
sky-high
sky·light
sky·line
slab-sid·ed
slake

slam-bang
slammed
slam·ming
slan·der
slan·der·er
slan·der·ous
slang·i·ness
slant·wise
slap·dash
slapped
slap·per
slap·ping
slat·ted
slat·tern
slat·ting
slaugh·ter·house
slave driv·er
slave·hold·er
slav·ery
slave trade
slav·ish
slay·er
slay·ing
slea·zi·er
slea·zi·ness
slea·zy
sled·ded
sled·der
sled·ding
sleek
sleep·i·er
sleep·i·ly
sleep·i·ness
sleepy·head
sleigh
sleight (cunning,
   skill; *see* slight)
sleight of hand

slen·der·ize
sleuth
sli·er (more sly)
sli·est
slight (slender, frail;
   see sleight)
slim·i·er
slim·i·ness (slimy)
slimmed
slim·mer
slim·mest
slim·ming
slimy
slip·case
slip·cov·er
slip·knot
slip·page
slipped
slip·per
slip·per·i·er
slip·per·i·ness
slip·pery
slip·ping
slip ring
slip·sheet (noun
   and verb)
slip·shod
slip stitch
slip-up (noun)
slob·ber
slob·bered
slob·ber·er
slob·ber·ing
sloe-eyed
sloe gin
slo·gan·eer
slo·gan·ize
slogged

slog·ging
slopped
slop·pi·er
slop·pi·ly
slop·pi·ness
slop·ping
slop·py
slot·ted
slot·ting
slough (swamp, to
   get rid of)
slov·en
slov·en·li·ness
slow·down (noun)
slow-mo·tion (adj)
slow-mov·ing
slow·poke
slow-wit·ted
slue (to turn)
slued
slug·gard
slugged
slug·ging
slug·gish
sluice
slum·ber·ous
slum·lord
slummed
slum·ming
slurred
slur·ring
slut·tish
sly·ly
sly·ness
small-mind·ed
small·pox
small-scale (adj)
small talk

small-time (adj)
small-town (adj)
smart al·eck (noun)
smart-al·ecky (adj)
smash·up
smat·ter·ing
smelled (past of
   smell)
smid·gen
smirch (to discolor
   or sully)
smirk (to smile
   complacently)
smit·ten
smog·gi·er
smog·gy
smok·able
smoke·less
smok·i·er
smok·i·ness
smoky
smol·der
smooth-shav·en
smooth-tongued
smor·gas·bord
smudge
smudg·i·er
smudgy
smug·ger (more
   smug)
smug·gest
smug·gle
smug·ness
smut·ti·er
smut·ty
snaf·fle
snagged
snag·ging

snag·gle·tooth
snag·gy
snail-paced
snake·bite
snake dance
snake pit
snake·skin
snaky
snap·back (*noun*)
snap-brim (*adj*)
snap·drag·on
snapped
snap·per
snap·pi·er
snap·pi·ly
snap·ping
snap·pish
snap·py
snap·shot
sneak·i·er
sneak·i·ness
snif·fle
snig·ger
snipped
snip·per
snip·pet
snip·pety
snip·pi·est
snip·pi·ness
snip·ping
snip·py
sniv·el
sniv·eled
sniv·el·er
sniv·el·ing
snob·bery
snob·bish
snob·bism

snoot·i·est
snoot·i·ly
snoot·i·ness
snor·kel
snor·keled
snor·kel·ing
snow (Compound
    words beginning
    with *snow* are
    written solid:
    snowman, except
    as otherwise
    shown below.)
snow-blind
snow blind·ness
snow blow·er
snow fence
snow line
snow pud·ding
snow tire
snow train
snow-white
snubbed
snub·ber
snub·bi·er
snub·bing
snub·by
snub-nosed
snuf·fle
snug·ger
snug·gery
snug·gest
snug·gle
so-and-so, *plural*
    so-and-sos
sobbed
sob·ber
sob·bing

so·ber-mind·ed
so·bri·ety
so·bri·quet
so-called
soc·cer
so·cia·ble
so·cial·ize
so·ci·ety
sock, *plural* socks
sod·ded
sod·den
sod·ding
soft·ball
soft-boiled
soft-cov·er (*adj*)
soft drink
soft goods
soft·head·ed
soft·heart·ed
soft-ped·al (*verb*)
soft-ped·aled
soft-ped·al·ing
soft sell (*noun*)
soft-sell (*adj*)
soft-shell (*adj*)
soft-shoe (*adj*)
soft-soap (*verb*)
soft-spo·ken
soft·ware
sog·gi·er
sog·gi·ness
sog·gy
soi·ree
so·journ
so·journ·er
so·lace
so·lace·ment
so·lac·er

so·lac·ing
so·lar
so·lar·i·um, *plural*
   solaria
sol·der
sol·dier
so·le·cism
sol·emn
so·lem·ni·ty
sol·em·nize
so·lic·it
so·lic·i·tor
so·lic·i·tors
   gen·er·al
so·lic·i·tude
sol·i·dar·i·ty
so·lid·i·fied
so·lid·i·fy
so·lid·i·fy·ing
so·lid·i·ty
sol·id-state (*adj*)
so·lil·o·quize
so·lil·o·quy, *plural*
   soliloquies
sol·i·taire
sol·i·tary
sol·i·tude
so·lo, *plural* solos
so·loed
so·lo·ing
so·lo·ist
sol·stice
sol·u·ble
solv·able
sol·ven·cy
sol·vent
som·ber
som·ber·ness

som·bre·ro, *plural*
   sombreros
som·er·sault
som·nam·bu·lant
som·nam·bu·lism
som·no·lence
som·no·lent
so·nar
so·na·ta
son·ic
son-in-law, *plural*
   sons-in-law
son·net
son·ne·teer
so·nor·i·ty
so·no·rous
soothe
sooth·say·er
soot·i·ness
soph·ist
so·phis·ti·cate
soph·ist·ry
soph·o·more
so·po·rif·ic
sopped
sop·pi·er
sop·ping
sop·py
so·pra·no, *plural*
   sopranos
sor·cer·er
sor·cer·ess
sor·cery
sor·did
so·ror·i·ty
sor·rel
sor·tie, *plural*
   sorties

sor·ti·lege
so-so
sot·tish
sot·to vo·ce
sou·brette
souf·flé
souf·fléed
souf·flé·ing
soul-search·ing
sound ef·fects
sound·ing board
sound·proof
sound track
sound truck
sound wave
source·book
sour·dough
souse
south (direction)
South (section of
   the country)
south·bound
south by east
south by west
south·east
south·east·er·ly
south·east·ern
south·ern
South·ern·er
south·land
south·paw
south pole
south-south·east
south-south·west
south·ward
south·west
South·west·ern·er
sou·ve·nir

239

sov·er·eign
sov·er·eign·ty
sowed (planted
   seed; *see* sewed)
sow·ing
space·craft
space·flight
space heat·er
space·man
space·port
space·ship
space sta·tion
space suit
space·walk
spa·cious
spade·work
spa·ghet·ti
span·gle
span·iel
spanned
span·ner
span·ning
spare·able
spared
spar·ing (spare)
spar·kle
sparred (spar)
spar·ring
spar·row
sparse
spar·si·ty
spasm
spas·mod·ic
spas·tic
spa·tial
spat·ted
spat·ter
spat·ting

spat·u·la
speak·able
speak·easy
spe·cial·ism
spe·cial·ize
spe·cial·ty
spe·cie (coins)
spe·cies (class,
   sing and *plural*)
spec·i·fi·able
spe·ci·fic
spec·i·fic·i·ty
spec·i·fied
spec·i·fy
spec·i·fy·ing
spec·i·men
spe·cious
speck·le
spec·ta·cle
spec·tac·u·lar
spec·ta·tor
spec·ter
spec·tral
spec·trum, *plural*
   spectrums
spec·u·la·tor
speech·i·fied
speech·i·fy
speech·i·fy·ing
speed·i·er
speed·i·ly
speed·i·ness
speed lim·it
speed·om·e·ter
speed trap
speed·up (*noun*)
speed·way
spell·bound

spell·down (*noun*)
spelled (*past of*
   spell)
spe·lunk·er (cave
   explorer)
spe·lunk·ing
spend·able
sperm
spew
spher·i·cal
sphinc·ter
sphinx
spic·i·er
spic·i·ness
spick-and-span
spicy
spied (*past of* spy)
spiel
spiel·er
spig·ot
spiky
spilled (*past of*
   spill)
spill·over
spin·ach
spi·nal
spin·dle
spin·dle-leg·ged
spin·dly
spin·et (musical
   instrument)
spin·na·ker
spin·ner
spin·ner·et
spin·ning
spin-off (*noun*)
spin·ster
spiny

spi·ral

spi·raled

spi·ral·ing

spir·i·tu·al·ism

spir·i·tu·al·ize

spir·i·tu·ous
(containing
alcohol)

spit·ted

spit·ter

spit·ting

spit·tle

spit·toon

splash·down (*noun*)

splat·ter

splay·foot

spleen

splen·dor

splen·dor·ous

sple·net·ic (spleen)

split de·ci·sion

split-lev·el (*adj*)

split sec·ond

split·ting

split-up (*noun*)

splurge

splut·ter

spoil·able

spo·li·a·tion

spong·i·er

spong·i·ness

spongy

spon·sor

spon·ta·ne·ity

spon·ta·ne·ous

spook·i·ness

spoon-fed

spoon-feed

spoon·fuls

spoor (animal track)

spo·rad·ic

spore (reproductive
cell)

sports·wear

sports·writ·er

spot check (*noun*)

spot-check (*verb*)

spot·ta·ble

spot·ted

spot·ter

spot·ti·er

spot·ti·ly

spot·ti·ness

spot·ting

spot·ty

spouse

sprad·dle

sprawl

sprayed

spray·er

spray·ing

spread-ea·gle (*verb*
and *adj*)

spri·er (more spry)

spri·est

spring·board

spring-clean·ing

spring fe·ver

spring·time

springy

sprin·kle

spry·ly

spry·ness

spu·mo·ne (ice
cream)

spu·ri·ous

spurn

spur-of-the-mo·
ment (*adj*)

spurred

spur·ring

spurt

sput·ter

spu·tum

spy·ing

squab·ble

squad·ron

squal·id

squall (storm)

squally

squa·lor

squan·der

square dance (*noun*)

square-dance (*verb*)

square deal

square knot

square-rigged

square-shoul·dered

square-toed

squat·ted

squat·ter

squat·test

squat·ti·er

squat·ting

squat·ty

squawk

squea·mish

squee·gee

squee·geed

squee·gee·ing

squelch

squig·gle

squint-eyed

squire·ar·chy

squirm
squir·rel
squirt
stabbed
stab·ber
stab·bing
sta·bil·i·ty
sta·bil·ize
sta·bi·liz·er
sta·ble
stac·ca·to
sta·di·um, *plural*
  stadiums
  (structure) or
  plural stadia
  (other meanings)
stage·coach
stage·craft
stage fright
stage·hand
stage·man·age
  (*verb*)
stage man·ag·er
stage-struck
stag·ger
stag·gered
stag·ger·er
stag·ger·ing
stag·nan·cy
stag·nant
stagy
staid (*adj*)
stake (piece of
  wood, prize, bet)
stake·out
stalk
stalk·er
stalk·ing-horse

stal·lion
stal·wart
stam·mer
stam·mer·er
stam·pede
stance
stanch (to stop; *see*
  staunch)
stan·chion
stand·ard
stand·ard-bear·er
stand·ard·ize
stand·by, *plural*
  standbys
stand·ee, *plural*
  standees
stand-in (*noun*)
stand·off (*noun*
  and *adj*)
stand·off·ish
stand·out (*noun*)
stand·pat (*adj*)
stand·pat·ter
stand·point
stand·still (*noun*)
stand-up (*adj*)
stan·za
sta·ple
stap·ler
star·board
star-crossed
star·gaz·er
starred
star·ring
star·ry
star·ry-eyed
star·tle
star·tling

sta·sis
stat·able
state aid
state·craft
State De·part·ment
  (U.S.)
state·li·er
state·li·ness
state·ly
state·room
state·side
states' rights
state-wide
stat·ic
sta·tion·ary (fixed,
  not moving)
sta·tion·er
sta·tion·ery
  (writing
  materials)
sta·tis·tic
stat·u·ary
stat·ue
stat·u·esque
stat·u·ette
stat·ure
sta·tus, *plural*
  statuses
stat·u·to·ry
staunch (*adj* sound,
  steadfast; *see*
  stanch)
stay-at-home (*noun*
  and *adj*)
stayed (*past of* stay)
stead
stead·fast
stead·i·er

stead·i·ly
stead·i·ness
steady
stealth·i·er
stealth·i·ly
stealth·i·ness
steam bath
steam·boat
steam boil·er
steam en·gine
steam fit·ter
steam heat
steam·roll·er
steam·ship
steam ta·ble
steel blue (*noun*)
steel-blue (*adj*)
steel gray (*noun*)
steel-gray (*adj*)
steel mill
steel·work·er
stee·ple
stel·lar
stemmed
stem·mer
stem·ming
stem·ware
stem-wind·er
sten·cil
sten·ciled
sten·cil·er
sten·cil·ing
ste·nog·ra·pher
sten·o·type
sten·to·ri·an
step (All compound
    words which
    begin with *step*

and express a
family
relationship are
written solid:
stepson.)
step-by-step (*adj*)
step-down (*noun*
    and *adj*)
step-in (*noun* and
    adj)
step·lad·der
steppe (vast, level
    land area)
stepped
stepped-up (*adj*)
step·per
step·ping
step·ping·stone
step-up (*adj*)
ster·e·o·pho·nic
ster·e·o·type
ster·ile
ster·il·ize
ster·il·iz·er
ster·ling
stern
stet (printing)
steth·o·scope
stet·ted
stet·ting
ste·ve·dore
stew·ard
stew·ard·ess
stewed (cooked)
stick·i·er
stick·i·ness
stick-in-the-mud
stick·ler

stick-to-it·ive·ness
stiff-arm (*noun* and
    verb)
stiff-necked
sti·fle
stig·ma, *plural*
    stigmata (religion)
    or *plural* stigmas
    (all other
    meanings)
stig·ma·tism
stig·ma·tize
sti·let·to, *plural*
    stilettos
still·birth
still·born
still life, *plural*
    still lifes
stim·u·lant
stim·u·la·tor
stim·u·lus, *plural*
    stimuli
stin·gi·er
stin·gi·ness
sti·pend
sti·pen·di·ary
stip·ple
stip·pler
stip·u·late
stip·u·la·tor
stirred
stir·rer
stir·ring
stir·rup
stock·ade
stock·bro·ker
stock ex·change
stock·hold·er

243

stock·i·er
stock·i·ly
stock·i·net
stock in trade
stock·pile
stock·room
stock-still
stock·yard
stodg·i·er
stodg·i·ness
stodgy
sto·gy (cigar)
sto·ical
sto·icism
stol·id
stom·ach
stom·ach·ache
stom·ach·ic
stone-blind
stone-broke
stone·cut·ter
stone-deaf
stone·ma·son
stone·ma·son·ry
stone·ware
stone·work
ston·i·er
stony
stony·heart·ed
stooge
stop·gap
stop·light
stop or·der
stop·over
stop·page
stopped
stop·per
stop·ping

stop·ple
stop street
stop·watch
stor·able
store·front
store·house
store·keep·er
store·room
store·wide
sto·ried (building
    level, famous in
    story)
storm·bound
storm door
storm·i·er
storm·i·ly
storm·i·ness
storm win·dow
sto·ry (level, tale)
sto·ry·book
sto·ry·tell·er
stout·heart·ed
stow·away (*noun*)
stowed
stow·ing
strad·dle
strag·gle
strag·gly
straight-arm
straight·away
straight·edge
straight·en
straight·en·er
straight face (*noun*)
straight-faced (*adj*)
straight·for·ward
straight-line (*adj*)
straight-out (*adj*)

strait (narrow
    passage)
strait·ened
    (distressed)
strait jack·et (*noun*)
strait-jack·et (*verb*)
strait-laced
stran·gle
stran·gu·late
strap·hang·er
strap·less
strap·pa·do, *plural*
    strappadoes
strapped
strap·per
strap·ping
strat·a·gem
stra·te·gic
strat·e·gist
strat·e·gy
strat·i·fied
strat·i·fy
strat·i·fy·ing
strato·sphere
stra·tum, *plural*
    strata
straw boss
straw flow·er
straw-hat (*adj*)
straw man
straw vote
strayed
stray·ing
streak·i·er
streaky
stream·lined
street·car
street·light

summed
sum·ming
sum·mit
sum·mit·ry
sum·mons,
   plural summonses
sump·tu·ary
sump·tu·ous
sun (Compound
   words beginning
   with *sun* are
   written solid:
   sunbaked, except
   as otherwise
   shown below.)
sun bath
sun·bathe
sun·bath·er
sun-cured
sun·dae (ice cream)
sun dance
sun deck
sun·der
sun·der·ance
sun·dog
sun-dried
sun·dries
   (miscellaneous
   items)
sun·dry (various)
sun-god
sun·lamp
sunned
sun·ni·er
sun·ning
sun·ny
sun·ny-side up

sun·tan
sun·tanned
sun·up
su·per (The prefix
   super is joined
   to following
   elements without a
   hyphen.)
su·per·able
su·per·abun·dance
su·per·abun·dant
su·per·an·nu·at·ed
su·perb
su·per·car·goes
su·per·cil·ious
su·per·e·rog·a·
   to·ry
su·per·fi·cial
su·per·flu·ity
su·per·flu·ous
su·per·in·ten·
   dence
su·per·in·ten·dent
su·pe·ri·or
su·pe·ri·or·i·ty
su·per·nu·mer·ary
su·per·sede
su·per·sed·ence
su·per·sti·tious
su·per·vene
su·per·ve·nience
su·per·vise
su·per·vi·sor
su·per·vi·so·ry
su·pine
supped
sup·per

sup·ping
sup·plant
sup·ple
sup·ple·ly
sup·ple·ment
sup·ple·men·ta·ry
sup·pli·ance
sup·pli·ant
sup·pli·cant
sup·pli·ca·tion
sup·plied
sup·pli·er
sup·ply
sup·ply·ing
sup·port·able
sup·por·tive
sup·pos·able
sup·pos·al
sup·po·si·tion·al
sup·pos·i·ti·tious
sup·pos·i·to·ry
sup·press
sup·press·ible
sup·pres·sor
su·prem·a·cy
sur·cease
sur·charge
sure-enough (*adj*)
sure-fire (*adj*)
sure-foot·ed
sur·e·ty
sur·feit
surf·rid·ing
surge (sudden
   increase; *see*
   serge)
sur·geon

Sur·geons
  Gen·er·al
sur·gery
sur·gi·cal
sur·li·er
sur·li·ness
sur·ly
sur·mise
sur·mount·able
sur·name
sur·pass
sur·pass·able
sur·plice (vestment)
sur·plus (extra)
sur·plus·age
sur·prise
sur·re·al·ism
sur·ren·der
sur·rep·ti·tious
sur·rey
sur·ro·gate
sur·round
sur·tax
sur·veil·lance
sur·veil·lant
sur·vey·or
sur·viv·al
sur·vi·vor
sus·cep·ti·ble
sus·pense
sus·pen·sion
sus·pen·so·ry
sus·pi·cious
sus·tain·able
sus·te·nance
su·ture
su·zer·ain

su·zer·ain·ty
swab
swabbed
swab·ber
swab·bing
swad·dle
swagged
swag·ger
swag·ging
swal·lowed
swal·low·ing
swal·low·tail
  (*noun*)
swal·low-tailed
swa·mi
swan dive
swan's-down
swan song
swapped
swap·per
swap·ping
swar·thy
swatch (sample)
swath (long strip,
  cut of a scythe)
swathe (to wrap)
swat·ted
swat·ter
swat·ting
sway·backed (*adj*)
sweat·band
sweat·box
sweat gland
sweat·i·er
sweat shirt
sweat·shop
sweep hand

sweep·stakes
sweet (Compound
  words beginning
  with *sweet* are
  written as
  separate words
  except as
  otherwise shown
  below.)
sweet-and-sour
sweet·bread
sweet·bri·er
sweet·ened
sweet·en·er
sweet·en·ing
sweet·heart
sweet·meat
sweet-talk (*verb*)
swell·head (*noun*)
swell·head·ed (*adj*)
swel·ter
swerve
swigged
swig·ging
swim·ma·ble
swim·ming
swin·dle
swin·dler
swirl
switch·blade knife
switch·board
switch-hit·ter
switch·man
switch·yard
swiv·el
swiv·eled
swiv·el·ing

swiz·zle
syc·a·more
syc·o·phan·cy
syc·o·phant
syl·la·bic
syl·lab·i·cate
syl·lab·i·fy
syl·la·ble
syl·la·bub
syl·la·bus, *plural*
  syllabuses
syl·lo·gism
syl·lo·gize
sylph
sylph·like
syl·van
sym·bol
sym·boled
sym·bol·ing
sym·bol·ize

sym·met·ri·cal
sym·me·try
sym·pa·thet·ic
sym·pa·thize
sym·pa·thy
sym·pho·ny
sym·po·si·um,
  plural
  symposiums
symp·tom
syn·a·gogue
syn·chro·nize
syn·chro·nous
syn·co·pate
syn·co·pa·tor
syn·di·cate
syn·di·ca·tor
syn·drome
syn·er·get·ic

syn·er·gism
syn·er·gis·tic
syn·er·gy
syn·od
syn·o·nym
syn·on·y·mous
syn·op·sis, *plural*
  synopses
syn·tax
syn·the·sis, *plural*
  syntheses
syn·the·size
syn·thet·ic
syph·i·lis
sy·ringe
syr·up
sys·tem
sys·tem·a·tize
syz·y·gy

T

tabbed
tab·bing
tab·er·na·cle
tab·leau, *plural*
   tableaus
ta·ble·cloth
ta·ble d'hôte, *plural*
   tables d'hôte
ta·ble-hopped
ta·ble-hop·per
ta·ble-hop·ping
ta·ble lin·en
ta·ble·spoon·fuls
ta·ble talk
ta·ble·top
ta·ble·ware
ta·boo, *plural*
   taboos
tab·u·lar
tab·u·la·tor
tac·it
tac·i·turn
tack·i·er
tack·i·ness
tack·le
tac·ti·cal
tac·ti·cian
tac·tics

tac·tile
tac·tu·al
taf·fe·ta
tag·board
tag day
tag end
tagged
tag·ger
tag·ging
tail·bone
tail coat
tail end
tail·gate
tail·gat·er
tail·light
tai·lor-made
tai·lor's goose,
   plural tailor's
   gooses
tail·piece
tail·pipe
tail·spin
tail wind
tak·able
take·down (*noun*
   and *adj*)
take-home pay
take-in (*noun*)

take·off (*noun*)
take·out (*noun*
   and *adj*)
take·over (*noun*)
take-up (*noun*)
talc
talcked
talck·ing
tale·tell·er
tal·is·man, *plural*
   talismans
talk·ing-to, *plural*
   talking-tos
tal·lied
tal·low
tal·ly·ing
tal·on
tam·able
ta·ma·le, *plural*
   tamales
tam·bou·rine
tam-o'-shan·ter
tan·dem
tan·gent
tan·gen·tial
tan·ger·ine
tan·gi·ble
tang·i·er

tang·i·ness
tan·gle
tan·go, *plural*
   tangos
tangy
tank·ard
tanned
tan·ner
tan·nery
tan·ning
tan·sy
tan·ta·lize
tan·ta·mount
tan·trum
tap dance (*noun*)
tap-dance (*verb*)
tap-danc·er
tape deck
tape mea·sure
ta·per (candle, to
   decrease)
tape-re·cord (*verb*)
rape re·cord·er
tape re·cord·ing
   (*noun*)
tap·es·try
tape·worm
tap·ing (tape)
tap·i·o·ca
tapped
tap·per
tap·pet
tap·ping
ta·ran·tu·la
tar·di·ly
tar·di·ness
tar·iff
tar·nish·able

tar·pau·lin
tar·ra·gon
tarred
tar·ring
tar·ry (delay,
   covered with tar)
tar·ry·ing
tar·tan (cloth)
tar·tar
tar·tar sauce
tas·sel
tas·seled
tas·sel·ing
tat·ter
tat·tered
tat·ting
tat·tle
tat·tler
tat·tle·tale
tat·too, *plural*
   tattoos
tat·tooed
tat·too·er
tat·too·ing
taunt
taut (tightly drawn,
   tense)
tau·tol·o·gy
taw·dri·er
taw·dri·ness
taw·dry
taw·ni·er
taw·ny
tax·able
tax-de·duct·ible
tax-ex·empt (*adj*)
taxi, *plural* taxis
tax·i·der·my

tax·ied
taxi·ing
teach·able
teach-in
tea·cup·fuls
tea·ket·tle
team·mate
team·work
tear·drop
tear gas (*noun*)
tear-gas (*verb*)
tear-gassed
tear-gas·sing
tear-jerk·er
tear sheet
tea·sel (*noun*
   and *verb*)
tea·seled
tea·sel·ing
tea·spoon·fuls
tech·ni·cal
tech·ni·cian
tech·nique
tech·nol·o·gy
te·dious
te·di·um
teen-age
teen-ag·er
tee·ter-tot·ter
teethe (*verb*)
tee·to·tal·er
tel·e·cast·er
te·leg·ra·pher
te·lep·a·thy
tel·e·print·er
tel·e·vise
tel·e·vis·ing
tel·e·vi·sion

tel·e·vi·sor
tell·able
tell·tale
tem·blor (earth-
    quake; *see*
    trembler)
te·mer·i·ty
tem·pera
tem·per·a·ment
tem·per·ance
tem·per·ate
tem·per·a·ture
tem·pered
tem·pest
tem·plate
tem·ple
tem·po, *plural*
    tempos
tem·po·ral
tem·po·rar·i·ly
tem·po·rary
tem·po·rize
tempt·able
temp·ta·tion
tempt·er
ten·a·ble
te·na·cious
te·nac·i·ty
ten·ant
ten·ant·ry
ten-cent store
ten·den·cy
ten·den·tious
ten·der·foots
ten·der·heart·ed
ten·der·ize
ten·dril
ten·e·ment

te·net (belief)
ten·or (purport,
    male voice,
    tendency)
tense
ten·sile
ten·sion
ten·sor
ten-strike
ten·ta·cle
ten·ta·tive
ten·u·ous
ten·ure (holding)
te·pee
tep·id
ter·cen·te·na·ry
ter·ma·gant
ter·mi·na·ble
ter·mi·nal
ter·mi·na·tor
ter·mi·nol·o·gy
ter·mi·nus, *plural*
    terminuses
ter·race
ter·ra cot·ta
ter·ra fir·ma
ter·rain
ter·ra·pin
ter·rar·i·um, *plural*
    terrariums
ter·res·tri·al
ter·ri·ble
ter·ri·bly
ter·ri·er
ter·ri·fic
ter·ri·fied
ter·ri·fy
ter·ri·fy·ing

ter·ri·to·ri·al
ter·ri·to·ry
ter·ror
ter·ror·ism
ter·ror·ize
terse
terse·ly
ter·ti·ary
test·able
tes·ta·ment
tes·ta·tor
tes·ti·er
tes·ti·fied
tes·ti·fi·er
tes·ti·fy
tes·ti·fy·ing
tes·ti·mo·ni·al
tes·ti·mo·ny
tes·ti·ness
test tube (*noun*)
test-tube (*adj*)
tet·a·nus
tête-à-tête
teth·er
tex·tile
tex·tu·al
tex·ture
T for·ma·tion
thawed
thaw·ing
the·ater
the·ater·go·er
the·at·ri·cal
the·ism
the·mat·ic
thence·forth
the·oc·ra·cy
the·ol·o·gy

the·o·rem
the·o·ret·i·cal
the·o·rize
the·o·ry
ther·a·peu·tic
ther·a·py
there·abouts
there·for (for that)
there·fore
    (consequently)
ther·mal
ther·mom·e·ter
ther·mo·nu·cle·ar
ther·mos
ther·mo·stat
the·sau·rus, *plural*
    thesauri
the·sis, *plural*
    theses
thes·pi·an
thick·en·ing
thick·et
thick·head·ed
thick-skinned
thick-wit·ted
thief, *plural*
    thieves
thiev·ery
thigh·bone
thim·ble·fuls
thing·a·ma·bob
thing·um·a·jig
think·able
thinned
thin·ner
thin·nest
thin·ning
thin·nish

thin-skinned
third base
third-class (*adj*)
third de·gree (*noun*)
third-de·gree (*adj*)
third es·tate
third per·son
third-rate (*adj*)
thirst·i·er
thirst·i·ly
thirst·i·ness
thir·ti·eth
thir·ty-first, etc.
thir·ty-one, etc.
this·tle
thorn·i·er
thor·ough
thor·ough·bred
thor·ough·fare
thor·ough·go·ing
though
thought-out (*adj*)
thou·sand·fold
thrall
thrall·dom
thread·bare
threat·en
threat·ened
threat·en·ing
three (Compound
    words beginning
    with *three* are
    written with a
    hyphen joining
    three to the
    second element:
    three-base hit,
    except as

otherwise shown
    below.)
three·fold
three R's
three·score
three·some
thresh·old
thrift·i·er
thrift·i·ly
thrift·i·ness
throat·i·er
throat·i·ness
throbbed
throb·ber
throb·bing
throe (pang, spasm),
    plural throes
throt·tle
throt·tle·hold
through
through·out
through street
throw·away (*noun*)
throw·back (*noun*)
thrummed
thrum·ming
thru·way
thud·ded
thud·ding
thug·gery
thug·gish
thumb in·dex
    (*noun*)
thumb-in·dex
    (*verb*)
thumb-in·dexed
thumb-marked
thumb·nail

253

thumb·print

thumb·screw

thumb·suck·ing

thumb·tack

thun·der·bolt

thun·der·er

thun·der·show·er

thun·der·storm

thun·der·stroke

thwart

thyme (herb)

thy·roid

ti·ara

tic (muscle spasm)

tick·le

tick·lish

tick·tack

tick-tack-toe

tick·tock

tid·al

tid·dly·winks

tide·land

tide·mark

tide ta·ble

tide wa·ter

tide·way

ti·di·er

ti·di·ly

ti·di·ness

tie·back (noun)

tied

tie-in (noun and
   adj)

tie·pin

tier (a row or series
   of rows)

tie-up (noun)

tight·en·er

tight·fist·ed

tight·fit·ting

tight-lipped

tight-mouthed

tight·rope

til·er

til·ing (tile)

till (all meanings)

till·able

till·age

till·er

tim·bal (drum)

tim·bale (food)

tim·bered

tim·ber·land

tim·ber·line

tim·ber right

tim·bre (quality of
   sound)

time and a half
   (noun)

time bomb

time cap·sule

time·card

time clock

time-con·sum·ing
   (adj)

time de·pos·it

time ex·po·sure

time-hon·ored

time·keep·er

time-lapse (adj)

time·li·er

time lim·it

time·li·ness

time loan

time lock

time-out (noun)

time·piece

time·sav·er

time·sav·ing

time·serv·er

time·shar·ing

time·ta·ble

time-test·ed

time·work

time·worn

time zone

tim·id

tim·ing (time)

tim·or·ous (fearful)

tim·pa·ni

tinc·ture

tinge·ing

tin·gle

ti·ni·er (smaller)

ti·ni·ness

tin·ker's dam

tin·kle

tinned

tin·ner

tin·ni·er

tin·ni·ness

tin·ning

tin·ny

tin plate (noun)

tin-plat·ed

tin·sel

tin·seled

tin·sel·ing

tin·type

tin·ware

tip-off (noun)

tipped

tip·per

tip·pi·er

tip·ping
tip·ple
tip·pler
tip·pling
tip·py
tip·si·ly
tip·si·ness
tip·ster
tip·sy
tip·toed
tip·toe·ing
tip·top
tis·sue
tis·sued
tis·su·ing
tith·able
tithe
tith·ing
tit·il·late
tit·i·vate
ti·tle·hold·er
ti·tle page
ti·tle role
tit·mouse, *plural* titmice
ti·trate
tit·ter
tit·u·lar
T-man
to-and-fro (*adj*)
to·bac·co, *plural* tobaccos
to·bac·co·nist
to·bog·gan
toc·ca·ta
toc·sin
to·day
to-do, *plural* to-dos

toe·cap
toed
toe dance (*noun*)
toe-dance (*verb*)
toe danc·er
toe·hold
toe·ing
toe·nail
tof·fee
togged
tog·gery
tog·ging
tog·gle
toi·let (grooming)
toi·let·ry
toi·lette (style of dress or costume)
to·ken
tol·er·a·ble
tol·er·ance
tol·er·ant
tol·er·a·tor
toll (charge, to ring a bell)
toll·booth
toll bridge
toll call
tolled (bell)
toll·gate
toll·ing
toll road
tom·a·hawk
to·ma·to, *plural* tomatoes
tomb·stone
tom·fool·ery
tom·my·rot

to·mor·row
tom-tom
ton·al
tone-deaf
tone po·em
tong (Chinese association)
tongs (grippers)
tongue
tongue-and-groove
tongued
tongue-lash
tongue-lash·ing
tongue-tied
tongue twist·er
tongue-twist·ing (*adj*)
tongue-ty·ing
tongu·ing
ton·ic
to·night
ton·nage
ton·sil
ton·sil·lar
ton·sil·lec·to·my
ton·sil·li·tis
ton·sure
tool·box
tool·house
tool·mak·er
tool·room
tool sub·ject (school)
tooth and nail (*adv*)
tooth·brush
tooth·i·er
tooth·paste

tooth·pick
tooth pow·der
to·paz
top brass
top·coat
top·dog
top-draw·er (*adj*)
top-dress (*verb*)
top dress·ing (*noun*)
top·er (drinker)
top·flight (*adj*)
top·full
top hat
top-heavy
top·i·cal
top·kick
top·knot
top-lev·el (*adj*)
top·lofty
top·mast
top·most
top-notch (*adj*)
top·notch·er
to·pog·ra·phy
to·pol·o·gy
topped
top·per
top·ping
top·ple
top·pling
top-se·cret (*adj*)
top·soil
top·sy-tur·vy
toque (hat)
to·re·a·dor
tor·men·tor
tor·na·do, *plural*
tornadoes

tor·pe·do, *plural*
torpedoes
tor·pe·doed
tor·pe·do·ing
tor·pid
tor·por
torque
tor·rent
tor·ren·tial
tor·rid
tor·sion
tor·so, *plural* torsos
tort (wrongful act)
torte (cake)
tor·til·la
tor·toise
tor·tu·ous (full of
twists and bends)
tor·tur·ous (torture)
toss·up (*noun*)
to·taled
to·tal·ing
to·tal·i·tar·i·an
to·tal·i·ty
to·tal·i·za·tor
(machine)
to·tal·ize
to·ta·liz·er
to·tem pole
tot·ter
touch-and-go (*adj*)
touch·back (*noun*)
touch·down (*noun*)
touch·stone
touch sys·tem
touch-type
tough·en
tough·en·er

tough-mind·ed
tou·pee
tour de force, *plural*
tours de force
tour·na·ment
tour·ney
tour·ni·quet
tou·sle
tout (tipster, to
praise)
tow·age
to·ward
towed (tow)
tow·eled
tow·el·ing (*noun*
and *verb*)
tow·er (structure,
one who tows, to
stand high)
tow·ered
tow·er·ing
tow·head
tow·head·ed
tow·ing
town clerk
town cri·er
town hall
town meet·ing
town·ship
towns·peo·ple
tow·rope
tow·truck
tox·e·mia
tox·ic
tox·i·col·o·gy
tox·in (poison)
toyed
toy·ing

trace·able

trac·ery

trac·ing

trac·ta·ble

trac·tion

trac·tor

trac·tor-trail·er

trad·able

trade-in (*noun*)

trade-last

trade·mark

trade name

trade se·cret

trades·man

trades·peo·ple

trade union

trade wind

tra·di·tion·al

tra·di·tion·ary

tra·duce

tra·duc·er

traf·fic

traf·ficked

traf·fick·er

traf·fick·ing

tra·ge·di·an (*masc*)

tra·ge·di·enne
  (*fem*)

trag·e·dy

trag·ic

trag·i·cal

train·able

train·ee

train·er

train·man

traipse

trai·tor

trai·tor·ous

trai·tress (*fem*)

tra·jec·to·ry

tram·mel

tram·meled

tram·mel·er

tram·mel·ing

tram·ple

tran(s) (The prefix
  tran(s) is not
  followed by a
  hyphen unless the
  second element
  begins with a
  capital letter:
  *transact, trans-
  American*.)

trance

tran·quil

tran·quil·er

tran·quil·est

tran·quil·ize

tran·quil·iz·er

tran·quil·li·ty

trans·ac·tor

trans·al·pine

trans·at·lan·tic

tran·scend

tran·scen·dence

tran·scen·dent

tran·scen·den·tal

trans·con·ti·nen·
  tal

tran·scribe

tran·scrib·er

tran·sect

tran·sept

trans·fer

trans·fer·able

trans·fer·al

trans·fer·ee

trans·fer·ence

trans·fer·or (law)

trans·ferred

trans·fer·rer

trans·fer·ring

trans·fixed

trans·fix·ing

trans·form·able

trans·form·er

trans·fuse

trans·fus·ible

trans·fu·sion

trans·gres·sion

trans·gres·sor

tran·sience

tran·sient

tran·sis·tor

tran·sis·tor·ize

tran·sit

tran·si·tive

tran·si·to·ry

trans·lat·able

trans·la·tor

trans·lu·cence

trans·lu·cent

trans·mis·si·ble

trans·mit

trans·mit·ta·ble

trans·mit·tal

trans·mit·tance

trans·mit·ted

trans·mit·ter

trans·mit·ting

trans·mut·able

trans·mute

trans·o·ce·an·ic

tran·som
tran·son·ic
trans·pa·cif·ic
trans·par·ence
trans·par·en·cy
trans·par·ent
trans·pire
trans·plant·able
trans·port·able
trans·pos·able
trans·ship
trans·ship·ment
trans·shipped
trans·ship·per
tran·sub·stan·ti·
   a·tion
trans·ver·sal
trans·verse
tra·peze
trapped
trap·per
trap·ping
trap·shoot·ing
trau·ma, *plural*
   traumas
trau·mat·ic
trau·ma·tize
tra·vail (toil)
trav·el agent
trav·eled (*verb* and
   adj)
trav·el·er
trav·el·ing
trav·el·ogue
tra·vers·able
tra·vers·al
tra·verse
trav·er·tine

trav·es·ty
trawl (fishnet)
trawl·er
treach·er·ous
treach·ery
trea·dle
tread·mill
trea·son
trea·son·able
trea·sur·er
trea·sury
treat·able
trea·tise
trea·ty
tre·ble
treed
tree house
tree·ing
tree·top
trek
trekked
trek·ker
trek·king
trel·lis
trem·ble
trem·bler (one that
   trembles; *see*
   temblor)
tre·men·dous
trem·o·lo, *plural*
   tremolos
trem·or
trem·u·lous
tren·chan·cy
tren·chant
tren·cher·man
trench mouth
trep·i·da·tion

tres·pass·er
tres·tle
tri·able
tri·ad
tri·al bal·ance
tri·al run
tri·an·gu·lar
trib·al
trib·u·la·tion
tri·bu·nal
trib·u·tary
trib·ute
trice
trick·ery
trick·i·er
trick·i·ness
trick·le
trick·ster
tri·corn
tri·cy·cle
tried (try)
tri·en·ni·al
tri·en·ni·um, *plural*
   trienniums
tri·er
tri·fle
tri·fling
tri·fo·cal
trig·ger fin·ger
trig·ger-hap·py
trig·o·nom·e·try
trill
tril·o·gy
tri·mes·ter
trimmed
trim·mer
trim ·mest
trim·ming

trim·ness
tri·month·ly
trin·ket
trio, *plural* trios
tri·par·tite
trip-ham·mer
tri·ple
tri·ple-space (*verb*)
tri·ple threat (*noun*)
trip·li·cate
tripped
trip·per
trip·ping
trip·tych
tri·um·phal
tri·um·phant
triv·et
triv·i·al
triv·i·al·i·ty
tri·week·ly
trod·den
trog·lo·dyte
troi·ka
troll (to sing, to fish, a giant or dwarf of fable)
trol·ley, *plural* trolleys
trol·ley bus
trol·lop
tro·phy
trop·i·cal
tro·pism
trot·ted
trot·ter
trot·ting
trou·ba·dour
trou·ble-free (*adj*)

trou·ble·mak·er
trou·ble-shoot·er
trou·ble-shoot·ing
trou·ble·some
trou·blous
trough (receptacle or drain for water)
trounce
troupe (group of actors, singers, etc.)
troup·er
trous·seau, *plural* trousseaus
trow·el
trow·eled
trow·el·ing
tru·an·cy
tru·ant
truck·driv·er
truck farm
truck·le
truck·load
truck trail·er
truc·u·lence
truc·u·lent
true bill
true-blue (*adj*)
true·born
treu·bred
true-false (*adj*)
true·heart·ed
true-life (*adj*)
true·love
true·ness
tru·ing
tru·ism
tru·ly

trumped-up (*adj*)
trump·ery
trum·pet·er
trun·cate
trun·cheon
trun·dle bed
trunk line
trust ac·count
trust com·pa·ny
trust·ee (manager)
trust fund
trust·i·ness
trust·wor·thi·ness
trusty (convict)
truth·ful·ness
try·ing
try-on (*noun*)
try·out (*noun*)
tryst
T-shirt
T square
tub·ba·ble
tubbed
tub·bi·er
tub·bing
tub·by
tu·ber (plant)
tu·ber·cu·lar
tu·ber·cu·lo·sis
tu·ber·ous
tub·ing
tu·bu·lar
tu·bule
Tues·day
tuf·fet
tugged
tug·ger
tug·ging

tug of war
tu·ition
tu·la·re·mia
tulle
tum·ble·down
tum·bler
tum·brel
tu·mes·cence
tu·mes·cent
tu·mor
tu·mor·ous
tu·mul·tu·ary
tu·mul·tu·ous
tun·able
tun·dra
tune-up (*noun*)
tung·sten
tu·nic
tun·nel
tun·neled
tun·nel·er
tun·nel·ing
tur·ban
tur·baned
tur·bid
tur·bo·fan
tur·bo·jet
tur·bo·prop
tur·bot
tur·bu·lence
tur·bu·lent
turf, *plural* turfs
tur·gid
tur·gor
tur·mer·ic
tur·moil
turn·about

turn·around
turn·down (*noun and adj*)
tur·nip
turn·key
turn·off (*noun*)
turn·out (*noun*)
turn·over (*noun*)
turn·ta·ble
tur·pen·tine
tur·pi·tude
tur·quoise
tur·ret
tur·ret·ed
tur·tle·back (*noun*)
tur·tle-backed (*adj*)
tur·tle·dove
tur·tle·neck
tus·sle
tu·te·lage
tu·te·lary
tu·tor
tu·to·ri·al
tut·ti-frut·ti
tux·e·do, *plural* tuxedos
twad·dle
twanged
twang·ing
tweak
tweed (woolen)
twee·zers
twelfth
twelve-tone (*adj*)
twen·ti·eth
twen·ty-first, etc.
twen·ty·ish

twen·ty-one, etc.
twen·ty-twen·ty (*adj*)
twice-baked
twice-laid
twice-told
twid·dle
twigged
twig·ging
twin bill
twin-en·gine
twing·ing (twinge)
twi·night (*adj*)
twin·ing (twine)
twin·kle
twinned
twin·ning
twin-screw
twirl
twit·ted
twit·ter
twit·ter·er
twit·tery
twit·ting
two, *plural* twos
two (In compound words beginning with *two*, the *two* is joined by a hyphen to the second element: *two-faced*, except as otherwise shown below.)
two-a-day (*adj*)
two-bit (*adj*)
two bits

260

two-by-four
two·fold
two·pen·ny
two·score
two·some
ty·coon
ty·ing (tie)
tyke (child)
typ·able

type·script
ty·phoid
ty·phoon
ty·phus
typ·i·cal
typ·i·fied
typ·i·fy
typ·i·fy·ing
typ·ist

ty·pog·ra·phy
ty·ran·ni·cal
ty·ran·ni·cide
tyr·an·nize
tyr·an·nous
tyr·an·ny
ty·rant
ty·ro, *plural* tyros

U

ubiq·ui·tous
ubiq·ui·ty
ug·li·er
ug·li·fied
ug·li·fy
ug·li·fy·ing
ug·li·ness
ukase
uku·le·le
ul·cer
ul·cer·ous
ul·te·ri·or
ul·ti·ma·tum,
   plural ultimatums
ul·tra·mod·ern
ul·tra·son·ic
ul·tra·vi·o·let
um·ber
um·bil·i·cal
um·bil·i·cus
um·brage
um·bra·geous
um·brel·la
un (The prefix *un* is
   not followed by a
   hyphen unless the
   second element
   begins with a

capital letter:
unfit,
un-American.)
un·abat·ed
un·ac·cent·ed
un·ac·cept·able
un·ac·com·pa·nied
un·ac·count·able
un·ac·count·ed
un·ac·count·ed-for
   (*adj*)
un·ac·cus·tomed
un·af·fect·ed
un·aligned
un·al·loyed
un·al·ter·able
una·nim·i·ty
unan·i·mous
un·an·nounced
un·an·swer·able
un·ap·peas·able
un·ap·proach·able
un·ap·proved
un·as·sail·able
un·as·sum·ing
un·at·tached
un·at·tain·able
un·at·tend·ed

un·avail·able
un·avoid·able
un·aware (*adj*)
un·awares (*adv*)
un·barred
un·bar·ring
un·bear·able
un·beat·able
un·be·liev·able
un·bi·ased
un·bid·den
un·blessed
un·bos·om
un·break·able
un·bridge·able
un·bri·dled
un·called-for (*adj*)
un·can·ny
un·capped
un·cap·ping
un·cared-for (*adj*)
un·ceas·ing
un·cer·e·mo·ni·
   ous
un·chal·lenged
un·change·able
un·char·i·ta·ble
un·chris·tian

un·clas·si·fied
un·col·lect·ible
un·com·fort·able
un·com·mit·ted
un·com·mu·ni·
　ca·tive
un·com·pli·men·
　ta·ry
un·con·cerned
un·con·quer·able
un·con·scio·na·ble
un·con·scious
un·con·sti·tu·
　tion·al
un·con·trol·la·ble
un·couth
un·crit·i·cal
unc·tion
unc·tu·ous
un·daunt·ed
un·de·ceived
un·de·ni·able
un·der (Words
　beginning with
　under are written
　solid: *underfed*.)
un·der·achiev·er
un·der·bid·ding
un·der·class·man
un·der·cut·ting
un·der·ling
un·der·ly·ing
un·der·pinned
un·der·pin·ning
un·der·priv·i·leged
un·der·propped
un·der·prop·ping
un·der·rate

un·der·run
un·der·sized
un·der·stand·able
un·der-the-count·er
　(*adj*)
un·der-the-ta·ble
　(*adj*)
un·de·sir·able
un·de·ter·min·able
un·dif·fer·en·ti·
　at·ed
un·dis·ci·plined
un·dis·cov·er·able
un·dis·guised
un·doubt·ed
un·drink·able
un·due
un·du·lant
un·du·late
un·du·la·to·ry
un·du·ly
un·dy·ing
un·eas·i·er
un·eas·i·ly
un·eas·i·ness
un·eat·able
un·em·ploy·able
un·en·dur·able
un·en·force·able
un·equaled
un·equal·ly
un·equiv·o·cal
un·ex·cep·tion·
　able
un·ex·plain·able
un·fa·mil·iar
un·fash·ion·able
un·fa·vor·able

un·feigned
un·fet·tered
un·fit·ness
un·fit·ted
un·fit·ting
un·flap·pa·ble
un·fore·see·able
un·for·get·ta·ble
un·for·giv·able
un·friend·li·ness
un·friend·ly
un·furl
un·gov·ern·able
un·gra·cious
un·gram·mat·i·cal
un·guent
un·hal·lowed
un·hap·pi·est
un·hap·pi·ly
un·hap·pi·ness
un·health·i·ness
un·heard-of (*adj*)
un·hoped-for (*adj*)
un·hy·gi·en·ic
uni·fi·able
uni·fied
uni·form·i·ty
uni·fy
uni·fy·ing
uni·lat·er·al
un·imag·in·able
un·im·peach·able
un·in·hab·it·able
un·in·hib·it·ed
un·in·tel·li·gent
un·in·tel·li·gi·ble
un·in·ter·rupt·ed
union·ize

unique
uni·son
uni·tary
uni·ty
uni·verse
un·jus·ti·fi·able
un·ken·neled
un·knot·ted
un·knot·ting
un·know·able
Un·known Sol·dier
un·li·censed
un·lik·able
un·like·li·est
un·like·li·ness
un·like·ly
un·lim·ber
un·liv·able
un·looked-for
un·lov·able
un·mail·able
un·man·age·able
un·manned
un·man·ner·ly
un·man·ning
un·mar·ket·able
un·men·tion·able
un·mis·tak·able
un·mit·i·gat·ed
un·mort·gaged
un·mov·able
un·muz·zle
un·nam·able
un·nat·u·ral
un·nec·es·sary
un·nerve
un·num·bered
un·ob·jec·tion·able

un·oc·cu·pied
un·of·fi·cial
un·os·ten·ta·tious
un·par·al·leled
un·par·don·able
un·par·lia·men·
    ta·ry
un·pas·teur·ized
un·per·ceived
un·per·suad·able
un·per·turbed
un·pinned
un·pin·ning
un·pop·u·lar
un·prac·ti·cal
un·prec·e·dent·ed
un·pre·dict·able
un·prej·u·diced
un·pre·pos·sess·
    ing
un·pre·sent·able
un·pre·ten·tious
un·prin·ci·pled
un·print·able
un·frof·it·able
un·pro·nounce·
    able
un·pro·pi·tious
un·qual·i·fied
un·quench·able
un·ques·tion·able
un·rav·el
un·rav·eled
un·rav·el·ing
un·read·able
un·read·i·ness
un·rea·son·able
un·re·gen·er·ate

un·re·li·able
un·re·lieved
un·re·mit·ting
un·re·turn·able
un·rhymed
un·righ·teous
un·ri·valed
un·roll
un·ruly
un·sad·dle
un·sal·able
un·sa·vory
un·sched·uled
un·sea·son·able
un·seem·ly
un·ser·vice·able
un·set·tled
un·shak·able
un·shrink·able
un·sink·able
un·skill·ful
un·snapped
un·snap·ping
un·so·cia·ble
un·solv·able
un·so·phis·ti·
    cat·ed
un·speak·able
un·spe·cial·ized
un·spec·i·fied
un·stop·pa·ble
un·stopped
un·stop·ping
un·strapped
un·strap·ping
un·sub·stan·tial
un·suc·cess·ful
un·suit·able

un·sur·pass·able
un·sus·pi·cious
un·sym·met·ri·cal
un·tam·able
un·teach·able
un·ten·a·ble
un·think·able
un·ti·di·ness
un·til
un·touch·able
un·trace·able
un·tram·meled
un·trav·eled
un·tu·tored
un·ty·ing
un·u·su·al
un·ut·ter·able
un·war·rant·able
un·war·rant·ed
un·wary
un·wear·able
un·wea·ried
un·wield·i·ness
un·wieldy
un·wit·nessed
un·wit·ting
un·world·li·ness
un·wor·thi·ly
un·wor·thi·ness
un·wrapped
un·wrap·ping
un·writ·ten
un·yield·ing

un·zipped
un·zip·ping
up (Compound
   words beginning
   with *up* are
   written solid:
   uphill, except
   as otherwise
   shown below.)
up-and-com·ing
up-and-down (*adj*)
up-bow (*noun*)
up·coun·try
up·heav·al
up·hol·ster·er
up·hol·stery
up·per case (*noun*)
up·per-case (*adj*)
up·per class (*noun*)
up·per-class (*adj*)
up·per·class·man
up·per crust
up·per·cut
up·per hand (*noun*)
up·per·most
up·pish
up·pi·ty
up·roar·i·ous
ups and downs
up·set price
up·set·ting
up·side down (*adv*)
up·side-down (*adj*)

up·take (*noun*)
up-to-date (*adj*)
up·ward
ura·ni·um
ur·bane
ur·ban·i·ty
ur·ban·ize
ur·chin
ure·ter
ur·gen·cy
ur·gent
uri·nal
uri·nary
urine
urn (vase; *see* erne)
us·able
us·age
us·ance
usu·al
usu·rer
usu·ri·ous
usurp
usurp·er
usu·ry
uten·sil
uter·ine
uter·us
utile
util·i·ty
uti·lize
ut·ter·able
ut·ter·ance
ux·o·ri·ous

V

va·can·cy
va·cant
va·cate
va·ca·tion·er
vac·ci·nate
vac·ci·na·tor
vac·cine
vac·il·late
vac·il·la·tor
va·cu·ity
vac·u·ous
vac·u·um, *plural*
  vacuums
vac·u·um-packed
vag·a·bond
va·ga·ry
va·gran·cy
va·grant
vague
vain·glo·ry
va·lance (drapery)
val·e·dic·to·ri·an
val·e·dic·to·ry
va·lence
  (chemistry)
va·let
val·iance
val·iant
val·id

val·i·date
val·id·i·ty
va·lise
val·ley, *plural*
  valleys
val·or
val·u·able
val·u·a·tion
val·u·a·tor
val·ue
val·ued
val·ue·less
val·u·er
val·u·ing
van·dal
van·dal·ize
vane (device to
  show wind
  direction)
van·guard
va·nil·la
van·i·ty
van·quish·able
van·quish·er
va·pid
va·por
va·por·ize
va·por·iz·er
va·por·ous

var·i·able
var·i·ance
var·i·ant
var·i·a·tion
var·i·cose
var·ied
var·ie·gat·ed
va·ri·etal
va·ri·ety
var·i·ous
var·mint
var·si·ty
vary·ing
vas·cu·lar
Vas·e·line
  (trademark)
vas·sal
vas·ti·tude
vat·ted
vat·ting
vaude·ville
vault
vaunt
vaunt·er
V-Day
vec·tor
veer (to change
  course)
veg·e·ta·ble

veg·e·tar·i·an
veg·e·tate
ve·he·mence
ve·he·ment
ve·hi·cle
ve·hic·u·lar
vein (blood vessel)
veined
ve·loc·i·pede
ve·loc·i·ty
ve·lour
vel·vet
vel·ve·teen
ve·nal
ve·nal·i·ty
vend·ee (buyer)
ven·det·ta
vend·ible
ven·dor (seller)
ve·neer
ven·er·a·ble
ven·er·ate
ven·er·a·tor
ve·ne·re·al
ven·ery
ven·geance
venge·ful
ve·ni·al
ven·i·son
ven·om
ven·om·ous
ve·nous (veins)
ven·ti·late
ven·ti·la·tor
ven·tri·cle
ven·tril·o·quist
ven·tril·o·quize
ven·tril·o·quy

ven·ture·some
ven·tur·ous
ven·ue
ve·ra·cious
ve·rac·i·ty
ve·ran·da
ver·bal
ver·bal·ize
ver·ba·tim
ver·bi·age
ver·bose
ver·bos·i·ty
ver·dan·cy
ver·dant
ver·dict
ver·di·gris
ver·dure
verge
ver·i·est
ver·i·fi·able
ver·i·fied
ver·i·fi·er
ver·i·fy
ver·i·fy·ing
ver·i·ly
ver·i·si·mil·i·tude
ver·i·ta·ble
ver·i·ty
ver·mi·cel·li
ver·mi·cide
ver·mil·ion
ver·min
ver·nac·u·lar
ver·nal
ver·sa·tile
ver·si·fied
ver·si·fi·er
ver·si·fy

ver·si·fy·ing
ver·sus
ver·te·bra, *plural*
  vertebras
ver·te·brate
ver·ti·cal
ver·tig·i·nous
ver·ti·go, *plural*
  vertigoes
ves·i·cal (*adj*)
ves·i·cle (*noun*)
ve·sic·u·lar
ves·per
ves·sel
ves·tib·u·lar
ves·ti·bule
ves·tige
ves·ti·gial
vest-pock·et (*adj*)
ves·try·man
vet·er·an
vet·er·i·nar·ian
vet·er·i·nary
ve·to, *plural* vetoes
ve·toed
ve·to·er
ve·to·ing
vet·ted
vet·ting
vex·a·tion
vexed
vex·ing
vi·a·ble
via·duct
vi·al (bottle)
vi·aled
vi·al·ing
vi·and

vi·bran·cy
vi·brant
vi·bra·to, *plural*
   vibratos
vi·bra·tor
vi·bra·to·ry
vic·ar
vi·car·age
vi·car·i·ous
vice ad·mi·ral
vice-chair·man
vice chan·cel·lor
vice-con·sul
vice-con·sul·ship
vice-pres·i·den·cy
Vice Pres·i·dent
   (U.S.)
vice pres·i·dent
vice-re·gent
vice·roy
vice squad
vice ver·sa
vi·chy·ssoise
vi·cin·i·ty
vi·cious
vi·cis·si·tude
vic·tim
vic·tim·ize
vic·tor
vic·to·ri·ous
vict·ual
vict·ualed
vict·ual·er
vict·ual·ing
vid·eo
vie
vied
vi·er

view·point
vig·il
vig·i·lance
vig·i·lant
vig·i·lan·te
   (member of a
   vigilance
   committee)
vig·i·lan·tism
vi·gnette
vig·or
vil·i·fied
vil·i·fi·er
vil·i·fy
vil·i·fy·ing
vil·lag·er
vil·lain (bad man)
vil·lein (feudal
   class)
vin·ci·ble
vin·di·ca·ble
vin·di·ca·tor
vin·di·ca·to·ry
vin·dic·tive
vin·e·gar
vin·e·gary
vin·ery
vine·yard
vin·tage
vint·ner
vi·nyl
vi·ol (music)
vi·o·la·ble
vi·o·la·tor
vi·o·lence
vi·o·lent
vi·o·let
vi·o·lon·cel·lo

vi·per
vi·per·ous
vi·ra·go, *plural*
   viragoes
vi·ral (virus)
vir·eo
vir·gin·al
vir·gin·i·ty
vir·ile (masculine)
vi·ril·i·ty
vir·tu·al
vir·tue
vir·tu·os·i·ty
vir·tu·o·so, *plural*
   virtuosos
vir·tu·ous
vir·u·lence
vir·u·lent
vi·rus
vi·sa
vi·saed
vis·age
vi·sa·ing
vis-à-vis
vis·cera
vis·cid
vis·cose (*noun*)
vis·cos·i·ty
vis·count
vis·cous (*adj*)
vis·i·ble
vi·sion·ary
vis·i·tant
vis·i·tor
vi·sor
vis·ta
vis·taed
vi·su·al

vi·su·al·ize
vi·su·al·iz·er
vi·tal
vi·tal·i·ty
vi·tal·ize
vi·ta·min
vi·ti·ate
vi·ti·a·tor
vit·re·ous
vit·ri·fied
vit·ri·fy
vit·ri·fy·ing
vit·ri·ol
vit·ri·ol·ic
vi·tu·per·ate
vi·tu·per·a·tor
vi·va·cious
vi·vac·i·ty
viv·id
viv·i·sec·tion
vix·en
vi·zier
vo·cab·u·lary
vo·cal·ize
vo·cal·iz·er
vo·ca·tion
vo·cif·er·ant

vo·cif·er·ate
vo·cif·er·ous
vogue
vogu·ish
void·able
void·ance
vol·a·tile
vol·ca·no, *plural*
  volcanoes
vo·li·tion
vol·ley, *plural*
  volleys
vol·ley·ball
vol·leyed
vol·ley·ing
vol·u·ble
vo·lu·mi·nous
vol·un·tar·ism
  (principle of
  relying on
  voluntary action)
vol·un·tary
vol·un·tary·ism
  (doctrine that
  schools and
  churches be

supported by
voluntary
contributions)
vol·un·teer
vo·lup·tu·ary
vo·lup·tu·ous
voo·doo
voo·doo·ism
vo·ra·cious
vo·rac·i·ty
  (greediness)
vor·tex, *plural*
  vortices
vot·able
vo·ta·ry
vouch·er
vow·el
voy·a·geur
voy·eur
vul·can·ize
vul·gar
vul·gar·i·an
vul·gar·ism
vul·gar·ize
vul·ner·a·ble
vy·ing (vie)

W

wad·ded
wad·der
wad·ding
wad·dle
waf·fle
waft (to float)
wage earn·er
wage lev·el
wa·ger
wa·ger·er
wage scale
wagged
wag·ger
wag·gery
wag·ging
wag·gish
wag·gle
wag·on·load
wag·on train
waif
wail (lament)
wain·scot·ed
wain·scot·ing
   (noun)
waist·band
waist·coat
waist-deep (adj)
waist-high (adj)

waist·line
wait·ress
waive (to give up)
waiv·er (act of
   giving up; see
   waver)
walk·away
walk-in (noun and
   adj)
walk-on (noun and
   adj)
walk·out (noun)
walk·over
walk-through (noun)
walk-up (noun and
   adj)
wall·board
walled-in
walled-up
wal·let
wall·eye
wall·eyed (adj)
wall·flow·er
wal·lop
wal·low
wall·pa·per
wall plug
wall-to-wall (adj)

wal·rus
wam·ble
wan (pale)
wan·der·er
wane (decrease)
wan·gle
wan·ing
wan·ner
wan·ness
want ad
wan·ton
wan·ton·ness
wany (wane)
war·ble
war chest
war crime
war cry
war dance
war·den
ward·er
ward·robe
war·head
war-horse
war·i·er
war·i·ly
war·i·ness
warm-blood·ed
warmed-over

warm front
warm·heart·ed
warm·heart·ed·
   ness
warm-up (*noun* and
   adj)
warp
war·path
war·plane
war·rant
war·rant·able
war·ran·tee
   (person)
war·ran·tor
war·ran·ty
   (guarantee)
warred
war·ren
war·ring
war·ri·or
war·time
war-wea·ry
wary (cautious)
wash (Compound
   words beginning
   with *wash* are
   written solid:
   washday, except
   as otherwise
   shown below.)
wash·able
wash-and-wear
wash draw·ing
washed-out (*adj*)
washed-up (*adj*)
wash·out
wash sale
was·sail

wast·age
waste·bas·ket
waste·land
waste·pa·per
waste pipe
waste prod·uct
wast·rel
watch·band
watch·case
watch chain
watch·dog
watch guard
watch·mak·er
watch·man
watch pock·et
watch·tow·er
watch·word
wa·ter (A majority
   of compound
   words beginning
   with *water* are
   written as
   separate words:
   water lily. Those
   written otherwise
   are shown below.)
wa·ter·borne
wa·ter·col·or
wa·ter-cool (*verb*)
wa·ter-cooled (*adj*)
wa·ter·course
wa·ter·craft
wa·ter·cress
wa·ter·fall
wa·ter-fast
wa·ter·fowl
wa·ter·front
wa·ter·less

wa·ter·line
wa·ter·logged
wa·ter·mark
wa·ter·mel·on
wa·ter·pow·er
wa·ter·proof
wa·ter-re·pel·lent
wa·ter-re·sis·tant
wa·ter·scape
wa·ter·shed
wa·ter·side
wa·ter-ski (*verb*)
wa·ter-skied
wa·ter-ski·er
wa·ter-ski·ing
wa·ter-soak (*verb*)
wa·ter-sol·u·ble
wa·ter·spout
wa·ter·tight
wa·ter·way
wa·ter·works
wa·ter·worn
watt (unit of
   electrical power)
watt·age
wat·tle
wave·length
wa·ver (to show
   doubt, falter;
   see waiver)
wa·ver·er
wav·i·er
wav·i·ness
wavy
waxed
wax·i·ness
wax pa·per
wax·work

waxy
way·bill
way·far·er
way·laid
way·lay
way·lay·ing
way-out (*adj*)
ways and means
way·side
way·ward
weak·en·ing
weak-kneed
weak·ling
weak-mind·ed
wealth·i·er
wealth·i·ness
wean (to withdraw)
weap·on·eer
weap·on·ry
wear·able
wear and tear
wear·ri·er
wea·ri·less
wea·ri·ly
wea·ri·ness
wea·ri·some
wea·ry
wea·sel
weath·er-beat·en
weath·er-bound
weath·er·cock
weath·ered
weath·er·man
weath·er map
weath·er·proof
weath·er strip
  (*noun*)

weath·er-strip
  (*verb*)
weath·er-stripped
weath·er strip·ping
  (*noun*)
weath·er·tight
weath·er vane
weath·er-wise
weath·er·worn
webbed
web·bing
web·by
web·foot
web-foot·ed
wed·ded
wed·ding
wedge
Wednes·day
week·day
week·end
weep·i·er
weep·i·ness
we·er
we·est
wee·vil
wee·viled
wee·vily
wei·ge·la (flower)
weigh
weight·i·er
weight·i·ly
weight·i·ness
weight lift·ing
weird
weld·er
wel·fare
wel·kin

well (Compound
  words beginning
  with *well* are
  written with a
  hyphen joining
  well to the second
  element: *well-
  being*, except as
  otherwise shown
  below.)
well·born
well·do·ing
well·head
well·spring
well-thought-of (*adj*)
well-to-do (*adj*)
well-wish·er
were·wolf
west by north
west by south
West·ern·er
west·ern·ize
west-north·west
west-south·west
west·ward
wet blan·ket
wet-bulb
wet cell
wet·land
wet-nurse (*verb*)
wet nurse (*noun*)
wet·ta·ble
wet·ted
wet·ter
wet·test
wet·ting
wet·tish

wet wash
whale·back
whale·boat
whale·bone
whammed
wham·ming
wharf, *plural*
   wharves
wheat bread
wheat cake
wheat germ
whee·dle
wheel·bar·row
wheel·base
wheel·chair
wheel·horse
wheeze
wheez·i·er
wheez·i·ly
wheezy
where·abouts
where·as
where·in
where·of
where·up·on
where·with·al
whet·stone
whet·ted
whet·ting
whim
whim·si·cal
whim·sy, *plural*
   whimsies
whin·ny (horse)
whiny (whine)
whip·cord
whip hand

whip·lash
whipped
whip·per
whip·ping
whip·poor·will
whip·saw
whip·stitch
whir
whirl·pool
whirl·wind
whirred
whir·ring
whis·key (bourbon,
   rye, and Irish)
whis·ky (Canadian
   and Scotch)
whis·tler
whis·tle stop (*noun*)
whis·tle-stop (*verb*)
white·bait
white·cap
white-col·lar (*adj*)
whit·ed sep·ul·cher
white-faced
white·fish
white-haired
white heat
white-hot
whit·en·er
whit·en·ing
white sale
white·wall (*noun*
   and *adj*)
white·wash
whit·tle
whiz, *plural* whizzes
whizzed

whiz·zer
whiz·zing
whole blood
whole·heart·ed
whole milk
whole·sale
whole-souled
whol·ly
whopped
whop·per
whop·ping
whore
whorl (fingerprint)
whose·so·ev·er
whos·ev·er
wick·et
wide-an·gle (*adj*)
wide-awake (*adj*)
wide-eyed (*adj*)
wide·mouthed
wide-open (*adj*)
wide·spread
wide-spread·ing
wid·get
wield
wigged
wig·gle
wig·gler
wig·gly
wig·wag
wig·wagged
wig·wag·ging
wild·cat
wild·cat·ter
wild·cat·ting
wild-eyed
wild·fire

wild flow·er
wild·fowl
wild-goose chase
wild land
wild·life
wild pitch
wild·wood
wile
wil·i·er
will·ful
will-o'-the-wisp
wil·low
will·pow·er
wil·ly-nil·ly
wily
wim·ple
wince (flinch)
wind·blown
wind-borne
wind-bro·ken
wind·burn
wind gauge
wind·i·er
wind·i·ness
wind·ing sheet
wind in·stru·ment
wind·jam·mer
wind·lass
win·dow box
win·dow-dress
   (verb)
win·dow dress·er
win·dow dress·ing
   (noun)
win·dow-dress·ing
   (verb)

win·dow en·ve·
   lope
win·dow·pane
win·dow seat
win·dow shade
win·dow-shop
   (verb)
win·dow-shop·per
win·dow-shop·ping
win·dow·sill
wind·pipe
wind·shield
wind·storm
wind·swept
wind tun·nel
wind·up (noun and
   adj)
wine cel·lar
wine-col·ored
wine cool·er
wine·glass
wine·grow·er
wine·shop
wine tast·er
wing·back
wing chair
wing col·lar
wing-foot·ed
wing·span
wing·spread
wing tip
win·na·ble
win·ner
win·ning
win·now
win·now·er

win·some
win·ter·feed
win·ter·ize
win·ter·kill (noun
   and verb)
win·tri·er
win·tri·ness
win·try
winy (wine)
wire cloth
wire·hair
wire-haired
wire pull·er
wire ser·vice
wire·tap
wire·tap·per
wire·tap·ping
wiry
wis·dom
wise·acre
wishy-washy
wis·te·ria
witch·craft
witch doc·tor
witch ha·zel
witch hunt
witch hunt·er
with·al
with·draw·al
with·ered
with·er·ing
with·hold
wit·ness stand
wit·ti·cism
wit·ti·er
wit·ti·ly

wit·ti·ness
wit·ty
wiz·ard
wiz·ard·ry
wiz·ened
wob·ble
wob·bly
woe·be·gone
woe·ful
wolf, *plural* wolves
wol·ver·ine
won·der·land
won·der-struck
won·der·work·er
won·drous
wood block (*noun*)
wood-block (*adj*)
wood·carv·er
wood pulp
wood screw
wood·sy
wood·turn·er
wood·turn·ing
wood·wind
wood·work
wooed
woo·er
woof (weaving)
woo·ing
wool·en
wool·gath·er·er
wool·gath·er·ing
wool·grow·er
wool·ly
wool·ly-head·ed
wooz·i·er

wooz·i·ly
wooz·i·ness
woozy
word·book
word class
word for word (*adv*)
word-for-word (*adj*)
word·i·est
word·i·ly
word·i·ness
word of mouth
    (*noun*)
word-of-mouth (*adj*)
word·play
work (Compound
    words beginning
    with *work* are
    written solid:
    workload, except
    as otherwise
    shown below.)
work·able
work camp
work·day (*noun* and
    adj)
worked-up (*adj*)
work farm
work force
work·ing class
    (*noun*)
work·ing-class (*adj*)
work·ing day
work·ing·man
work sheet
work stop·page
world-beat·er

world·li·ness
world·ly-mind·ed
world·ly-wise
world pow·er
World Se·ries
world-shak·ing
World War I
World War II
world-wea·ry
world·wide
worm-eat·en
worm·hole
worm·i·er
worm·wood
worn-out
wor·ried
wor·ri·er
wor·ri·some
wor·ry·ing
wor·ry·wart
wors·en
wor·ship
wor·shiped
wor·ship·er
wor·ship·ful
wor·ship·ing
wor·sted (beaten,
    cloth)
wor·thi·er
wor·thi·ly
wor·thi·ness
would-be
wrack (destruction,
    to disturb,
    torture)
wraith

275

wran·gle

wran·gler

wrap·around

wrapped

wrap·per

wrap·ping

wrap-up (*noun* and *adj*)

wrath

wreak (inflict)

wreath (*noun*)

wreathe (*verb*)

wrench (all meanings)

wrest (to turn, take by force)

wres·tle

wres·tler

wretch (miserable one; *see* retch)

wri·er

wri·est

wrig·gle

wrig·gler

wring·er

wrin·kle

wrink·ly

wrist·band

wrist·watch

write-down (*noun*)

write-in (*noun* and *adj*)

write-off (*noun*)

write-up (*noun*)

writhe

writ·ten

wrong·do·er

wrong·head·ed

wrought (formed)

wrought-up

wry·ly

wry·neck

wry·ness

X

xen·o·phobe
xen·o·pho·bia

x-ray (all uses)
xy·lo·phone

Y

yacht
yachts·man
yam·mer
yam·mer·er
yap
yapped
yap·ping
yard·arm
yard·bird
yard goods
yard·man
yard·stick
yawl (boat)
year·book
year·ling
year·long

yearn
year-old (*adj*)
year-round (*adj*)
yel·low-dog (*adj*)
yel·low jack·et
yenned
yen·ning
yeo·man
yeo·man·ry
yes, *plural* yeses
yes man
yessed
yes·ses (*verb*)
yes·sing
yew (evergreen)
yield

yipped
yip·ping
yo·del
yo·deled
yo·del·er
yo·gurt
yoke (*noun,* frame
    for joining animals,
    bondage; *verb,* to
    join, put to work)
yo·kel
yolk (egg)
yo-yo
yule·log
yule·tide

Z

za·ni·er
za·nies
za·ni·ly
za·ni·ness
zeal
zeal·ot
zeal·ot·ry
zeal·ous
ze·bra
zeph·yr

ze·ro, *plural* zeros
ze·ro hour
ze·ro-ze·ro
zig·zag
zig·zagged
zig·zag·ging
zincked
zinck·ing
zincky
zipped

zip·per
zip·pi·er
zip·ping
zip·py
zith·er
zo·di·ac
zon·al
zo·ol·o·gy
zwie·back